SOCIAL ECONOMY

SOCIAL ECONOMY

International Debates and Perspectives

Eric Shragge,
Jean-Marc Fontan,
editors

Montréal/New York
London

Black Rose Books No. DD287
Hardcover ISBN: 1-55164-163-1 (bound)
Paperback ISBN: 1-55164-162-3 (pbk.)

Canadian Cataloguing in Publication Data
Main entry under tile:
Social economy : international debates and perspectives

Includes bibliographical references.
Hardcover ISBN: 1-55164-163-1 (bound)
Paperback ISBN: 1-55164-162-3 (pbk.)

1. Economics--Social aspects. 2. Economic history--1990-
I. Fontan, Jean-Marc II. Shragge, Eric, 1948-

HM548.S63 2000   330.9'049   C99-901588-5

Cover design by Associés libres, Montréal

C.P. 1258	2250 Military Road	99 Wallis Road
Succ. Place du Parc	Tonawanda, NY	London, E9 5LN
Montréal, H2W 2R3	14150	England
Canada	USA	UK

To order books in North America:
(phone) 1-800-565-9523 (fax) 1-800-221-9985
In Europe: (phone) London 44 (0)20 8986-4854 (fax) 44 (0)20 8533-5821

Our Web Site address: http://www.web.net/blackrosebooks

A publication of the Institute of Policy Alternatives of Montréal (IPAM)
Printed in Canada

The Canada Council | Le Conseil des Arts
for the Arts | du Canada

Contents

Notes On Contributors

Eric Shragge teaches social policy and community organization at the School of Social Work, McGill University. He is the editor of *Community Economic Development: In Search of Empowerment*, (Montréal: Black Rose Books, 1997) and *Workfare: Ideology for a New Underclass*, (Toronto: Garamond, 1997). He is able to escape from the university by working with grassroots community organizations.

Jean-Marc Fontan has a Ph.D. in sociology from the University of Montréal. He is a professor-researcher at the department of sociology at the University of Québec in Montréal. He works mainly on local development and community economic development. He co-published, in 1994, an important book on local development in Québec. He is a member of the Collectif de recherche inter-universitaire sur les transformations et les régulations économiques et sociales (CRITERES).

Enzo Mingione is professor of rural and urban sociology at the University of Messina, Italy. He is author of *Fragmented Societies: A Sociology of Economic Life Beyond the Market Paradigm*, (Oxford: Basil Blackwell, 1991) and *Urban Poverty and the Underclass: A Reader*, (Oxford: Basil Blackwell, 1996).

Michele Cangiani teaches economic sociology at the Universitá di Venezia, Italy. He is the author of *Economia e democrazia*, (Padova: Il Poligrafo, 1998) and the editor of *The Milano Papers. Essays in Societal Alternatives*, (Montréal: Black Rose Books, 1997).

Jack Quarter is a professor at the Ontario Institute for Studies in Education of the University of Toronto specializing in the study of community economic development, co-operatives and democratic workplaces. His most recent books include: *Canada's Social Economy: Co-operatives, Non-Profits and Other Community Organizations* (Lorimer); *Crossing the Line: Unionized Employee Ownership and Investment Funds*, (Lorimer); (with Paul Wilkinson) *Building a Community-Controlled Economy: The Evangeline Co-operative Experience*, (University of Toronto Press); (with Uri Leviatan, Hugh Oliver, eds.) *Crisis in the Israeli Kibbutz*, (Praeger); and forthcoming, *Beyond the Bottom Line: Socially Innovative Business Owners*, (McGill-Queen's).

Paul Leduc Browne is Senior Research Fellow at the Canadian Centre for Policy Alternatives. Before joining the Centre in 1994, he worked as a translator and taught at several universities and colleges. He holds a doctorate in social and political thought from the University of Sussex. His publications include *Love in a Cold World? The Voluntary Sector in an Age of Cuts*, (CCPA), 1996.

Andrea Levy has a Ph.D. in History from Concordia University in Montréal. A freelance writer and scholar, she has been active in urban politics for many years, publishing articles on the peace movement, the New Left, and the ecology movement.

Kathryn Church is an independent researcher based in Toronto. She has worked for many years in the areas of mental health and economic development. She holds a Ph.D. from University of Toronto, and is the author of *Forbidden Narratives: Critical Autobiography as Social Science*, (Gordon and Breach, 1995). She is the curator of the exhibition *Fabrications: Stitching Ourselves Together*, an intimate autobiography of working women and wedding dresses in Central Alberta. The exhibition is touring Canada.

Benôit Lévesque has a Ph.D. in sociology. He teaches sociology at the Université du Québec à Montréal. Specialist on economic sociology and social movements, he co-published several books on social economy and socio-economic development in Québec. He is the coordinator of an important inter-university research team, the Collectif de recherche sur les innovations sociales dans les entreprises et les syndicats (CRISES).

William A. Ninacs is an independent trainer and researcher working out of a worker co-operative in Victoriaville, Québec. He has been an active practitioner in the field of the social economy for twenty-five years as both an organizer and a manager. He currently teaches Business Development at New Hampshire College's Community Economic Development (CED) Program, while pursuing a Ph.D. in social work at the Université Laval in Québec City.

Jean-Luc Souchet graduated in social sciences from l'Université de Nantes (1996). He is an independent researcher and a journalist on social economy. He works mainly on the French department of Loire-Atlantique. He published several books on mutuality and social economy in the Loire-Atlantique department or on the city of Nantes.

Louis Favreau is a social worker and has a Ph.D. in sociology. He is professor in social work at the Université du Québec à Hull. Specializing in the field of social movement and community development, he co-published several books on community development and social work in Québec. He is Rédacteur en chef of Économie et Solidarités and a member of CRISES.

Michael Toye is a Montréal-based activist. He is currently involved in a number of cooperatives, including the worker cooperative Interface which does research, consulting and training on issues of local development and the social economy.

Chapter 1

Tendencies, Tensions and Visions in the Social Economy

Jean-Marc Fontan and Eric Shragge

This book grew out of the Polanyi Conference of November 1996. We organized a session on the social economy debate as a way to bring together commentators and present the debate that was current in Quebec in particular to a wider audience. The contents of this book are based on some of the presentations at the panel plus other papers related to this theme that were presented at the wider conference. In addition, we have included several additional chapters from individuals who have contributed to the social economy debate. Our goal is to present a wide perspective. The common theme that underlies all of the essays is that capitalist societies, particularly advanced industrialized capitalist societies are in the process of undergoing some important changes, shaped by globalization of the economy and related changes in the state. As a consequence and related to the specific context of each country or region, new practices have emerged and new importance is accorded to the "third sector" or social economy.[1] It is the significance of this sector and the role it plays in the changes that is debated in these essays.

In recent years, social economy as a concept and a practice has taken on new significance in Europe and Quebec. In the rest of North America, as several of the contributors to this book point out, the "third sector," has taken on a similar significance and revival. It is difficult to construct a clear image of these organizations because of their diversity. Many types of organizations co-exist under the general category-social economy/third sector ranging from those involved primarily in economic activities such as cooperatives to others providing a variety of local services. The essays in this collection do not share one common perspective but come at the social economy from different vantage points and raise questions which reflect them. We hope that these essays will open the debate and raise more critical questions.

In this introduction, we will briefly trace the long historical tradition of the social economy, its rise and fall and subsequent re-emergence in a renewed form. The wider contexts are always important in shaping the role of this sector and we shall look at the links between the wider context and the practices associated with the social economy. We will also look at two tendencies that have crossed historical periods: pragmatic/reformist and utopian/social change. We will see how these tendencies are played out in the current period. We will then turn to some of the key issues and questions in the social economy debate. Finally, a brief outline of the content of the book will be presented.

The debate on the social economy—what it is, its social and economic role is complex and difficult. It is complex because there is no one accepted definition that delimits its field of practice. It is difficult because we are not only dealing with a wide range of practices and traditions but also with their emergence in a period of rapid social and economic change in which the social economy in many countries is being redefined and has a growing significance. Thus the field both in theory and in practice is in flux. The authors in the chapters that follow grapple with both definitions and with the role of the social economy. For the purpose of this introduction we can begin our discussion of the social economy through looking at a couple of elements in its practice. The first is that in their origins the projects associated with the social economy are neither controlled directly by the state or the private sector, and second, they play either or both a social or an economic role. As the essays in this book demonstrate there is not a consensus on the definition of the social economy. The following are some examples from the literature.

- Desroche uses organizational criteria to define the key characteristics of the social economy-cooperative structures for example (D'Amours 1997).

- Vienney examines the logic of those involved as well as their activities and regulations to develop his definition (D'Amours 1997).

- Defourny uses the concepts of citizenship, solidarity, and autonomy as his starting points (D'Amours 1997).

- Marée and Saive associate themselves with a practice approach, one associates social economy with any practice that rejects the maximization of profit and builds democratic decision-making processes (Fontan 1992).

The consistency in the definitions is the acknowledgment of the continuity with practices that come out of the last century, plus a recognition of the new social practices of the 1960s and 1970s, such as those developed in France and Quebec and elsewhere that can be described as the new social economy (Lévesque, Bourque, Forques, 1998) or the solidaristic economy (Laville,1994). We will pick up this historical thread later in the discussion. It is not that the current practices differ greatly from historical antecedents that is important, but their place and significance in the redefinition of the functions and responsibilities of both the state and the wider market economy that creates this renewed interest in the social economy.

Competing Perspectives

Throughout its long history there have always been two competing visions of the social economy. The first can be described as pragmatic/reformist. It regards the social economy as playing a role in the management of individual and group social welfare through initiatives which target and are limited to specific problems and groups, for example agricultural cooperatives or mutual societies. Those promoting these projects are not concerned with changing the social order, but with making changes that would ameliorate specific problems.

A second position links the social economy with the fundamental change, or the building of a new society-utopian/social change. Propositions to this end go back as far as the work of Plocboy, Bellers or Pestalozzi in the 18th century (Leclerc, 1982). This voice which was a counter-cultural current, was actively repressed or marginalized by the dominant class and supporters of their ideology because their vision and practice constituted an attack on the social order. This perspective can be situated in relation to the traditions of social change movements of the left.

By the end of the 19th century three perspectives on social change were taking their place. These formed the debate on the left for most of the following century. The social democratic movement wanted to attack social and economic injustice through the electoral system and build the strength of the working class through political parties, often linked to the trade union movement. The revolutionary Marxists such as Lenin and his followers that believed that fundamental change was possible through the seizure of power by the working class under the leadership of a vanguard party. Both of these traditions saw a strong centralized state as the vehicle to bring about change. In contrast, anarchists believed that power should be radically decentralized into neighbourhood or factory councils, with seizure of power at the local level. Within this position, is the belief that direct democratic organizations could be created within capitalist societies that would allow self-managed production. This position is closely linked with the social change/utopian perspective on the social economy, and has a thread that runs through the current discussion. It embodies the traditions of Proudhon and Kropotkin, Owen and Cabot. Their vision was not limited to the local alone but sought to build a new society from the bottom up. Decentralized institutions could be federated to create a new society in the shell of the old one. The radical side of the cooperative movement was influenced by this position arguing that cooperatives were not only about democratic production and consumption but were the seeds of social change, a form of organization that would be the basis of shift in power. We will pick up these themes in the discussion of the historical development of the social economy.

Historical Development of the Social Economy

The social economy has very early origins, dating back before the period of industrialization or the modern state. It has been with us as long as humans have worked communally and shared in the results of their labour. Collective practices such as the management of risk-death and sickness benefits—associated with religious and secular movements converged in the period of the birth of the of modern society and the state in the late 18th century. This period of social effervescence, brought with it debates on the principals and orientations of the nation state, particularly new rights which allowed the appearance of a variety of organizations such as those that defend social interests, and collective organizations such as cooperatives. These organizations embodied both a continuity and a rupture with the earlier period. The rupture was created by the far greater scope for action that the new period permitted. The right of association permitted the possibility for individuals to choose to associate with a variety of collectivities, thus creating new forms of action.

Another important element was the passage from an agricultural economy to one based on industry. Labour was recruited from a wider market, shifting the process of employment from work in extended family units and guilds to that of individuals in a market. With the emergence of a market-based economy, the role of the social economy was the defense of and the promotion of collective interests through services related to consumption, savings and credit as well as directly in production. The underlying beliefs of the social economy clashed with the emerging creeds of capitalism. The fundamental distinction between the concepts liberal and social economy were taken up in 19th century debates through a discussion of the relationship between the economy and the social sphere. For those who were supporters of the liberal economy like Adam Smith and Malthus, the social was to be subordinated and was there to service economic development (Vienney, 1994). The market and the state were the two institutions of regulation, based on the nation state and the national market. For those who supported the early ideas on the social economy, the central precept was that the economy should serve social ends. Their support for this idea was linked to their desire to establish an order based on egalitarianism. Examples of this approach were discussed earlier. Within this general position there is diversity and complexities (Baslé, Benhamou, Chavance, Gélédon, Léobal, Lipietz, 1988).

One important characteristic of the social economy in this period is the blurring of the boundary between the economy and the national state. If the traditional liberal economy is defined within a national framework, the social economy is defined fundamentally within a local framework, with international linkages between local initiatives (for example, Proudhon's concept of an international federation of cooperatives). From this perspective the nation is understood as an instance that permits exchanges between federated societies and not as the body that shapes the society. This perspective was central in the formation of international institutions such as the International Association of Workers of 1864, and contributed as early as the 19th century to the vision of a world-wide civil society.

With the beginning of the 20th century, the concept of the social economy lost ground. Social reform was made possible by improvements in economic conditions in more developed capitalist countries. Belief in social progress was accompanied and supported by economic growth. The split between economy, politics and social grew with autonomy for each of these three spheres. The traditions of the more radical social economy that linked these spheres disappeared and the institutions of the social economy such as cooperatives were treated as part of the economy. Reformist tendencies emerged in the trade union movement with their focus on economic gains and workplace struggles, which eclipsed both the utopian concepts of the social economy and revolutionary workers' organizations. As the economic system grew, it found ways to absorb the grievances of the working class, particularly in periods of economic growth. Taylorism in the workplace with its division of labour was mirrored in the wider society with the representation of workers in politics by social democratic parties, and a wide variety of grouping competed in the social sphere, for example the many religious or secular non-profit organizations.

From the end of the first world war through to the 1970s, the practice of the social economy remained at the margins as a practice and conceptual framework. It specialized in specific economic practices mainly in the cooperative movement. This movement encompassed a variety of experiences and domains, including consumption, banking and saving, production and agriculture. Many of these cooperatives had their origins at the beginning of the twentieth century, and grew in size as they succeeded in the marketplace. The cooperatives had political and social links to both reform movements, the church, and social democratic parties. Yet, despite the success of these organizations, in economic terms, the welfare state and related economic policies shaped by Keynesian ideas, dominated in the period after the second world war as the approach for social provision. The state became a technocratic manager of the social with little participation from the community sector in the planning and control of these welfare state programs.

It was not until the end of the 1970s that the notions of the social economy were rehabilitated. These were not in the form of radical, utopian ideas of the previous century, but as a moderate approach promoted not by intellectuals or social activists, but by those in public institutions who were responding to the growing crisis of the state. The governments of France and Belgium began to talk about the concept of social economy in the early 1980s and then by the late 1980s the European Union involved itself in the discussion. Thus the social economy did not have an element of social change in any kind of fundamental way; the discussion was controlled by those in the cooperative, mutualist movements and those in state bureaucracies concerned with decentralization of services and new ways to address the problems associated with state cutbacks and unemployment. The context of the renewed social economy is shaped by the long period of high unemployment in all developed capitalist countries beginning in the 1980s, by a wide restructuring of the world economy, and a generalized attack on the welfare state with a reduction in state spending in the social sphere. These changes while diminishing the social gains of the Keynesian welfare state, created a space in which new initiatives from the community sector were both necessary and possible.

Competing Perspectives Revisited

There are two contemporary crises that are central in our understanding of the role of the social economy. The first is the crisis of work itself. This is expressed not only through unemployment, as a cyclical phenomenon, but as a growing and permanent feature of industrial capitalist societies. The second crisis is the redefinition of the role of the state, particularly the withdrawal of many social programs and the redefining of relations between the community or voluntary organizations and the state. Both of these crises, have created a new space for the social economy, and it is in this context the current practices defined within the social economy have increased significance.

The relationships that have emerged are complex. The community sector has played an innovative role in trying to find solutions to the consequences of unemployment and related poverty. It has turned entrepreneurship on it head, by using it as a tool to ameliorate social conditions rather than traditional private gains, and confronted the cutbacks in the health and social services with new forms of social provision. But there are many questions, particularly about the social and political role played by this sector in the current context. Along with the questions there are strong positions that have already been taken by those who see the social economy as a way out of the current crisis, on one end and by those who argue that the social economy masks the underlying problems and acts as a manager of those marginalized by the changes in the labour market and the reorganization of the welfare state. Two aspects of the activities of those organizations involved in the social economy can be used to help us understand the nature of these diverse practices: 1) the objectives of the organizations and groups; 2) the issue of democratic functioning and processes.

Objectives

If we return to the historical perspective raised earlier, we argued that there are two tendencies—the dominant one a reformist version that seeks limited, progressive changes within the dominant order. The second tendency, the utopian vision sees a new society growing out of new practices within the social order and in opposition to it. The dominant view in the current period, is linked to the reformist position. It defines the objectives of the social economy as social integration particular for those excluded from the labour market and particularly wider social relations because of the restructuring of the economy and the reduction of state programs. Changes in economies and government strategy have led to privatization of resources and services, a polarization of wealth and poverty, and a shift to greater responsibility for the community sector. The consequences of theses changes has brought about a crisis and the need for new strategies of socio-economic management/reform. The social economy has been one of the tools that the government has jumped on as long as the objectives remain social integration rather than social change, the costs are low, and it does not become a point of confrontation.

The reasons that the social economy has become attractive for government, are not only the micro-social practice that have put in place a variety of community based businesses and services but also as a model for orienting wider social development. If conditions are supportive, the social economy permits the combination of public and private strategies to manage social problems. The related processes draw upon the institutional forms of both the market and the state in attempting to achieve social peace, while allowing power and wealth to remain concentrated in the hands of the few. Our position, that we will develop in more detail below is that despite the complex practices of the social economy, the underlying current is one of pragmatic social reform within the dominant power arrangements of capitalist societies.

Democratic Functioning

One of the claims of the social economy and one of its defining characteristics is that it functions within democratic processes. However, the reality is much more complex. Given the wide range of experiences, it is difficult to argue that as a sector it is inherently democratic. We would argue that the social economy is more of a zone in which there is democratic experimentation rather than a place in which a strong, permanent, successful democratic tradition has been established (Bidet 1997). Democratic participation requires that individuals learn to work in new ways. The socialization and education processes in most countries do not prepare individuals to act in this way (Sainsaulieu, Tixier, and Marty, 1983). Further, existing collectivities function through the provision of service for individuals and groups by professionals who control expertise; for example unions provide workplace protection with agents and a bureaucratic structure representing and negotiating on behalf of workers. In practice, democracy is carried out by the delegation of responsibility. In the milieu of the social economy, democracy implies direct involvement of the individuals, and in order to do this effectively, there has to be a tradition of democratic workplaces, so that learning of new ways of organizing work becomes a training ground for the social economy.

Democratic processes in organizations are not necessarily part of the tradition of the older social economies such as cooperatives and mutual societies. Often the democratic functioning is limited to formal structures with day to day processes delegated to managers. Democracy in organizations necessitates ongoing work in the creation of an environment of individual support that enables the building of group process. As well, democracy generates a cultural dynamic in the organization which extends both creative powers and the voices of the individuals involved. As the new social economy has evolved a new cadre of professionals is taking their place as it managers. This has contributed to the recognition of this practice but also the separation of those at the provision end and those receiving, thus reducing democratic processes. Thus democratization is difficult and requires a commitment of changing both organizational structures, and processes, and implicitly challenges the control of the practices of the social economy by both funders and professionals.

What's at Stake: Social Change or Social Control in a Global Economy

We opened the discussion by referring to the reformist and utopian approaches. These have new expression in the current debate. The reformist position is based on social compromise and consensus building within the liberal market place, and defines its practice within those limits, but adding the extension of democratic participation within new socially-oriented projects. This perspective is most clearly articulated by the promotion of a new social contract which uses the social economy as a central tool in combating poverty and social exclusion (Vaillancourt and Lévesque 1996). This position is attractive at a one level because it puts forward an alternative to the Keynesian welfare state which is seen as *dépassé* and irretrievable. But the limits to this position reside in the barriers of the localism of the social economy itself, which does not have the redistributive power of the state. A critique of the more orthodox left position has denounced the attempt by the state to integrate and institutionalize the practices of the social economy. There is concern that the social economy will become the economy of the poor, of women and of the marginalized, and act through the provision of and the organization of minimal welfare type programs to replace those withdrawn by government. As well, the democracy of the social economy will be the poor managing themselves on the economic margins. The role of this position tends to be oppositional and critical, while falling back on the traditions of older left positions. (Boivin and Fortier, editors: 1998)

It is politically dangerous to promote locally based solutions in a period when power is further and further removed from the local. Without the traditional left demand for economic redistribution through the state, the social economy will be relegated to the role of a social manager of poverty at the local level. In the context of globalization and the resulting polarization of wealth and income, the reformists favour the development of micro-economic tools such as financial and production cooperatives and community organizations which are subject to the pressures of playing an integrative role within the liberal economy. The possibilities of a gradual social transformation through these programs and micro-economic development is an illusion.

The radical/utopian perspective promotes the social economy as an alternative form of socio-economic development that breaks with the liberal economy. It suggests a new model of society in which the liberal market economy will be replaced by a socially-oriented one. There are many examples of this type of practice such as the LETS system or barter and exchange at a community level. (Dobson: 1993) This new localism believes in constructing a practice outside of both the state and mainstream economy. It has a tradition, influenced by anarchist thought, that can be seen in attempts at urban change through neighbourhood development and the creation of alternative, ecological, and feminist approaches and practice in economic development. There is a continuity with the past utopian traditions mentioned above insofar as the emphasis is on the creation of alternatives within the society with an eye on the extension of these practices and their federating being the strategy of social change. This position supports the autonomy of practice from the state, and its practice has created some new forms designed to meet human need, but the practice tends to be limited to experimental and new forms of democratically managed local activities. There are dangers of isolation of these projects and therefore a self-marginalization, and in addition, local empowerment is prioritized instead of a political program involving claims-making on the state and the private sector.

As we enter the 21st century, the nature of the evoling institutional framework that manages modern and modernizing societies is more and more transparent. The recent work of Boyer and Hollingsworth (1997) clarifies the nature of the institutional arrangements that have been put in place by the "western elites" during the last fifty years. These have made the social relations of capitalist societies hegemonic almost everywhere. These constitute a system of regulation for the planet which imposes the same logic of management on all governing structures, on all states and their societies. Along with the homogenization of economies and states, cultural differences and regional distinctions are maintained giving the appearance of variation. These differences cloud the increasingly unified system, and no longer constitute the dynamic force that shape the development of local organizations and their wider societies. Within this framework, there is a general tendency. The state through its programs and policies has two sets of practices, one that deals with those in, around and out of the labour market and another designed to promote the interests of the elite in a world market.

Perhaps it is time to renew and redefine the historical project of the utopians. However, the utopian tradition, focuses on building new institutions from below. This processes is a central aspect but it also requires a wider political program. Giddens (1994) uses the concept of "utopian realism" to define in defining a framework of radical politics. He discusses four orienting concepts-combating poverty-absolute and relative; redressing the degradation of the environment; contesting arbitrary power; reducing the role of force in and violence in social life. There is a clear need to have a political and social vision that is neither limited to the local nor ignores the importance of local practice. The development of the social economy has to be linked to a vision of social change that is at once the creation of new democratic social institutions and at the same time is able to be part of wider mobilizations for social and economic justice, making claims on the state and the private sector.

It is inadequate to just situate the social economy within the liberal framework on a global scale. A social economy implies the basic reorientation of the whole economy and related social institutions. Instead of thinking of the social economy as a set of micro-economic tools, the utopian tradition proposes the building of a wider cultural framework devoted to the elimination of social divisions built through the control of the wealth and power. We need to begin with a basic reconception of the role of the economy, one that starts with the social utility of each individual. We need to oppose the current view that the individual is considered a resource that can be used and disposed of at the discretion of the economy. In contrast the social economy should be a means of promoting a vision in which economic development should be in the service of human need; this should be the beginning point of the discussion.

In this overview of some the issues in the social economy debate, we have built on the contrast between a reformist and a utopian view. This has helped us through our analysis, but the implications of practice are at best vague. To conclude this section, we thought that some clarification would help us avoid the trap of writing off the emerging practice as simply part of the reformist position. Practice is always complex and takes into account the political and economic conjuncture, both the opportunities and limits it presents and the demands of the constituency with whom the projects engage. Practitioners face growing poverty, limited funding choices, and a wider environment which is not sympathetic to the type of broad social reform that is necessary to ameliorate deteriorating social and economic conditions faced by the poor. The social economy, whose specific practices are described in many of the chapters that follow, has been a site for innovations in social practice that seems to make some difference in this period. The question then becomes is it possible for the practices of the social economy to play a role in moving toward an alternative vision or is it condemned to remain within the liberal framework. Practice that promotes social change has to live in a tension between its engagement in the complexities of the community sector, and a longer-term social vision.

Several elements can facilitate the linking of practice and an alternative vision. The first is to make the vision explicit both in statements made, and in affiliation with groups with similar viewpoints. It is important that alternative visions are affirmed publicly, so the traditions can be maintained as a legitimate point of view. Next, there is a tendency in the practices of the social economy to separate the building of social programs and services from the more overtly political dimension such as resisting attacks on the poor and on social programs, and raising new political and social demands. Linking the more explicitly political with the creation of the social economy is a means of looking for a new approach in which the state still plays a central role but in which the local can begin to build power and process of controlling those organizations and programs identified with the social economy. It is necessary to acknowledge the complex relationship between the social economy and the state.

In this period of redefinition, tension and uncertainty are elements in the renegotiating of the respective role of the state and the social economy/third sector. The interests of the state is to find new ways to manage social problems, without resorting to expensive, unionized, bureaucratic structures. At the same time new community services are being created both to compensate for the withdrawal of government and to build new groups that can provide services that are locally controlled. With these changes, the state has found new ways to build legislative and policy frameworks to encourage the emergence of these new community initiatives, which can lead to their institutionalization. Many supporting the social economy are demanding this recognition and the legitimation. The contradictions are evident and the questions of who will control the processes and the role of the social economy are central. Providing recognition and funding, the state can also shape the social economy as a sector to manage the poor while allowing the tendencies of unregulated international capitalism and economic polarization to continue. Clearly, new policies are required that give the necessary support to the social economy, but the consequence of this support should not mean that the this evolving practice is swallowed up by the state and becomes yet another quasi-governmental program for specific populations. Support for this sector will then become an excuse for not replacing the state social and income maintenance programs, and ignoring the growing inequalities. The organizations of the social economy must also participate in the promotion of a program for social change and not allow themselves to be turned into economic and social managers of the new poverty. Negotiation with the state and the related funding bodies are required, in which the organizations of the social economy can go beyond limited self-interest and promote a wider social vision.

Finally, practice needs to put social processes in the forefront. Processes are about the ways that organizations are created, how decisions are made, and who holds power and control. The social economy on a small scale should be the training ground in how people can act to control and manage their own organizations. However, limited this might be, perhaps the strongest social change role that organizations in the social economy can play is to be a training ground in which the control of organizations is shared democratically. As people gain control over some aspects of their lives they will be more able to demand more of it in wider spheres. Thus, a broad vision coupled with political demands and democratic process will be the key elements if the social economy is to become more than the management of the poor by local leaders through inexpensive programs. Together, these practices can build an alternative, counter-culture, that stand against the dominant assumptions that the social should be subordinated to the economic, and at the same time create points of local counter-power to corporate rule.

Content of the Book

The first essay by Enzo Mingione does not directly discuss the social economy but examines how the market economy itself is a social construction and cannot exist as an independent entity, independent of other institutions. In the context of a shift from what he calls welfare capitalism to global capitalism, the market has been presented as living free from social constraints. He demonstrates the fallacy of this argument attacking it both logically and historically. He sites Polanyi's argument that there are three basic forms of the social relation of exchange-the competitive market, reciprocity and redistribution. With the shifts in the economy we face a reconfiguration of these relationships. These changes include a growing importance of cultural diversity, small firms, working life instability, changes in family and the emergence of social exclusion as a social question. It is in this context that we can understand the role and place of the social economy. Mangione closes as a proponent of the need to renew cooperative behavior and other reciprocal networks that have long been overshadowed by the market economy. Thus the local and a new economic diversity becomes the counter-weight to globalization and the spread of the market ideology.

Cangiani traces the emergence of neo-liberalism as a dominant approach of the state, freeing the market from constraints and restrictions. He introduces the "third sector" through the work of several authors, and explores the wide-ranging European debate. He argues that the roots of the third sector as an oppositional force or utopian vision have their origins in the social movements of the 1970s. The continuity of these traditions is developed particularly on the question of work and the crisis of unemployment. He concludes by raising fundamental questions and contradictions faced by proponents of the third sector. He asks if the third sector can be a vehicle for progressive social change and if so, how. These are the key questions for this book. If the social economy or the third sector is only a decentralized manger of poverty and the consequences of globalization then in whose interest is the development of this sector?

Jack Quarter is one of the few authors in English Canada who has used the term social economy in his writing. In this chapter, he situates its development in a context of the withdrawal of government from service provision and social development, and in their place the emergence of alternative service delivery. He presents a typology of the social economy with three sub-sectors: entrepreneurial, mutual associations and financially dependent. He argues that their common feature is that they form social as opposed to private property. He then turns to several of Rifkin's proposals for the development of the third sector to see if they can be useful to the building of this sector. He concludes that there are opportunities but these cannot be isolated from wider political struggles for greater social equality and the redistribution of wealth.

Andrea Levy's chapter touches the core question of the consequences of globalization—the absence of waged work. She starts with the crisis of work itself and looks at how the social economy touches this issue. Interwoven in this discussion is a critique of economic growth as a solution, primarily because of its ecological limits. She also examines Rifkin's work and is critical of some of the limits of his propositions. She argues that for the social economy to be an effective means of countering the crisis of work it has to be connected to other policies such as work-sharing and a reduction in the hours of work. She concludes her discussion with an argument that freeing time is a necessary precondition for renewed democracy at the local level. With this essay, our attention moves from the social economy to a wider social vision with the question of whether or not the third sector can contain within it the seeds for a redefinition of work itself.

Paul Leduc Browne takes an explicitly critical stance on the social economy/third sector debate. He situates the emergence of this sector in the context of the shift in social policy perspectives that have been shaped by neo-liberal beliefs, and the dismantling of the welfare state. Further, and this is a point often forgotten in the debates on the social economy, the third sector is not independent of the state but intertwined with it, and part of the reconfiguration of the welfare state. Browne argues these points by examining the growth of third sector organizations in Ontario, and their relation to government programs, particularly workfare. He concludes by drawing parallels between 19th century charities and the current growth of the third sector, and asking if large sectors of that sector will be transformed into "unwitting agents of the neo-liberal order."

Louis Favreau's chapter compares emerging practices of the social economy in the North, and in the South. He describes the common context of globalization and the impact that it has had in both hemispheres. He then turns to a discussion of the traditions of both. In the north a combination of the decline of the welfare state and the emergence and responses of social movements, has created conditions for a new "solidarity-oriented society." These changes have the potential of leading to a reconfiguration of economic and social relationships, that can open up new opportunities for the extension of democracy into new spheres. In the South, three forms of practice contribute to their equivalent of the social economy: micro-project support work, defense of social rights, and measures designed to integrate socio-economic development. His argument turns to some of the convergence and the potentials of this sphere for social change, within a context of international solidarity and cooperation.

Jean-Luc Souchet presents the social economy in one region in France. He describes the development of mutual societies in the Loire-Atlantique region over two centuries of growth and decline and rebuilding. Throughout each of the periods, he discusses tensions and debates, particularly those over control of these societies, and their relationship to social security programs and the state. One of the recurring themes is whether or not mutual societies can be seen as vehicles for social change on a larger scale or whether they were restricted to a particular socio-economic role. With reduction in the scope of state programs in the 1980s, new possibilities for mutual societies has been created, particularly in health care.

In Quebec, the debate on the social economy has moved from the community movement into the centre of social and economic policy debates with the economic summit of 1996. There has been a lot at stake as the government has supported the development of the social economy in the context of its zero deficit policy. Two chapters examine issues and questions faced in Quebec's social economy. The first by Benoît Lévesque and William Ninacs present the state of discussion in Quebec. Beginning with a summary of definitions of and approaches to the social economy, the authors examine what they describe as the Quebec model of development. They trace the historical evolution of practice, and the institutions and organizations that currently support these practices. Finally, they raise some of the issues and challenges this sector faces, in particular the relation with government. William Ninacs contributes further to this discussion, looking at Quebec's social economy from a practitioners point of view. This bottom-up analysis looks at the viewpoints of the major stakeholders-women's groups, the communitarian, co-operative and labour movements in the context of the specific government policies and the organizations that deliver them. In his conclusion, he examines the dilemmas faced by practitioners in the social economy and the potential of that sector to do if it can take its place as an equal player with the traditional economy.

Kathryn Church's chapter looks at one example of social economy from below. She discusses the emergence of businesses in Toronto established by people who have survived the psychiatric system. Democratic management and flexible work conditions in the context of a functioning business demonstrate that the social economy can help people redefine their lives through work in a democratic context. However, these new businesses do not exist in isolation from the state and social policy debates. She explores the complex inter-relationship between practice and state policy.

Finally, Mike Toye's chapter offers a review of books and web sites that are useful for analysis and discussion of the social economy.

NOTES

1. Some of the authors use the third sector and others use the social economy. The term social economy tends to be used more by those from France and Quebec, and the third sector by those writing from Anglo-Canadian traditions and from the United States. We will generally use the term social economy in the discussions that follow.

BIBLIOGRAPHY

G. Allaire, "Le développement rural et la politique agricole de transition: quel paradigme alternatif au productivisme?," *Revue internationale d'action communautaire*, # 22/62, 1989.

M. Baslé, F. Benhamou, B. Chavance, A. Gélédan, J. Léobal, and A. Lipietz, *Historie des penseurs économiques*. Paris: Sirey, 1988, tome 1, 373 p, tome 2, 556 p.

J. Bennet, *La mutualité française, des origines à la révolution de 1789*. Paris: Coopérative d'information et d'édition mutualiste, 1981.

E. Bidet, *L' économie sociale*. Bruxelles: Le Monde Éditions, 1997.

L. Boivin and M. Fortier, (eds.), *L'économie sociale: l'avenir d'une illusion*. Montréal: Fides, 1998.

R. Boyer and J.R. Hollingsworth, (eds.), *Contemporary Capitalism, the embeddedness of Institutions*. Cambridge: Cambridge University Press, 1997, 493 p.

B. Brandt, *Whole Life Economics: Revaluing Daily Life*. Gabriola Island, British Columbia: New Society Publishers, 1995.

M. D'Amours, *L'économie sociale au Québec*. Montéral: Institut de formation en développement économique communautaire, 1997, 80 p.

M. D'Amours, *Présence de l'économie sociale au Québec, une illustration dans six secteurs et sept régions*. Montreal: Institut de formation en développement économique communautaire, 1997.

J. Defourny and J.L. Monzon Campos, *Économie sociale, entre économie capitaliste et économmie publique/The Tird Sector, Cooperative, Mutual ans Non-profit Organizations*. Bruxelles: CIRIEC, De Boeck université, 1992.

H. Desroche, *Pour un traité d'économie sociale*. Paris: Coopérative d'information et d'édition mutualiste, 1983.

H. Denis. *Histoire de la pensée économique*. Paris: Presses universitaires de France, Thémis économie, 1993, 739 p.

R.V.G. Dobson, *Bring the Economy Home from the Market*. Montreal: Black Rose Books, 1993.

J.M. Fontan, *Les corporations de développement économique communautaire montréalaises : du développement économique communautaire au développement local de l'économie*. Thèse de doctorat, Université de Montréal, département de sociologie, les Presses de l'IFDEC, Montréal, 1992, 585 pages.

J.M. Fontan and E. Shragge, "CED in Montréal: Community versus State Control," in E. Shragge, (ed.), *Community Economic Development, in Search of Empowerment*. Montreal: Black Roses, 1997, pp. 87-109.

J.M. Fontan and E. Shragge, "Chic Resto Pop, New Practive in Quebec," *Community Development Journal*, Volume 31, No. 4, October 1996, pp. 291-301.

A. Giddens, *Beyond Left and Right: The Future of Radical Politics*. Stanford, California: Stanford University Press, 1994.

J.J. Gislain and C. Deblock, "L'économie sociale en perspective: émergence et dérive d'un projet de société," in B. Lévesque et.al., *L'autre-économie une économie alternative ?*. Quebec: Presses de l'Université du Québec, 1989.

J. Godbout, (in collaboration with Alain Caillé), *L'esprit du don*. Paris: La Découverte, 1992.

A. Leclerc, *Les doctrines coopératives en Europe et au Canada*. Sherbrooke: IRECUS, 1982.

J.L. Laville, (ed.), *L'économie solidaire. Une perspective internationale*. Paris: Desclée de Brouwer, 1994.

B. Lévesque, G. Bourque and E. Forgues, "La sociologie économique de langue française: originalité et diversité des approches," *Cahiers internationaux de sociologie*, Vol. CIII, 1997, pp. 265-294.

J. Plant and P. Plant, *Putting Power in its Place*. Gabriola Island, British Columbia: New Society Publishers, 1992.

R. Sainsaulieu, P.E. Tixier and M.O. Marty, *La démocratie en organisation, vers des fonctionnements collectifs de travail*. Paris: Librairie des Méridiens, 1983.

E. Shragge,(ed.), *Community Economic Development, In search of Empowerment*. Montréal: Black Rose Books, 1997.

E. Shragge and J.M. Fontan, "Employability Approaches in CED Practice: Case Studies and Issues," in J. Hudson and B. Gallaway, (eds.), *Community Economic Development: Canadian Research and Policy Perspectives*. Toronto: Thompson Educational Publishing, 1994, chapter 14, p. 144-152.

D.G. Tremblay and J.M. Fontan, *Développement économique local: la théorie, la pratique, les expériences*. Quebec: Presses de l'Université du Québec, 1994, 579 pages.

Y. Vaillancourt and B. Lévesque, "Économie sociale et reconfiuration de l'État-providence (éditorial)," *Nouvelles Pratiques Sociales*, Volume 9, numéro 1, Printemps 1996, p.1-13.

C. Vienney, *L'économie sociale*. Paris: La Découverte, 1994, 125 p.

Chapter 2

Market and Society: The Social Embeddedment of the Economy

Enzo Mingione

The Critique of the Market Paradigm and the Social Construction of the Economy
The profound changes that have swept through economic life in industrial
countries since the crisis of the Seventies have helped to relaunch the laissez-faire
approach. It is accompanied by an asocial vision of the economy characterized by
increasing impatience with bureaucratization, state intervention and social
support and integration policies, and large hierarchical organizations. The talk is
of globalization and flexibility, of opportunities created by utilitarian behaviour in
contexts where regulation freed from the burden of welfare provides efficiency
and innovation. We are said to be passing from *welfare capitalism*, a system
centred on the coupling of large manufacturing units and national states, to
global capitalism, a less organized system dominated by financial and data flows,
in which people's working careers and family biographies are unstable and the
capacity of nation states to control their economies is very limited. Underlying
this vision of the new economic world order is the old market paradigm that
accompanied the stages of industrial history as a means of conditioning it and
providing a distorted interpretation of economic life. The idea is that competition
between individuals free from constraints gives rise on its own to collaboration
and organization, a dense fabric of social ties indispensable for improving one's
own life conditions without compromising those of others. Moreover, it is
believed that society is created by the market and competition, that the universal
goals of rational behaviour are far stronger than cultural traditions, and that
economics is more a utilitarian than a social science. These are dangerous
notions, above all because we are in the middle of a complicated transition from
one dominant regulative system to another; it is therefore important to
understand how cooperational balances are achieved, which are not at all
generated by utilitarian competition. In order to provide alternative
interpretations, we need to start from the critique of the market paradigm and
build up a picture of the economy embedded in social contexts.

The market paradigm was the product of a long period of transformations,
becoming more intense in the XVIII century, and of optimistic views on the
emancipation of man from myth and prejudice through *doux commerce*
(Hirschman, 1982), a universal practice grounded in the individual interests of
free *homo economicus*. Trade was considered to be "gentle" because it entailed

benefits in terms of life conditions without any big sacrifices. Until the founding of neo-classical economics, this paradigm remained a philosophical vision lacking analytical depth. It was with the "dogma of the fixed wage fund,"[1] based on the assumption that the labour market operated without considering how workers lived, that a true logical paradigm was formulated, making it possible to universalise economic understanding and put it forward as independent from local or sectorial[2] social and cultural factors. Industrial societies are supposed to be organized through exchange relations within individual atomized competition, which are not conditioned by exogenous factors.

The paradigm has been much criticized for its lack of correspondence with reality but never in terms of its logical consistency. This is the real question, for any interpretative paradigm is an abstract construct that never corresponds with reality. It rests on two foundation stones: its internal logical consistency and its capacity to explain a reality more complex and articulated than its own grounding elements. The theory of embeddedment that is put forward here attacks the paradigm's logical consistency. From this perspective, the reality of industrial development models and dynamics is necessarily very varied since it is conditioned by the play of sociality factors that absorb the spread of rational utilitarian behaviour in a differentiated manner.

The ideal market of perfect competition is inconsistent because it is founded on the absence of organized sociality relations—atomized competition between anonymous sellers and buyers. At the same time, however, it postulates given social conditions—the possibility for buyers and sellers to interact—and automatic effects of an organizational kind—social repercussion of prices, competition, efficiency, productive innnovation and so on. The paradigm's inconsistency does not lie in its asocial nature but in the fact that it also presupposes theoretically impossible sociality conditions. The paradigm can be made consistent only by removing its assumptions regarding sociality. The market exists only in the way it is embedded in various specific combinations of sociality and its impact is mediated through the re-forming of cooperative links by social institutions. This reformulation of the paradigm maintains its explanatory force but has important consequences for the interpretation of economic life. Economic behaviour has a limited autonomy with respect to social and cultural conditions. The point to be underlined is that the modes of development are not always the same but vary according to the way social institutions adapt and react innovatively. This "defect" in the reformulation helps to explain why the paradigm in its inconsistent formulation has resisted criticism so well. Furthermore, its capacity to explain reality was high in the case of the, culturally dominant, industrial countries for a long period up to the oil crises of the 1970s.

The epistemological critique of the market paradigm entails redefining the confines between economics and sociology in industrial societies starting from two basic assumptions: 1) market relations are embedded in social rules and conditions that make them possible but are not generated directly by the market itself; 2) the question of embeddedment is incompatible with the notion of a self-organizing market. Market exchange does not constitute an autonomous organizational form of industrial societies; rather, it has to be related to organizational forms of society that lie outside the market. The market is not at the same time both a regulating and a regulated entity.

The Question of the Market's Social Embeddedment

The question of embeddedment was first posed by Karl Polanyi (1957)[3] in connection with the anthropological theory of pure forms of exchange-based social interaction: those universal phenomena that explain society (on the front of organizational models of social life) and the economy (on the front of procurement, distruibution and use of resources). Recently, the question has been put forward again by the American sociologist Mark Granovetter (1985).

According to Polanyi (1944; 1977) market-competitive behaviour is one of the three basic forms of the social relation of exchange, the other two being reciprocity and redistribution.[4] It is thus important to underline the difference between market exchange on one side and the conceptual axioms of reciprocal exchange and redistribution on the other. The former makes sense only if it is assumed that the market operates free of any social constraint, while the latter are meaningful only when considered within specific forms of social organization. Reciprocity is a form of exchange based either on uncertain or delayed restitution or on restitution to somebody other than the actual donor. Therefore, actions of reciprocal exchange reflect given organizational systems in which givers and receivers act according to pre-established ratonales, rules and times. Similarly, redistributive exchange cannot take place without rules for determining what resources are taken from the direct producers for redistribution, who they are allocated to and in what ratios, who carries it out and the reasons that justify it.

Market exchange, on the contrary, makes sense as an abstract concept only if it is perceived as a finished transaction between actors unaffected by other kinds of organized social relations. The idea that the market is an organizational system confuses the possible results of a set of atomized interactions—defined under abstract conditions that cannot exist in *social* reality—with the operational conditions for this specific set of interactions. As Albert Hirschman has noted, the ideal markets of perfect competition with their large numbers of anonymous buyers and sellers postulated by the market paradigm:

> [F]unction without any prolonged human or social contact between the parties. Under perfect competition there is no room for bargaining, negotiation, remonstration or mutual adjustment and the various operators that contract together need not enter into a recurrent or continuing relationship as a result of which they will get to know each other well (1982:1473).

The different degree of abstraction of the three pure kinds of exchange-based social interaction is evident. Reciprocity and redistribution are meaningless unless they refer to a social order; hence they have to be automatically associated with rules of action that have a common general rationale but diverse contents from case to case. The rationale of reciprocity is made up of the collective interests of a small group with strong direct social bonds, for example the family or a group of friends. The rationale of redistribution, in contrast, consists of the interests and power relationships of a wider and more complex group where social bonds are not so direct, for example tribes, clans or, more generally, national communities. Conceptually incompatible with social organization, market exchange presents itself as a universal instrument without any social substance and for which, as a consequence, socio-cultural variables are unimportant. In other words, embeddedment is a constituent of the concepts of reciprocity and redistribution, whereas the market is conceptually disembedded and thus at a higher level of abstraction. It follows from this that it is only the market that has an inner conceptual tension, in the sense that, unlike the other two pure forms of exchange, it cannot be directly an organizational form of society; and, being grounded in a logical matrix incompatible with social organization, it presupposes an explanation, beyond its own conceptual logic, as to how a growing number of market-based interactions can be reconciled with a social order. Besides, though in an abstract vision an interactive phenomenon can be assumed without any organizational forms, in the concrete world systematic market exchanges cannot take place outside of a favourable social fabric that allows buyers and sellers to meet. Given that these organizational forms cannot spring from the market itself, in order to understand industrial societies we have to explain how a system of market relations is embedded in specific social orders.

The fact that market relations do not constitute an autonomous socio-organizational system does not undermine the usefulness of the abstract model of the market. Neither is it detrimental to the idea put forward first by Weber and then by Braudel that the diffusion of market relations acted as a powerful economic multiplier in the standardization of price-cost ratios and the establishment of rational economic accounting. In fact accounting cannot be equated with organization. The point is that market exchanges do not take place either within the abstract model of an inconceivable atomized society or in a self-organized system involving a set of discrete and contingent competitive relations. They do take place, on the contrary, within contexts of social organization that are built up historically through variable combinations of socio-organizational relations. These combinations undergo great changes so that they can adapt to the disorganizing impact from the spread of individualistic and competitive behaviour, but they have not been replaced by an organizational system deriving directly from the market.

The problem of the social construction of the market, as indicated above, involves addressing certain questions: 1) the main analytical factors in identifying the construction of the market; 2) the impact on interpretational paradigms from failure to address the last question; 3) the ways in which the social construction of the market can be used to interpret processes and trends of the, above all

contemporary, economy as an alternative to the distorted visions produced by the
market paradigm.

The Rationales of Social Cooperation

If we consider that far from being the most important organizer of social life in
the industrial age, the market is on the contrary a disorganizer, the system for
interpreting economic phenomena undergoes a radical change. Now we must
address the question as to how various disorganizing tensions from the diffusion
of market-competitive activities are accomodated within an organization shaped
by other factors.

The interpretation of economic life in the industrial age consists in
combining three complex sets of independent variables: reciprocal relations;
associative/redistributive components; market-competitive tensions. These
variables are based on two pure types of socio-organizational factors expressing
diverse rationales of social cooperation. The first is based on the priority given to
the collective interests of a small group, the second on individual interests
common to a large number of people in the same social condition in terms of
employment or property. All social contexts are characterized by complex
combinations of the two factors, which shape behavioural patterns of
cooperation and economic competition. In this sense the rationales behind social
organizations are never solely inspired by a pure principle of association or
reciprocity, not even in organizations that see themselves as founded on
associative interests, such as trade unions, or on the priority given to an interest
group, such as the family. Associative factors become increasingly important with
industrialization and the spread of individualism because they take on a crucial
role in determining the rules of economic redistribution typical of industrial
societies, where the direct production of resources is separated from their
utilization. Contextually, however, reciprocity-based behaviour continues to
condition economic life.

The question of the social construction of the market is posed in all
societies in the industrial age, characterized by a great density of interactions
based on exchange and the separation between the production and utilization of
resources. Put more precisely, in all those societies in which a large part of
production is not destined for direct consumption by producers and distribution
goes on outside of cooperation within small fixed groups, the problem arises of
explaining how competitive interaction is able to take place in an organized
context and, consequently, how it is regulated by a specific sociality mix.

It is important to underscore that the complex interplay of the three sets of
independent variables functions contextually on two levels. The first is constituted
by the impact of market tensions in a given organizational framework, articulated in
historical combinations of associativity and reciprocity. The second level derives
from the fact that the spread of these tensions produces in turn an unstable
reordering of the social system. The two levels can be distinguished on a logical
basis but, in as much as integrated into a unified process, they do not appear as

distinct phases, which makes analysis more difficult.[5] Market tensions are generated by the diffusion of competitive behaviour, varying with the different social contexts in which it arises. The impact is therefore indirect and contextual with the respective organizational system and this serves to avoid erroneous deterministic explanations by emphasizing the persistence, through change, of strong tensions. In other words, on one side organizational reactions embed competitive behaviour in the social context more effectively and, on the other, they stifle its capacity to spread further. In tandem, the adaptation of associative and reciprocal systems magnifies eventual incompatibilities since the two systems possess different organizational rationales and the greater force of modern associative rationales is unable to eliminate reciprocity-based orientations.

The same result is reached if one applies the theory of the social embeddedment of the market in an analysis based on the motivations for individual actions, as preferred by Weberian-style sociology and most economists. Economic actions grounded in market exchange are based on opposing interests. The buyer wants to buy at the lowest while the seller wants to sell at the highest possible price. It is not plausible to assume that atomized actors, who do not know and trust one another, reach a compromise for reasons of "natural justice"—the whole community will benefit from the "fair price"—or because they in any case foresee the favourable intermediary result. This is demonstrated by the fact that as soon as the opportunity arises, exchange is characterized by swindling. It is all the more likely, the weaker both the associative and reciprocal socio-organizational contexts are. A retailer may demand too high a price if not obliged to display fixed prices (weak associative context) or from an occasional customer (weak reciprocal context). Conversely, it is highly improbable that a buyer will steal a product from a big store equipped with advanced security systems or from a corner store, where reciprocal ties are stronger. From a theoretical standpoint, atomized market behaviour is an abstract model with no rules. In reality, market behaviour occurs according to rules fixed by socio-regulative factors. Concrete actions are, therefore, never atomized but conditioned by the specific context of social regulation.

Strands of Theoretical Reformulation

In order to examine closely the theoretical approach based on the social embeddedment of the economy and before looking at interpretations of economic life, it is worth going back to Polanyi. In his view, a system founded on a self-regulating market is incompatible with any form of sociality bond and ends up destroying society itself. Nevertheless, it is risky to look to Polanyi for inspiration without careful revision of the methodological ambiguities in his approach. In The Great Transformation (1944) he combines micro-analytical tools, typical of anthropology, with a historical reading of economic change in English society between the end of the XVII and the beginning of the XX century. He uses these anthropological tools to demonstrate the natural incompatibility between extended and dominant, generalized competition and any form of social organization. Macro-historical analysis allows him to highlight two forms of transformation that take place in social contexts of industrialization. First, there is the adaptation of traditional sociality contexts due not only to the onslaught of individualistic competition but also to various reactions to this form of aggression. Second, he records the formation of new sociality relations specifically oriented to stemming the damage to society from the unchecked spread of individual competitivity (trade unions, monopolies, cartels, laws and regulations governing economic and professional activities, direct government intervention in the economy and so on). What we have is not an inert combination of the weakening of traditional forms of solidarity and the advent of new contexts of sociality more equipped to resist disintegration induced by rampant individualism. It is, rather, a transformation of sociality contexts as an independent factor in the process of industrialization. For Polanyi, the ways in which these contexts are changed are both the results of and the conditions for industrial transformation.

Consideration of the methodological flaws in Polanyi makes it necessary to readapt the anthropological concepts of reciprocity and redistribution to a different kind of analysis and to see to what extent these same concepts correspond to those of community and association. Unlike other social theorists, the merit of Polanyi is that he directly attacks the paradigm of the self-regulating market. If it is true that industrial societies are founded on economic behaviour becoming independent from traditional conditioning, then the question must also be put as to how far this autonomy from factors of sociality in general can extend. He underlines the fact that full independence of a market-regulated economy means the subordination of society to the laws of the market and that such subordination is incompatible with the very survival of society.

A self-regulating market demands nothing less than the institutional separation of society into an economic and political sphere. Such a dichotomy is, in effect, merely the restatement, from the point of view of society as a whole, of the existence of a self-regulating market...Such an institutional pattern could not function unless society was somehow subordinated to its requirements. A market economy can exist only in a market society...A market economy must comprise all elements of industry, including labour, land and money...To include them in the market mechanism means to subordinate the substance of society to the laws of the market (1944/75:71).

Labour, land and money are not true commodities, he notes, but in order to function the market has to commodify these elements; hence it is based on three fundamental fictitious commodities. To carry out this operation, the market needs regulatory institutions in industrial societies where exchange becomes the predominant form of economic behaviour. It is this fictitious commodification, however, that is incompatible with the working of the other two institutional forms of complex social regulation, reciprocity and redistribution. The historical evidence in *The Great Transformation* is wholly aimed at demonstrating that the history of industrialization is based, on one side, on the spread of the market into the sphere of true commodities and, on the other, on the reaction of socio-regulative contexts to impede the complete subordination of the fictitious commodities or, in other words, to save society from certain death.[6] For Polanyi too, therefore, the problem of the social embeddedment of the market presents itself as the market's need to *generate*, though not automatically, institutions of social organization.

The reason for his choice of methodology can be found in the posthumously published *The Livelihood of Man* (1977). In this work he attempts to incorporate conceptual tools from structuralist anthropolgy into an economic analysis based on the paradigm of atomized individual action. The methodological shortcoming lies in his failure to do just this; however it does not vitiate the adapting of anthropological concepts to the different perspective of macro-social research.

Polanyi's approach is based on two concepts: forms of integration and supporting structures. The first comprise reciprocity, redistribution and exchange and are defined as follows:

> Forms of integration thus designate the institutionalized movements through which the elements of the economic process—from material resources and labour to the transportation, storage, and distribution of goods—are connected (Polanyi, 1977:35).

Supporting structures are the equivalent of what I have defined as the socio-organizational factors underlying relations of reciprocity and redistribution. According to Polanyi, "the supporting structures, their basic organization, and their validation spring from the social sphere"(p.37). The question is why exchange, defined as a movement "between any two dispersed or random points in the system,"(p.36) is in need of a supporting structure. His answer is that,

> ...exchange, as a form of integration, is dependent on the presence of a market system, an institutional pattern which, contrary to common assumptions, does not originate in random actions of exchange (p.37).

It is an unconvincing answer, and not only because it invalidates analogy with the other two concepts in as much as the socio-organizational form is included in the definition of reciprocity and redistribution but not in that of market exchange. While symmetry or hierarchy cannot exist without an organized system, chance is by definition the contrary of such a system. It is unconvincing also because it ends by adapting a conceptual tool to existing reality. In other words, the fact that a widespread exchange system does not exist outside of socio-institutional contexts cannot be inserted a posteriori into an abstract model that is by definition incompatible with them. On the other hand, it is precisely Polanyi's historical analysis that demonstrates there is no need to invent an impossible supporting social structure generated by the market in order to explain its forms of institutionalization. It is enough simply to combine changes in the other two forms of sociality. If we did not have families, different community systems, associations, the state and trade unions, exchange would not be regulated but neither would a market society exist. Even those economic institutions, such as enterprises, the stock exchange and banks, that are normally held to be creatures of the market are in reality inspired, in as much as organizations based on cooperation, by criteria of sociality rather than by competitive goals.

What Polanyi considers as the market's social institutions can be traced back to socio-organizational factors of the mainly associative kind. As we will see shortly, he transplants the anthropological concept of redistribution into a macro analysis and as a consequence overlooks the continuity between socio-organizational factors, above all and increasingly of the associative kind, and redistributive processes.

Reciprocity and Social Structuring of Industrial Economies

As we have seen above, the abstract concept of market exchange is incompatible with forms of social organization while in the real world systems of market exchange prove to be conditioned by behavioural rules, without which they would not be feasible. This question has given rise to a series of solutions that are inadequate because they attribute sociality to elements inherent in the very concept of market. Whether in the structural versions of Marx, Durkheim and Polanyi or in the Weberian methodology of action the concept of market becomes a *monstrosity*: an abstract construction grounded on real assumptions (the rules of cooperation that permit competition and the social market system) which are its negation. The starting-point for overcoming this impasse is the interplay of the three sets of independent variables which I began to illustrate above. But first it is necessary to clarify how the concepts of reciprocity and redistribution work as interpretational tools for macro analysis of the social embeddedment of the economy.[7]

The anthropological approach is useful because it allows us to identify a typology of social exchange relations that are significant in terms of organizational rationale or the lack of one. It is a question of adapting the concepts formulated for the anthropological methodology so that they are compatible with an approach oriented to the analysis of social organization. Market exchange has already been discussed. Before moving on to reciprocity, it is worthwhile to discard explicitly the possibility that passing from a micro- to a macro-approach entails on the one hand losing the socio-organizational significance of the concepts or, on the other, neglecting any other pure typologies of social relations associated with different organizational systems.[8] The socio-organizational significance of the concepts is illustrated below. Also the possible existence of other pure typologies is resolved in the discussion below of the homologation in principle of the concept of redistribution with that of associative relation. As Weber maintains, at a purely conceptual level there are no organizational relations other than associative or communal ones.

Reciprocity is a type of social relation that only has meaning within an organizational system, because exchange is not concluded in a single act, transactions are potentially inequitable and the commitment to reciprocate is vague or only implicit.[9] For this reason, reciprocity refers to forms of social organization involving a limited number of individuals who know specifically of one another's existence, engage in personal contact and share a common collective goal. Both in the case of reciprocity and in that of association the sense of the social relationship is given by common interests, their orientation being reflected in the difference in underlying organizational form. To take this distinction to its extreme limit, one could say that whereas in reciprocity the defence of a group interest requires some members to make individual sacrifices, associative relations directly promote and defend the individual interests of all members in an association as against non-members. The difference is manifest if instances from opposite ends of the spectrum are compared, less prone to assuming a mixed meaning, such as the family and the trade union. The common interest of the family assumes a meaning independently of individual interests and involves unequal sacrifices and exchanges. The common interest of the trade union is not separate from that of its members and whenever some of them systematically benefit more than others from union activity, this weakens the organization and can in the long run lead to its break-up.

The question of the priority of group interest over the immediate individual interests constitutes the core of the concept of reciprocity as a factor of social organization. From this also derives the fact that the interaction between reciprocity and market is substantially different from that between association and market. We are here entering a domain of analysis where pure concepts no longer exist but are transformed into tools for interpreting a complex and hence mixed reality. An example will clarify this point. Consider the difference between the economic strategy of a family business, in which the reciprocal factor is strong, and that of a large enterprise, organized in line with associative factors, such as obtaining maximum profit, the institutionalized conflict between the interests of the owner and management and those of the workers, and the formal separation of roles. Studies of family farming have highlighted many elements in this difference (Friedmann, 1979; Shanin, 1987; Mottura 1988). From the perspective of the theories founded on the market paradigm, what emerged from these studies was viewed more as something specific to the nature of agriculture than as a starting-point from which to build a different model of the interface between industrial development and socio-organizational factors. More recently, we have begun to understand the importance of this interaction between reciprocity and market through the attention paid to ethnic entrepreneurship and to the success of more community-based variants of capitalism, as in Japan or the third Italy.

Before making some brief historical comments on the varying role played by reciprocity in the construction of the models of social embeddedment of the economy, it is useful to mention the great variety of reciprocal systems and their internal power relations. Each individual is involved in many different and changing systems of reciprocity, from the nuclear household to the kinship network, from one or more circles of friends to the neighbourhood or village, from the workplace and workmates to school and fellow-students. These systems may be more or less powerful in subordinating immediate individual interests to the commonly shared group goal. Furthermore, reciprocal systems may dispose of more or less resources for achieving collective aims. Systems rich in resources are also more powerful in the sense that compensation is seen to be more likely. But the reverse is not true: a poor family is often, though not always, a powerful system with few resources.

Reciprocal systems may be voluntary (friends) or ascriptive (the family). This variability is important and plays a different role at different times and under different conditions. By way of example, territorial mobility tends to lessen involvement in reciprocal networks, but emigration can be a source of new economically very important networks, as is the case with ethnic entrepreneurship and the migratory chain.

In as far as they are socio-organizational contexts, reciprocal networks are power systems in the sense that they are endowed with the force to impose cooperation even on the unwilling. Family and patriarchy are the most studied themes. The point to underline is that even in terms of power reciprocal contexts differ from associative ones. Not only is a father-boss different from a foreman, but his power also tends to change along different lines with the development of technologically advanced modern family businesses, the urbanization of the poor rural strata in developing countries, and the growth of the informal sector. Likewise, managers and foremen have a different power, exercised in different ways, in more reciprocity-oriented enterprises than in those characterized more by associative divisions, as shown by Dore's comparative studies (1986 and 1987) on the difference between Japan and the UK.

The diversity of and the changes in the power structure of reciprocal systems is connected with both the meaning and importance of common goals and with some general conditions. In theory, it is true that reciprocal patterns of organization are far removed from the individual autonomy that emerged with the development of industrial society. For this reason, the structuring of power based on reciprocity can be extremely authoritarian. In voluntary organizations, by contrast, the power structure can be loose. The best example is that of a group of friends. But in this case too, whenever the group goal is more demanding, the power structure can change and become more authoritarian and hierarchical. Take a group of friends on an adventurous holiday in a difficult environment. The most able and expert will become the leader while those who are most in difficulty will end up in a condition of subordination. This may lead to a weakening or even break-up of their friendship.

Following these considerations, we should not idealize reciprocal social organizations as being reflected in less authoritarian power structures than those in bureaucratic organizations. Nevertheless, reciprocal patterns of social organization are more disposed than large bureaucracies to change their internal power structure in order to accomodate a growing need for individual autonomy and self-fulfilment, at least under certain conditions. The best example is the, still incomplete, transformation of family power structure in industrial countries. Age and gender discrimination have decreased and organizational goals are more often negotiated than imposed by the family head. Individual vocations and aspirations are taken into account even when they conflict with traditional ways of safeguarding family objectives.

A greater flexibility of reciprocal systems in supporting individual autonomy compared to large bureaucratic organizations is not a paradox if we consider that individuals are closer to the centre of decision-making and thus in a better position to influence collective action strategies. Correspondingly, the decision-making apparatus may be more receptive to individual expectations. This flexibility is found only in industrial societies when the diffusion of competitive behaviour and the concomitant emergence of individual identity in a comprehensively changing social context, dominated by associative patterns, leads to the dismantling of the social order grounded in a strict subordination of individual interests to those of groups based on reciprocity. Moreover, this process is conditioned by the fact that the opportunities open to such groups to achieve their objectives must not be too limiting. For instance, negotiation of the power structure is more likely to occur in families with a wide range of opportunities than in those condemned to struggle for bare survival.

During the history of industrial society orientation towards reciprocity has declined and changed considerably, but it has continued to play a role of prime importance in generating the propensity to cooperate. Elsewhere (Mingione, 1997), I have examined the historical tempi and typologies of this transformation, so here I will confine myself to some pertinent observations aimed at putting social substance back into the analysis of contemporary economies.

The persistence of reciprocity rationales has affected all spheres of economic life, including those formalized and bureaucratic contexts that in theory are totally structured by associative orientations. However, the propensity towards reciprocity rationales is manifest in two areas: the organization of household economies and of family reproductive strategies (in the broad sense that covers the importance assumed by kinship and friendship networks in structuring both entrepreneurship and work opportunities); and the organization of small enterprises and local economic systems. Starting from the organizational and cultural rationales of peasant families, reciprocal orientations have introduced into industrial economies patterns conflicting with the utilitarian and productivist models of the big economic and political apparatuses, which are more extended and flexible and less sensitive to immediate profit and industrial concentration but not always resistant to economic innovation.

More attention is now being paid to economic organizations where reciprocal orientation is very important—from networks (Castells, 1996) to the systems of small firms, from ethnic entrepreneurship to the Japanese organization of the *keiretsu* (Dore, 1986 and 1987)—and the question of mutual trust and share capital (a local ambience with a large communal predisposition for cooperation) is under discussion. This has crucial theoretical consequences. Orientation towards reciprocity is by no means a traditional organizational factor that is incompatible with the development of individualized societies. On the contrary, this orientation has undergone substantial transformation and regeneration as a prime regulator of economic life. Moreover, the present post-Fordist transition is characterized by a more complex mix of associative and reciprocal patterns than the preceding transition, in which institutionalization, formalization, bureaucratization, economies of scale and concentration seemed to restrict the economic role of reciprocal organization more and more and confine it to the private affective sphere of nuclear families (Parsons and Bales, 1955). As I will further point out in my concluding remarks, understanding of current transformations cannot be achieved without once again paying full attention to reciprocity as a factor in the embedding of the economy in society.

Associative Sociality and Redistributive Processes in the Industrial Age

Homologation of the anthropological concept of redistribution and the sociological concept of associative system is destined to remain incomplete.[10] From the perspective of macro analysis, redistributive processes do not constitute an autonomous system of social organization. Like the market, the process of redistribution is regulated in different ways by the complex and changing interaction between the two socio-organizational systems. In this sense, it is inexact to reduce redistribution conceptually to the associative system. First, it excludes the play of reciprocal factors in orienting the rationales of redistributive processes and, second, there is the risk of neglecting the partially independent role played by political processes in regulating economic life. On the other hand, for the sociologist there is a problem with making redistributive processes into a totally independent factor in social organization since this does not explain the social matrix of the forms of power. Although the concept is not fully worked out, I will try to show that the associative rationale takes on an economic meaning only if related to redistributive processes and that in industrial societies these processes are mainly inspired by associative principles.

In an anthropological approach, redistribution takes place within a closed and limited organizational context. In the areas traditionally studied by anthropologists—primitive societies, tribes and isolated villages—the dominant factor is reciprocity. A varying share of resources is withdrawn from the narrower reciprocal contexts in which they are directly produced and redistributed by the community's political chiefs. The latter are chosen according to power rationales consistent with the rationales that originate in the reciprocal systems themselves and which are often, though not always,[11] inspired by an intertwining of patriarchy and gerontocracy. Redistribution is carried out following rules laid down by tradition, which in general reflect three requirements: to put off consumption of excess resources in anticipation of periods of scarcity; to privilege and underscore the power structure and by means of the latter finance the community's plans for expansion, in many though not all cases through wars and territorial conquests; to assist community members who are not sufficiently protected by the narrow system of reciprocity, such as widowers, the childless elderly, the disabled, orphans and so on. From the micro perspective of the anthropological approach, this form of exchange takes on a different significance from that of reciprocity in the narrow sense. For those interested in macro analysis, it is simply a question of a broader vis-à-vis a narrower sphere of reciprocity.

The question of redistributive processes is posed differently in industrial societies. The latter are characterized by the separation between the sphere of direct production of resources and that of their consumption, by complex forms of the division of labour, by the diffusion of market exchange relations and the random interaction of strangers, and by the bureaucratization and formalization of political relations. The typology of final ends for a part of the redistributive process is not very different from that identified by the anthropological approach, just wider and more complicated. It is the socio-organizational context underlying the rationales behind these ends that is substantially different, just as the ways of producing resources are different. It is, in fact, the industrial methods of production that lead to a new redistribution of the product between the different subjects involved in creating it: not only capital and labour but also different types of workers, representatives of capital and those working in the indirectly productive sectors. Both redistribution by the state, the kind that in some of its ends-oriented rationales still resembles the anthropological redistributive process, and private redistribution are no longer controllable by reciprocal factors, or only to a very limited extent. Hence the expansion and growing importance of associative factors.

Associative sociality takes on a socio-economic meaning only under two conditions: first, there are common individual interests to defend; second, the defence of these interests impacts on redistributive processes, whether public or private. The sociological tradition has accumulated a considerable store of knowledge on the contextual growth of associative sociality and the industrial economy and on the meaning of organizational factors in relation to redistributive processes. I have in mind not only the Marxist line of class struggle but also the Durkheimian vision of organic solidarity and Weber's theory of rationalization, bureaucratization and the spread of associations of individuals linked by common individual interests. However there is the danger that this approach will continue to overshadow the persistent role of reciprocal factors in redistributive processes; this also goes for the internal inconsistencies and the complexity of the socio-organizational mixes that the different associative and reciprocal systems continue to produce in response to the tensions arising from the spread of market-competitive behaviour. For all these reasons, the conceptual coupling of associative factors and redistribution is plausible as a simplification on condition that the analysis focuses sufficiently on the importance of reciprocity also with respect to redistributive processes.

Within this approach we need to define the area of autonomy that the political system carves out in relation to associative interests and instances of reciprocity. It is therefore important to mention the question of power inside associative contexts and of their presumed monopoly on the representation of political interests. The idea that associative contexts always express a power structure founded on the best possible defence of the interests at stake is simplistic and does not take into account that the influence of reciprocal relations extends into associative contexts. Hence the sundry forms of nepotism and particularism. In addition, the political system in individualized societies carves out wide areas of autonomy with respect to the mechanical representation of interests. This happens both because the political and bureaucratic apparatus develops its own interest in retaining power and because political practice imposes compromise regarding legitimation or hegemony also on interests that are not directly represented by the classes in power. For the same reasons, the reduction of the redistributive dynamic to associative sociality, though useful, will always remain incomplete.

Furthermore, it is worthwhile to point out that almost all political systems in the industrial age have equipped themselves to represent and therefore govern associative interests, which are divided and compete for the redistribution of resources. Reciprocal systems come into play as elements inside the associative organizational context: nepotism and networks in the political class or in the bureaucracy. Present-day societies are characterized by the growing importance of innovative and dynamic reciprocal contexts that interfere with and fragment associative interests. The question of the future of socio-political systems concerns precisely the kinds of reaction to this transformation.

Conclusion

The majority of social scientists see the market as an autonomous sphere of modern social life that with the development of individualism becomes dominant and conditions all aspects of our life.[12] As a consequence we have approaches that, whatever the discipline or method, are grounded in the unqualified dominance of atomized individual competitive behaviour. This is the case of economists of neo-classical derivation for whom a social context exists only as a sub-product of market relations. However, in a less explicit fashion, the market paradigm has penetrated deep into all the approaches adopted by social scientists, in particular in their ways of interpreting economic relationships.[13] In broad outline, the subordination of dominant social theories to the market paradigm has systematically led to various interconnected analytical distortions. The tendency for industrialization and modernization to move along homogeneous, standardized lines has been exaggerated. Not enough attention has been paid to the preservation of customs and traditions even within processes of change. The economic importance of material reproduction relations and the population's life conditions and strategies has been pushed into the background. The social conditions and combinations that differ from those in the hegemonic patterns first of the UK and then the US have been underestimated, in particular the combinations where reciprocal factors maintain a relatively greater importance. In other words, the dominance of the market paradigm has magnified out of proportion the importance of certain phenomena, such as monetary consumption, regular employee jobs, large firms and financial relations. Conversely, it has practically ignored other phenomena viewed as economically immaterial or dying out: unpaid work (domestic and care work), self-employment, family businesses, non-monetary or informal consumption relations, subsistence economies. All of this has also been reflected in a marked overvaluation of the universalistic tendencies of social homogenization, with little importance being given to the role of persistent differences also within the processes of modernization.

In reality, the development of industrial economies has been discontinuous throughout historical cycles (Pirenne, 1953; Arrighi, 1996; Mingione, 1997) and diversified into a growing number of social and political regimes (Esping-Andersen, 1990; Mingione 1991 and 1997) in which different combinations of reciprocity and associative sociality have materialized. Market tensions have given a powerful thrust in a single progressive direction, while the renewal of sociality and indispensable cooperative behaviour, varying according to the conditions and resources found in the diverse contexts, has consolidated differences and discontinuities. It is perfectly understandable that different kinds of social visions and the market paradigm have united, leading to acritical subordination to uniform models centred on the inevitability of technological progress, economic growth, the monetization of social ties and the superiority of individual utility over other relations. Indeed, the construction of modern social theory took place in tandem with western industrial societies and it has always demonstrated a greater power to explain these compared to other societies and cultures. In this sense, the overvaluation of industrial tendencies is built into the theoretical approach since throughout a long historical phase it was an effective tool for simplifying the complexity typical of those environments in which the social sciences were taking shape.[14]

The union of social visions and the market paradigm assumed particular forms during the "thirty glorious years" from the end of the second world war to the oil crises in the 1970s, a period subsequently called Fordist or welfarist. Economic and social analysis concentrated on the virtuous connection between economic growth and the importance of economies of scale and the big bureaucratic and organizational apparatuses. It is in this very regard that the iron link between the market paradigm and associative systems, representation of organized interests and full formalization of social relations was forged. What has been interpreted as organized capitalism (Offe, 1985; Lash and Urry, 1987) is in part the result of a shortsighted ethnocentric view and the predominance of the market paradigm and in part a real phenomenon. A prolonged phase of economic transformation subsidized by global market penetration under conditions favourable to the advanced countries allowed them to attenuate the inconsistencies inside the social organization systems. The latter leaned increasingly too far in the associative/redistributive direction and were oriented towards promoting forms of social selection based on productivity and consumerism. It was on these conditions that the Fordist social and employment regimes were founded, centred on the powerful economic role of nation-states, the institutionalization of worker, employer, artisan and professionals' organizations, the containment of industrial strife, full adult male employment and the success of breadwinner regimes. From this derived the fact that for many years increasingly regulated markets stayed competitive and there were apparently unending trends towards the development of forms of industrialization that were conflictual, divided and unequal but organized.

Let us shift our gaze onto the last twenty years and adopt a less ethnocentric methodological approach, focussing also on the contribution of reciprocal factors. The immediate impression we have is of a marked increase in the inconsistencies both within the socio-organizational processes, where what are defined as informal activities are one indicator of tensions, and between these processes and the market's disorganizing tendencies, reflected in the spread of laissez-faire policies that magnify inequalities and social privation.

Even looking at only the advanced industrial countries, societies of the present day are neither disorganized nor less organized than those of the 1950s or 1960s. Social-organizational balances have recently become more complicated because the play of reciprocal factors is more manifest and important, though often in new ways compared with the contexts of reciprocity typical of pre-industrial traditions. What we have is a process that has taken society's interpreters by surprise and which is accompanied by wide organizational rifts, different from those characteristic of societies in the preceding phase. But observation of the globalization processes and the spread of informational and telematic networks, and financial conglomerates and various forms of economic consortia and networks could lead one to maintain that capitalism today is as organized as ever. Nevertheless, the internal tensions characterizing the diverse reorganizational processes in present-day society must also be taken into consideration. Not least is the fact that societies where associative contexts are weaker are less conflictual but also less governable by a central power, more fragmented and afflicted by new fissures, with a growing part of society being excluded from the life chances and conditions enjoyed by the majority of their fellow citizens.

Phenomena of growing importance at present include the role of cultural diversity and small firms in the structuring of different patterns of local economy, the impact of working career instability and of the increasing heterogeneity of family systems undergoing profound changes, and the emergence of the question of social exclusion (Castel, 1995; Mingione, 1996). In order to understand them and what other phenomena like globalization, neo-localism and computerization effectively consist of, we need to emphasize that the renewal of socially cooperative behaviour, useful for increasingly unstable social, family and work biographies, intertwines with the decline in forms of regulation that developed during the golden age of Fordism. That is to say, the complex play of social embeddedment of the economy has to be brought to light starting with the areas that have long remained in the shadows: from the economic role of social reproductive relations to the importance of reciprocal networks, from the question of persistent diversity to the problem of the discontinuity of processes of economic development.

NOTES

1. The "dogma of the fixed wage fund" allows one to assume that wages and employment levels depend solely on labour market competition and the dynamic of the economic cycle.

2. As Hirschman maintains, this operation serves to provide economic legitimacy to the detriment of sociological legitimacy, which "it could rightfully have been claimed for the way, so unlike the perfect-competition model, most markets function in the real world." (1982: 1473)

3. Polanyi maintains that "the human economy, then, is embedded and enmeshed in institutions, economic and non economic. The inclusion of non economic is vital. For religion or government may be as important for the structure and functioning of the economy as monetary institution or the availability of tools and machines themselves that lighten the toil of labour." (1957: 250)

4. Anthropology studies systems of social organization that are relatively closed and homogeneous from a cultural point of view and not particularly affected by outside interference, social mobility and intense interaction with strangers. In this sense, as will be seen, in order to be used for macro social analysis the tools of anthropology have to be adapted. In any case, generally speaking, the anthropological classification of pure forms of exchange constitutes a useful starting-point in interpreting factors of social organization. Even if other classifications are possible (see, for example, Davis, 1972; Cheal, 1988) they all derive from the "pure" rationales of reciprocity, redistribution and the market.

5. As will be seen, Polanyi, who talks of "forms of integration" rather than socio-organizational mixes, explicitly raises the problem and maintains that " ... the forms of integration do not represent 'stages' of development. No sequence in time is implied. Several subordinate forms may be present alongside of the dominant one, which may itself recur after a temporary eclipse." (1957:256)

6. "Social history in the nineteenth century was thus the result of a double movement: the extension of the market organization in respect to genuine commodities was accompanied by its restriction in respect to fictitious ones." (1944/75: 76)

7. The compatibility between reciprocity and community is easy to explain because the distance between sociology and anthropology in respect of the methods used to study the phenomenon is not great. The closeness of the terms and the greater precision of the concept of reciprocity in evoking the socio-organizational rationale are not enough to explain the preference expressed herein for the anthropological term. The decisive factor is that the term "community" takes on a wide range of meanings both in everyday language and in sociology. In common language "community" defines not only small organizations based on reciprocal exchanges but also a nation, large town, political party and so on. In sociological terminology the family is not a community, but thousands of sociologists and economists scattered throughout the world and strangers to one another constitute a scientific community. In this sense, the use that I make of the concept is more clearly defined by the organizational orientations evoked by the term "reciprocity."

8. The fact that in the real world we almost always find complicated mixes of reciprocity and association does not affect the significance of the concepts, but rather how they are used to interpret different forms of social organization in which now reciprocity now associativity predominates or the organizational orientations strain against one another. For instance, a worker may decide not to join in a strike so as not to put his job at risk and his family in difficulty; or an employer may choose to make concessions to his workers against the employers' association line in order not to weaken the good climate of cooperation in his firm.

9. Among many others, let me mention the following definitions of "reciprocity" and "redistribution" by the American anthropologist Marshall Sahlins (1988), explicitly inspired by Polanyi: "On a very general view, the array of economic transactions in the ethnographic record may be resolved into two types. First, those 'vice-versa' movements between two parties known familiarly as 'reciprocity.' The second, centralized movements: collection from members of a group, often under one hand, and redivision within this group, this is 'pooling' or 'redistribution' ... Their social organizations are very different. True, pooling and reciprocity may occur in the same social contexts—the same close kinsmen that pool their resources in household commensality, for instance, also as individuals share things with one another—but the precise social relations of pooling and reciprocity are not the same. Pooling is socially a *within* relation, the collective action of a group. Reciprocity is a *between* relation, the action and reaction of two parties. (pp.188-9)

10. In a recent contribution inspired by Polanyi, Cella (1997) uses the Polanyian concept of redistribution in a different way: he considers it to be independent and equates it with the political sphere. For this reason, to the three forms of exchange formulated by Polanyi—market, redistribution and reciprocity—he adds a fourth generated by association. As in Streeck and Schmitter (1985), this last form is limited to the impact at a private level of the associative organizations representing the economic interests of employers, workers, artisans, retailers and so on. As is explained here and more fully in the first chapter of Mingione (1997), Cella's approach is wrong since it attributes to politics full autonomy from the social contexts that give rise to power relationships. In my case, what still remains to be defined is how the political sphere carves out its own autonomous space to prevent it being prey to complete social determinism. (Poggi, 1992)

11. In reality, the selection procedures of the political class reflect the most useful features for achieving the goal of the greatest wellbeing for the community, thereby recalling also Weber's concept of charisma.

12. According to Granovetter, "the majority view among sociologists, anthropologists, political scientists, and historians, sees the economy as an increasingly separate, differentiated sphere in modern society, with economic transactions defined no longer by the social or kinship obligations of those transacting but by rational calculation of individual gain. It is sometimes further argued that the traditional situation is reversed: instead of economic life being submerged in social relations, these relations become an epiphenomenon of the market."(1985: 428)

13. Hirschman (1970 and 1977) has very effectively criticized economic approaches for their incapacity to take into account the independent impact of political power. A similarly trenchant criticism can be based on the independent impact of factors of social organization.

14. As Granovetter rightly says, "the idealized markets of perfect competition have survived intellectual attack in part because self-regulating economic structures are politically attractive to many. Another reason for this survival...is that the elimination of social relations from economic analysis removes the problem of order from the intellectual agenda, at least in the economic sphere."(1985: 484) These arguments are even more convincing if supplemented by the consideration that in any event the modern social sciences have been characterized by a marked ethnocentrism.

BIBLIOGRAPHY

G. Arrighi, *The Long XX Century*. London: Verso, 1994.

R. Castel, *Les métamorphoses de la question sociale. Une chronique du salariat*. Paris: Fayard, 1995.

M. Castells, *The Rise of Network Society*. Oxford: Basil Blackwell, 1996.

G. Cella, *Tre forme di scambio*. Bologna: Il Mulino, 1997.

D. Cheal, *The Gift Economy*. New York: Routledge, 1998.

J. Davis, "Gifts and the UK Economy," *Man*, 7, No.3, 1972, pp. 408-29.

R. Dore, *Flexible Rigidities. Industrial Policy and Structural Adjustment in the Japanese Economy 1979-80*. London: The Athlone Press, 1986.

R. Dore, *Take Japan Seriously. A Confucian Perspective on Leading Economic Issues*. London: The Athlone Press, 1987.

G. Esping-Andersen, *The Three Worlds of Welfare Capitalism*. Cambridge: Polity Press, 1990.

H. Friedmann, "World Market, State and Family Farm: Social Bases of Household Production in the Era of Wage Labour," Cologne, *Comparative Studies in Societies and History*, No. 20, 1979, pp. 545-86.

M. Granovetter, "Economic Action and Social Structure: the Problem of Embeddedness," *American Journal of Sociology*, 91, No.3, 1985, pp. 481-510.

A.O. Hirshman, *Exit, Voice and Loyalty. Responses to decline in Firms, Organizations and States*. Cambridge, MA: Harvard University Press. 1970

A.O. Hirshman, *The Passions and the Interests*. Princeton, NJ: Princeton University Press, 1977.

A.O. Hirshman, "Rival Interpretations of Market Society: Civilizing, Destructive of Feeble?," *Journal of Economic Literature*, 20, No. 4, 1982 pp. 1463-84.

S. Lash, and J. Urry, *The End of Organized Capitalism*. Cambridge: Polity Press, 1987.

E. Mingione, *Fragmented Societies: A Sociology of Economic Life beyond the Market Paradigm*. Oxford: Basil Blackwell, 1991.

E. Mingione, *Sociologia della vita economica*. Roma: NIS, 1997.

E. Mingione, (ed.), *Urban Poverty and the Underclass: a Reader*. Oxford: Basil Blackwell, 1996.

G. Mottura, "La persistenza secolare. Appunti su agricoltura contadina ed agricoltura familiare nelle societa industriali," *Materiali di Discussione*, 38, Modena: Università degli Studi, 1988.

C. Offe, *Disorganized Capitalism: Contemporary Transformations of Work and Politics*. Cambridge: Polity Press, 1985.

T. Parsons and R. Bales, *Family, Socialization, and Interaction Process*. New York: The Free Press, 1955.

H. Pirenne, "Stages in the Social History of Capiatlism," in R. Bendix, S. Lispet (eds), *Class, Status and Power: a Reader in Social Stratification*. Glencoe, IL: The Free Press, 1953, pp. 501-17.

G. Poggi, *Lo stato: natura, sviluppo, prospettive*. Bologna: Il Mulino, 1992.

K. Polanyi, *The Great Transformation*. Boston: Beacon Press, 1944/1975.

K. Polanyi, "The Economy as Instituted Process," in K. Polanyi; C. Arensberg and H. Pearson (eds) *Trade and Market in the Early Empires. Economies in History and in Theory*. Glencoe, IL: The Free Press, 1957.

K. Polanyi, *The Livelihood of Man*. New York: Academic Press Inc., 1977.

M. Sahlins, *Stone Age Economics*. Chicago: Aldine, 1988. [Repr. 1980, London and New York, Routledge].

T. Shanin, (ed.), *Peasants and Peasant Societies*. Oxford: Basil Blackwell, 1987.

W. Streeck and P. Schmitter, "Community, Market, State and Associations?," in W. Streeck and P. Schmitter (eds) *Private Interests Government. Beyond Market and State*. London: Sage, 1985.

Chapter 3

About the Possibility of Reversing the Process of Commodification: The Scope of the "Non-Profit Economy"

Michele Cangiani

The debate over "non-profit" activity and the "third sector"—"third" in relation to capitalist enterprises and to the state—has widened over the last few years. It is essential to try to understand the situation that has aroused this interest, since the phenomenon in itself is not new, and stirred up theoretical and political discussions also in the past. In the following pages I will refer in particular to Italy, where the interest in the third sector revived later than in other countries, but has recently greatly accelerated. There, in 1996, bills which determine the characters, the juridical status and the fiscal standard of non-profit organizations and the newly institutionalized bank-foundations were drawn up. A pool of organizations constituted an "ethical bank" dedicated to financing non-profit activities. Numerous conferences, exhibitions and publications concerning the third sector were launched. Several associations such as the "Forum of the third sector" were created with the purpose of coordinating non-profit organizations and representing their interests. Yet, the character and the very definition of non-profit activity are still theoretically and *politically* at stake.

The Neo-Liberal Age
We now live in an age dominated by a neo-liberalist ideology. (According to Ignacio Ramonet, editor of *Le Monde Diplomatique*, it has in fact become the *"pensée unique,"* the only way of thinking.) This domination is a result of the crisis of the institutional system that came into being during the post-war years, generally described as Fordist-Keynesian. The technical and organizational characteristics of this system, as adopted by industrial mass-production during the first half of the century, have been backed up by neo-corporative consent and state-intervention, which serves to guarantee both the development of the economy and the social-democratic compromise. The "warfare-welfare state" (O'Connor 1973, p. 171) has become a complement of the Fordist method of market expansion based on the increase of the volume of production and the number of wage-earners, and of productivity and (in lesser measure) wages. In the state budget, costs that depend on development and on its complex consequences as they affect society as a whole are 'socialised'. In general, state spending aims to promote development, in the form of capital accumulation. The

breakdown of such spending—as well, obviously, as that of state revenues—is the result of the struggle between different classes and groups, representing different interests. From the post-war period to the seventies, economic growth and the respective strength of the different classes allowed a level of state spending high enough to support aggregate demand, as well as budget composition able to satisfy different interests. Then this 'golden age' of capitalist development entered into crisis.

The crisis is at once a precondition and a result of the new exigencies of capitalist accumulation. Such exigencies are both political (the need to deprive the working classes of power) and economic (the need to slow down inflation and reduce the cost of the labour-force). With this end in mind, companies are, on the one hand, trying to reduce wages, supplementary benefits and job-stability, as well as the rights and autonomy won by workers in factories, the job-market and society. On the other hand, they are engaged in a technological and organizational shake-up, based on computerization. Labour-saving investments are being made; labour-processes and industrial relations are in the process of changing; decentralization, sub-contracting and various forms of partnership, also made possible by new technologies, are tending to expand on a global level. Global competition compels companies to save labour in order to increase productivity. Technological unemployment cannot be reabsorbed, to the extent that the global market remains too narrow, owing to the twofold tendency to lower wages and to invest profits in financial and speculative activities.

The slowing down of economic development and the decline of employment (regular employment, at least) bring about a reduction of fiscal revenue and compulsory contributions. Reducing the public debt and balancing the budget become, for the state, more difficult. A solution to this problem is sought by means of a restructuring of the state budget, the privatization of state activities, and the deregulation of the market economy. In the state budget, what is called for is an increase in spending and investments that are at least indirectly productive (infrastructures, services, education and all scientific research directly serving economic growth, in addition to transfers and concessions on taxes and contributions benefitting businesses). At the same time, non-productive spending (mainly for welfare and social security) must be reduced. The intention is to guarantee a satisfactory level of profit, justifying it with the (fallacious) argument that only in this way can unemployment be absorbed.

In addition to the prospect of profit, capitalist investment requires the opening up of new areas. This explains both the privatization of economic activities and services managed by the state and the dismantling on a global scale of all the safeguards, limitations and guidelines that public authorities had laid down in relation to what is called the free play of the market, but which is, in fact, the freedom of action of big business and financial capital.

In order to achieve all these results—but also simply in sheer revulsion at the very idea—any development of the social democratic compromise in the direction of a "popular government" (I have taken this expression from Karl

Polanyi's *The Great Transformation* [1944], to underline the recurrence of similar reactions to the crisis) is fiercely contested—even with methods that are far from pacific, legal or open.

The neo-liberal remedy for the "fiscal crisis of the state" is thus the very reverse of that proposed by O'Connor (1973, p. 291), which consisted in socialising profits at least in part and passing from the "use of political and social means to achieve individual goals" to "a socialist perspective that must attempt to define needs in collective terms." Almost a quarter of a century has passed since O'Connor elaborated his ideas, and we still have to face—as Federico Caffè points out (1979, p. x) in the preface to an Italian edition of O'Connor's book—"the real process of cultural regression that is under way with constant invocations of the 'market,' wholly ignoring its failures in actual practice."

In the USA, with the reform programme endorsed by President Clinton in the autumn of 1996, social security, which has suffered numerous cutbacks, is passing from the federal state to lower level administrations; the latter are expected to entrust it to various companies, which will make a profit by managing public funds. (In his book, O'Connor raises the spectre of a "social-industrial complex," within which private companies, financed with public funds, will be entrusted with the management of hospitals, homes, prisons, entire cities, anti-pollution projects, and so on.) The ideological pressure of neo-liberalism remains strong in Italy too; it has nullified all attempts to discuss the functioning of state administration and, in particular, the state budget. *Laissez-faire* fundamentalism, or rather, the subjection of society to the "economic rationality" that the companies *judge* indispensable for their own existence, finds its pretexts in world competition and in the commitments that have to be fulfilled before Italy can become part of the European Union. These are purely monetary commitments, concerning the rate of inflation, interest rates, exchange rate stability, the public debt and the state budget, as laid down by the Treaty signed on 7 February 1992 at Maastricht: a European version of the "structural adjustment" imposed in many countries by the IMF. In order to attract capital on the occasion of the reunification with the DDR, Germany had raised interest rates, thus throwing into crisis not only Italy's currency but also that of Great Britain, both of which were compelled to leave the European Monetary System for a time. Germany has helped to lead the way in monetary intransigence and the attack on he welfare state. The President of the Bundesbank, Tietmeyer, has summed it up as follows: welfare expenditure, taxes, and "the rigidities of labour market" must be reduced, in order to augment investors' confidence (*Le Monde*, October 17, 1996).

Despite economic growth, most of humanity became poorer during the 1980s, the years of neo-liberal recovery. Inequality and unemployment (and thus poverty) all continued to grow, and it is impossible to ignore the problems caused by the over-exploitation and destruction of the natural environment, and the degradation of the social environment.

In Italy, as elsewhere, rising unemployment, social hardship, public corruption coupled with private economic criminality, the financial difficulties of independent workers and small-scale entrepreneurs exploited by the monopolistic sector, could easily be considered a failure of the 'market,' revealing the urgent need to react to the political and cultural crisis, but instead the only effect is to deepen this crisis and reinforce the "constant invocations of the 'market'." In addition there is a concern with the enormous public debt accumulated over the years (this *exceeds* the GNP by 20 percent), which is forcing the government to adopt a deflationary policy in an attempt to enter the European Union as a full partner from the very start. This financial situation has further eroded confidence in the public administration, from which no one expects the benefits enjoyed in the past, but rather a heavier burden of taxes (or some timid attempt to reduce large-scale tax-evasion).

The development of the state sector has been functional to the expansion of the private economy (as O'Connor has pointed out). However, this does not prevent people—particularly the 'competitive' and/or petit-bourgeois sector—from now attacking the state, even to the extent of threatening a tax-revolt. This attack, together with Italy's international commitments, is drastically reducing the range of economic policy, and of politics in general. It is an attack directed, on the one hand, against the welfare state and the universalistic social rights that are to some extent embodied in it, and, on the other hand, against the rules and safeguards that regulate labour-relations, a legacy of the "Fordist age" (Revelli 1996, p. 9). These rules and regulations testify to the strength of the working class in that age and also to the system of "macro-concertation" (Regini 1991)—the political regulating of industrial relations and of the economy itself, with the intervention of mass union organizations and of the state.

Monetarist ideology and the pressure to free the market from all restrictions and 'safeguards,' and in particular to render the labour market more 'flexible,' are formally justified in Italy, as elsewhere, by the pressure of international competition and the rising unemployment rate. The 'activity rate' (the relation between the employed and the working-age population) is particularly low in Italy (at least according to official figures, without taking into account 'informal' work): slightly over 50 percent compared with the 60 percent average in Europe, 72 percent in the USA and 74 percent in Japan. Two recent studies of the European Union Commission and the OECD shows that, in European countries, there exists an inverse relation between the activity rate and the restrictions that discipline labour-relations and dismissals in particular (Galimberti 1996). In the Italian debate, this would seem to represent a good reason for the "post-Fordist" liberalization of the job-market. The reduction of unemployment in Great Britain and the USA is ascribed to neo-liberal policies. Hence the proposal that wage differentiation should be introduced to promote employment in under-developed areas, and that wage-bargaining should once again be carried out within the confines of individual companies. It is admitted that this may lead to a rise in contingent and deregulated work, distributed possibly by private agencies that hire workers for short periods. Furthermore, there may be only a partial legalization of informal and black-market work, supplied not only by immigrant workers but also by the unemployed, the under-employed, the employed, pensioners, and children.

In short, there is a growing propensity to agree with Friedrich Hayek's (1944) statement that preventing an individual from selling his own labour at a price and under conditions that permit him to find a purchaser—no matter what this price and these conditions are—means restricting his freedom, along with everyone else's. As a matter of fact, the real watchword is 'low wages'; this constitutes the true objective. For some time now the Confindustria (Confederation of Italian Industries) has been attacking the incomes policy agreed upon by the workers' unions in July 1993, according to which the workers were no longer automatically protected against inflation, but could subsequently recover the reduction of real wages caused by the rise in the cost of living. Now, not only is this policy being questioned, but also the very principle of collective bargaining, which is said to grant excessive protection to the "caste of the employed."

Monetarist policies and low wages have slowed down not only inflation but also growth, which came to a full stop in the course of 1996. The consequent impossibility of increasing fiscal revenue makes it difficult to balance the state budget, in spite of the reduction of spending and interest rates on the national debt. An improvement in the state accounts could come from a fiscal reform, which would combat tax evasion and reduce investment income. But no innovations of this kind are envisaged *at present* (1997) in the policy of the government—a liberal government, in which left-wing parties predominate. Furthermore, no efficacious industrial policy has been drawn up to foster innovation and lay down all the conditions—infrastructures, services, research, relations with foreign markets—that might make industry more innovative and competitive, at the same time making it possible to alleviate (not to resolve) the problem of unemployment. State investments remain scarce and ill-directed, especially in sectors such as hydro-geological projects and town planning; conservation of the nation's natural and artistic heritage; education, artistic and cultural activities; and scientific research: all fundamental sectors, if we wish to achieve both a rise in employment and a better use of resources from the point of view of the ecological equilibrium and collective welfare.

The "Third System"

These considerations lead to a problem with broader implications than the ability of the Italian economy to remain among the central economies of the world-system. The problem is that society does not appear to be facing up to the 'substantive' issue of the economy, which—as Giorgio Ruffolo observed in a book which draws on Karl Polanyi's theories—is the choice of how to "allocate *resources* for the improvement of the ecosphere as a *social environment*"

(Ruffolo, 1985, p. 166). The discussion about the third sector was originally concerned mainly with this problem; currently, however, it is mainly focused on the so-called crisis of the welfare state and the systematic rise of unemployment. *The non-profit sector could, in fact, bring budget relief to the state and private companies, since it allows for cheaper services and lower labour costs.*

Ruffolo's book came out when neo-liberal ideologies and policies were already prevalent; however, it was informed by once widespread alternative viewpoints, based on criticism of capitalistic development. Ruffolo criticises not only the drastic reduction of the role of politics, which monetarist theories imply, but the very ideology of economic growth and the market. Increased production does not necessarily correspond to increased benefits for society as a whole. The market does not take into account the costs of economic growth. Moreover, many need remain unsatisfied or even unrecognised; furthermore a "social shortage" is produced, a kind of congestion due to the increase in the quantity of goods, especially those which are the object of competition as status symbols, rather than a source of satisfaction.

It is also possible to find in Ruffolo's book an anticipation of the more recent awareness that the exploitation of resources taken from the natural and *social* environment, on which the post-war development was based, was so massive in scale that it provoked a rise in costs and, at a certain point, held back development. This, according to O'Connor (1992), is the "second contradiction of capitalism" (the first being the more classically Marxist one, according to which the rise in the rate of exploitation tends to provoke excessive accumulation and makes it difficult to realize profits).

The neo-liberal demand that market mechanisms be freed from all restraints and that these mechanisms be extended to all aspects of social life is unfounded, according to Ruffolo, because it ignores the role that state policy has played: support for accumulation on the one hand, and a guarantee of social consensus on the other. He agrees in part that the crisis of the "État-Providence" (Rosanvallon 1981) must not be forgotten, nor the need to reform public administration and the welfare system, with the aim of minimising bureaucratic and parasitic costs, authoritarianism and the protection of vested interests. However, the scope, the necessity and the peculiarity of public policy cannot be disavowed. Milton Friedman's proposal to substitute public social services with a "negative tax"—that is, with subsidies to the have-nots, who could then buy services on the market—fails to grasp "the essence of the problem, which is not that of guaranteeing everyone a minimum starting point *in the market*, but of removing *from the market* certain decisions regarding the basic conditions of social welfare" (Ruffolo 1985, p.239). However, only a 'basic protection,' free for everybody, should be guaranteed: beyond that, the supply of social services would be liberalised in the form of a 'welfare market' "formed by public companies, private companies and voluntary associations, in free competition among one another, and subject to state control" (*ibid.,* p. 240). The state could, if necessary, intervene in this market on the demand side, providing citizens with 'social benefits,' such as an allowance for such essential goods and services as housing, education and health care. If we add to these considerations Ruffolo's wish that production should be directed increasingly "towards *cultural assets* and towards *co-operative activities*," superseding the "market-form" (*ibid.*, p. 169) for these activities, it can come as no surprise that he devotes a paragraph to what he calls the "third system."

The idea of the "third system" had been developed in a 1977 report drawn up by a group of experts for the Commission of the European Communities. The group included Michel Albert and Jacques Delors, and Ruffolo himself as chairman. Ruffolo recalls that the report was ignored, but that similar ideas were put forward at the time by other people (a few precursors include): Weisbrod 1975 and 1977; and, in Italy, Donati 1978 and Ardigò 1981].

Ruffolo (1985, pp. 197 ff.) observes that both the market and bureaucratic organs function in an increasingly costly way, while their ability to satisfy personal and social needs does not grow at all. On the other hand a new value is being accorded to self-sufficient activities, whether individual, domestic or social, as a consequence of various factors: computerization, which makes "cottage-industries" viable once again; the spread of education, which expands the range and heightens the quality of people's needs; a "return to disinterested social solidarity," from leisure associations to voluntary social work. This latter may be motivated by religious or political ideals, or even by "pure existential activism," and finds an outlet in various fields of activity from aid work to ecology, from the upkeep of public facilities to recreational and creative activities.

Thus a system of direct economic and social relations is developing outside the market and state administration: "a *third system* of activities not aimed at profit and which are direct producers of use values" (Ruffolo 1985, p. 199). It possesses certain aspects of the "conviviality" desired by Ivan Illich (1971), but on the basis of more up-to-date techniques and a more modern mentality. Quoting Schumacher (1974) and Toffler (1980), Ruffolo counts on two characteristics of the new computer technologies: the miniaturization of techniques, which would permit the organization of businesses based on auto-production and auto-consumption, businesses that would be small and efficient at the same time; and the creation of communication networks able to deal with a great quantity of information for a great number of users. He claims that this could lead to a complex but egalitarian interdependence, which would mean that both the hierarchical forms of organization (private and public) and the market as an integrating mechanism (in the sense in which Polanyi meant it) had been superseded. Self-managed markets could be organised, within which social enterprises would arise, devoted both to a local auto-production of energy and to permanent education and training. Encouragement would be given to the production and reproduction of ideas, an autonomous expression of needs, an economy oriented towards use value.

The analysis of the "reticular global structure" of the economy carried out by Robert Reich (1991) documents how differently the new technologies have been applied, in accordance, obviously, with capitalist organization and, in particular, with the institutional order that it has gradually begun to assume in the "post-Fordist" age.

Ruffolo too realised that the new form of social organization, which the third sector could represent, was not a necessary and irreversible development. In his view, a political initiative is required; a series of questions must be confronted. First, there is the question of how to set matters on a formal juridical basis, organising safeguards, limits and controls, distinguishing different kinds of activities and associations (which might, for example, provide services for the associates or for non-members). The relationship with the public administration must be regulated, in all matters ranging from technical assistance to contracts and commissions. Finally there is the problem of financing, the way to channel resources from the market and the state towards the third system. The most obvious methods, according to Ruffolo, are state contributions and contracts, and getting big businesses to redistribute surpluses resulting from increased productivity. Suitable fiscal legislation, furthermore, could encourage forms of entrepreneurial patronage, such as "foundations for social development." Even more interesting would be a fund of capital managed by the unions that would channel wage-earners' savings into non-profit and self-managed activities.

It is worth revisiting these ideas that Ruffolo conceived over ten years ago, since they sum up the first phase of the debate on the third sector. On the one hand, we can see that many elements of the present discussion are not new; on the other hand, it is clear that the passage of time has caused many illusions and ambiguities to fade away. Different and even opposing ways of conceiving the third sector have come to light.

Aspects and Phases of the Debate on the Third Sector

A driving force in the debate on the third sector arose within some social movements in Italy during the seventies; these movements underscored he value of autonomous subjectivity, in opposition both to the market and the state, and foreshadowed the criticism both of utilitarianism and of statism and bureaucracy. Such criticism was also directed at "the social democratic model of the workers' movement" (Bihr 1991, chap. 1), in both its reformist and revolutionary forms. The movements of the seventies are referred to by André Gorz in books (1980, 1988, 1994) that are well known in Italy, and which are a source of one of the currents of thought pertaining to the development and potential of the third sector, a tendency that we can call 'utopian'. Gorz not only criticises the intrusion of commercialism (and the profit motive Polanyi would add) into all fields of life, and the welfare state but also rejects productivist ideology, observing that development entails an ever sharper division between a small minority, which carries out skilled work and wields all power, and a growing number of individuals obliged to carry out marginal, contingent and "servile" work. The alternative might consist in the redistribution of *both* necessary work (the volume of which is decreasing with technological development, and could decrease much more rapidly), and the work of caring for children, the elderly, the sick and households. As a result, the time 'freed' from work and given over to autonomous cultural development would be redistributed too. Cultural development, in suitable conditions and with the right logistical and organizational instruments, would take the form of activities belonging to the "sphere of autonomy." The market and the state constitute, by contrast, the *"sphère hétérorégulée de la mégamachine industrielle-étatique"* (1988, p. 53).

In a recent article, Gorz and Robin (1996) have once again evoked the slogan that was coined in Italy twenty years ago, *"lavorare meno, lavorare tutti"* (work less so all can work). They maintain that the extensive development of technology ought to constitute the basis for a different form of social organization, in which wealth, produced in modes that are increasingly independent from labour time, should be enjoyed in an equally independent fashion. Time freed from the constriction of work should be devoted "to social production, to the production of self and the production of meaning." A basic income, guaranteed to everyone in exchange for a few hours work, would make it possible to carry out, without remuneration, "artistic, sporting and political activities, assisting those in need," tending to the natural and urban environment. In this fashion, the "social bond" could be reconstructed autonomously. The designers of this utopia are sufficiently realistic to specify various essential preconditions: first of all, the redistribution of socially produced wealth and of the labour time necessary to produce it, but also, for example, restructured cities, an organization to distribute work, alternative monetary and banking arrangements.

According to Jeremy Rifkin, in order to reach the utopian "Post-Market Era" in the twenty-first century, it is essential that productivity gains resulting from the introduction of new time and labour-saving technologies should be shared out; in other words, there should be a reduction in working hours, a rise in wages, and a financing of the third sector—"that of the economy of the non-market," of the "social economy" (Rifkin 1995, pp. 349-350).

All of this is as utopian as it is incompatible with the capitalist organization of production. The fiscal crisis of the state resulted precisely from the state's inability to appropriate a bigger share of the surplus generated by higher productivity. Rifkin himself ends by suggesting other more plausible ways to finance the third sector, such as the decreasing of state welfare and warfare expenditure, cutting subsidies to multinational corporations, consumption taxes (with the drawback of a regressive fiscal effect).

There exist theories to explain this incompatibility; even those who consider them out of fashion cannot deny the facts. For example, in the USA, the average wage of unskilled workers is at present 13 percent lower than in 1973 (Pollin 1996). Even if we accept that a period of over twenty years can be considered short, in the long term the widening gap between the rise in productivity, on the one hand, and, on the other, the rise in wages and/or the reduction in working time, is even more striking. Gorz, too, takes this as his starting point, together with the systematic growth of unemployment and the tendency of capital to seek new fields of investment, gradually commercialising all areas of human life. We must then conclude, as Gorz himself admits, that the potential (in terms of time, resources and available fields) of the third sector (in its utopian version) depends on a "collective project," which has yet to be forged and even if it were it would come up against the resistance of capitalism, for which it would constitute a threat.

This does not alter the fact that the non-profit sector has continued to grow: it now represents, according to recent estimates, a percentage of the total workforce that ranges from the 6.8 percent in the USA to 1.8 percent in Italy (3 percent if one takes into account voluntary work; but it does not make much sense to consider the latter as employment) (Barbetta 1996, p. 154). People working in social services—the most important field of non-profit activities—increased in Italy by 33 percent (in the USA, 25.9 percent) from 1980 to 1990, while the number of employed increased overall by 4.3 percent (in the USA, 8.7 percent) (cfr. Borzaga, Gui, Schenkel 1995). What is the historic significance and what are the limits of this growth? Just *what kind* of third sector is it, and, in particular, what is its relationship with the utopian prospect outlined above? Why is it stirring up a debate?

I will now deal briefly with a few aspects of this debate as it has taken shape in Italy.

The economist Giorgio Lunghini has suggested that promoting "socially useful jobs" could be a remedy for that typical contradiction of our epoch, the simultaneous presence of unemployment and unsatisfied or even unexpressed needs.

Lunghini takes his cue from John Maynard Keynes's lecture on the "Possibilities for our Grandchildren," in which "technological unemployment" appears as the perverse effect of technical progress and capitalist accumulation; the effect, that is, of those characteristics of the modern world that should help us to solve the economic problems of humanity within a century. As a consequence of technical progress, along with scarcity, the problem of economics itself would disappear; in its stead the problem of how to employ leisure time would arise.

It is worth bearing in mind two particular elements in Keynes's lecture. The first is that he envisages a cultural revolution, vital if humanity is to readjust to the wholly new condition of an absence of economic necessity. Premodern, traditional principles would make a come-back, in a new context and thus with a new meaning: "avarice is a vice," "love of money detestable." "We shall once more value ends over means and prefer the good to the useful." Furthermore, "to be economically useful to others" will continue to have a meaning, to constitute a motive, even when we are free from the need to act for our own advantage. The second aspect is the typically technocratic one of Keynes's thought, which stipulates that, in order to reach "our destination of economic bliss," what is required is not only demographic control and peace, but also "our willingness to

entrust to science the direction of those matters which are properly the concern
of science" (Keynes 1972, p. 331).

Basing himself on Marx's theory, Lunghini shows that the actual tendency
of capitalist development is not abundance, but waste. The anomaly of the
simultaneous presence of unemployment and penury, attributed by Keynes to the
crisis, has become a long-term trend. On the one hand, the present forms of
technological and organizational change systematically produce unemployment;
on the other hand, even within the limited confines of that part of the world
where economic prosperity reigns, pockets of poverty remain, along with
"unsatisfied social needs in the field of education and culture, the tutelage of
individuals and the fabric of society, the preservation of the environment and
nature" (Lunghini 1995, p. 15).

In the market system production is for profit, not for use. Only 'productive'
labour can be employed, that which produces goods and services to satisfy needs
that possess purchasing power, so that a profit can be made. Given the laws of
capitalist accumulation and the present irreversibility of technological
unemployment, a solution to the problem of unemployment needs to be sought
outside the market: employing the inactive labour-force "in the production of
those goods and services that society demands and which the market does not
supply" (Lunghini 1995, p. 60). In this way, the definition of what kind of work
is "productive," and thus actually gets done, would not be left only to the market
and to the profit motive, but would depend on social and political dynamics. This
is a condition of democracy, according to Lunghini, along with the economic and
political autonomy of individuals, that can be guaranteed only by the availability
of an income *from work*—work that could be carried out occupying "that no
man's land of economics and society in which goods are not paid for," in spite of
their social utility (as is already happening with volunteer work, associations,
environmentalist movements, co-operatives, social centres); "concrete" work,
socially useful, destined directly to the production of use value, to satisfying needs
"that lack individual purchasing power" *(ibid.,* pp. 74-76). In this area outside the
market it would be possible to create "democratic forms of needs assessment,
local control of demand, and decentralised organization of supply" *(ibid.,* p. 76),
and communal and reciprocal relations could be recreated in a modern form,
taking autonomous individuals as their starting point.

Lunghini considers the question of how the third sector could be *gradually*
created, posing two problems: how to finance "concrete work" (or rather socially
useful work), and how to manage the relationship with the market-sector and,
when necessary, the redistribution of "concrete" work and capitalist work among
individuals. The solution to the latter problem depends on a long-term process of
growing cultural and political maturity. The former could be solved, at least
temporarily, and within the context of capitalist society, with a fiscal
transfer—not by imposing tax-increases, however, but by fighting evasion and
tax-avoidance. The limited nature of the solutions that Lunghini offers probably

results from the fact that the question of the third sector is framed—which is rare—within a theory of capitalist society and of its present phase.

There are those, like Gorz, who continue to consider a drastic reduction in working time essential in order to eliminate unemployment and to give everyone, in egalitarian fashion, the possibility *also* to do "socially useful" work. For Lunghini, as for Keynes, this is a utopian prospect worth bearing in mind: but he considers it impractical in this society, especially at this stage. Both Michel Albert (1982) (cited above as the author, together with Ruffolo, of the report for the European Community) and Gorz claim that the reduction of working time could be effected by reducing wages proportionately; then the only problem would be to find a way to pay the workers the difference, or at least a good part of it. Guy Aznar (1993) calls this difference a "second cheque" (*deuxième chèque*), and proposes a series of detailed and apparently realistic strategies to finance it.

Alain Lipietz (1989; 1997) holds that the development of a new sector of activity characterised by "non-market social relations" could provide a way out from the deep crisis of "Fordism as a regime of accumulation" and a "mode of regulation"; and it could thus be an aspect of the inevitable "new transformation" (a reference to the "great transformation" that began in the 1930s, and, according to Polanyi (1944), allowed the capitalist system to overcome the crisis of the liberal institutional structure). The development of the new sector would correspond to an opportunity to improve the quality of life rather than the quantity of available goods, with the possibility of more free time and a greater cultural capacity to enjoy it. Furthermore, the limitation of the market would render regional economies less subject to disturbances stemming from international competition. The reduction of working time would solve the problem of unemployment. Finally, superseding productivism would mean that ecological constraints could be taken into account as well. According to Lipietz, in "the new economic sector" useful activities would be undertaken which are currently carried out by the welfare state in excessively expensive or authoritarian ways, or which are not done at all. Hesees it as important that new social relations may come about as a result: a new form of self-managed co-operation, and the possibility to define and democratically control the social usefulness of activities.

The French intellectuals cited above, along with numerous others, launched two appeals in June 1995 and October 1996 (this latter was published in Italy in the newspaper *Il Manifesto* on 27 October). In them they point out the inadequacy of all traditional economic policies, the breakdown of society and the need for democracy. They therefore propose to reduce working time and to share out employment; to guarantee everyone a minimum income level; to develop a "third sector" consisting in a "economy of solidarity," partly by using public finances. They see these measures as "immediately attainable," and oppose the utilitarian and 'market' logic which gives rise to the creation of marginal jobs, the deregulation and destabilization of work, the creation of a separate sector of activities (generally obligatory and underpaid) for the unemployed.

What Third Sector?

The difference between these two types of strategies is important and must be borne in mind as a starting point for a critical review of the problem of the third sector. For the reasons laid out above, however, one may question the immediate feasibility of the French intellectuals' proposals, at least so long as production continues to be organised in the present fashion. Reducing working time and sharing out income is problematic precisely because it contrasts with the aims and method of capitalist accumulation. This is occurring in an unfettered way at the present historical moment, which is characterized by global competition and the general, perhaps definitive, defeat of the workers' movement. There is no need to point out that these features are among the basic causes of unemployment, the persistence of a long working day, and the devaluing of the labour force.

This does not mean that the third sector cannot be developed in a limited way. A recent report (Associazione Lunaria 1996) concludes that, with adequate measures (tax concessions, new forms of financing, ethical banking, a supply of contracts and services) 200,000 new jobs could be created in the non-profit sector in Italy over the next two years. It is thus worth taking this development seriously, and posing the question of its *quality*.

If we consider the reality of the non-profit sector, it is clear that it presents, or at least foreshadows, only in part the characteristics of an alternative economy, and that it rarely corresponds to the utopian prospect outlined in various forms and degrees by the authors considered so far. Furthermore, there is too little realistic economic assessment of the resources available for the third sector, taking into account the organization of the economic system in its current phase. Finally, the question of the third sector is not discussed in relation to the institutional and cultural crisis of state policy and politics itself. The underpinnings and the boundaries of the debate are rather the so-called crisis of the welfare state, and the increase of unemployment and casual, irregular and 'moonlight' work.

The problem of the different types and meanings of non-profit organizations is overlooked in an important enquiry into this sector in Italy, which was carried out in the context of an international research project directed by scholars from Johns Hopkins University (see Salamon and Anheier 1994), and published recently (Barbetta 1996). The non-profit sector is defined functionally, on the basis of the formal constitution of the organizations, their legal status, self-government, use of voluntary work, and, obviously, the non-distribution criterion. On this basis, estimates are made of the number of people employed and the number of volunteers in the various sectors of activity (social services, education, health care, culture and leisure, environmentalism, professional and union organizations, international activities, civil rights). The different sources of funds are analyzed. The historical traditions of non-profit organisations in Italy are discussed, along with the legal and fiscal regulations which are either already in effect or are desirable, and relations with government. However, no theoretical distinctions are made with regard to the significance of the *different types* of non-profit organizations within present-day society. The emphasis is placed—and here an attempt at evaluation can be perceived, behind the apparent sociological detachment—on the potential for expanding the sector as a result of privatization and the contracting-out of public welfare progrmmes.

Another collection of essays in third-sector sociology in Italy (Donati 1996) appears to lend even further support to the "subsidiarity principle," according to which state intervention is desirable only in cases in which no other provision is made for social needs. Appealing to the generally "humane" motives of voluntary organizations and associations, and to a hazily defined societal vision, Donati reassesses the solidarity rooted in family ties, typical of premodern organic societies. The third sector, a producer of "relational goods," contrasted with "statism," considered an Italian tradition, without distinguishing between the totalitarianism of the Fascist state and the modern conquests of citizens' rights and welfare.

Italian students of the third sector generally come from a Roman Catholic background. Some are from the Università Cattolica, a non-profit institution financed by the Italian state. This by no means implies that their point of view is uniform. Similarly a variety of aims and political positions are found among the various non-profit organizations of Catholic origin (over 40 percent of the total).

It is this diversity of positions that makes it necessary to distinguish different tendencies among non-profit activities. A commission headed by the economist Stefano Zamagni (Commissione Zamagni, 1995) has formulated proposals for a law that would provide the sector with a legal and fiscal framework. In the debate that ensued, certain voices, speaking on behalf of the most powerful Catholic organizations, with close ties to the Vatican hierarchy, asked for very broad criteria to be applied in deciding what constitutes a non-profit organization, with all the related benefits and concessions envisaged by the law. The same voices, in an attack against the "omnivorous state," asked for a wide-ranging privatization programme for health and education. Luigi Scapicchio, who ran a private asylum for many years, declared: "I believe that priests do not have an adequate market culture. They have not realised that they could provide a viable solution in many fields of aid-work: psychiatry is, in fact, the least remunerative of all pathologies" (Il Manifesto, 13 October 1996, p. 9).

The most important factor in explaining the smaller size of the third sector in Italy, in comparison with other countries, is the absolute dominance of the state in the fields of health and education; health care constitutes over 60 percent of the third sector in the USA, and education almost 50 percent in Great Britain (Gui 1996, pp. 175-76). This Italian peculiarity is the principal reason why opinions about the third sector and strategies for it are so divided in the present debate.

Some reject any other criteria than that of "non-distribution," and insist on the "subsidiarity principle" (see Vittadini [ed.] 1997). *They seek to abolish or alter that Italian peculiarity.* Others, however, react to this viewpoint, which they view as an assault of the Catholic forces and the supporters of a thorough privatization of social security, medical benefits and welfare services. They claim that it is important to assess those cases in which public agencies are more efficacious and efficient than private initiatives. They point, by way of example, to education, where state administration guarantees educational freedom, pluralism, and equality among users. *As for health care, there are instances of non-profit organizations which choose their customers, as well as the field and kind of activity, according to market criteria.* Finally, there is the problem of the relation of non-profit organizations to the market. Some participants in the debate are concerned with the cases in which the special conditions granted to organizations formally defined as non-profit constitute unfair competition (it should be remembered, in this regard, that more than a third of the revenue of the non-profit sector in Italy derives from contracts, and almost another third by the sale of goods and services [Barbetta 1996, p. 165]). Others observe that those special conditions allow a reduction of wages, guarantees, contributions to social security and union protection for workers; as a result, the labour market will be modified according to the demands of neo-liberal deregulation.

It would be useful to take into account critical reflections on the third sector in other countries. Based on his studies of the U.S. education and health care systems, Charles Clotfelter suggests that "by their nature, nonprofit organizations will be less redistributive than government agencies"; "to the extent that they serve more affluent clients, [these organizations] are no more than a symptom of a country's decision to allow unequal consumption of public and quasi-public goods" (Clotfelter 1996, pp. 162-63; see also Weisbrod 1996). Clotfelter (1996, p. 164) insists on viewing "the nonprofit form" as "an instrument for the pursuit of ultimate social objectives, not an end in itself."

A further problem is that any general legal definition and regulation of non-profit activities could not, in any case, make the relevant distinctions with regard to a political, *partisan* evaluation of non-profit activities and their capacity to constitute an alternative to the predominant tendencies in today's society. For this purpose, it is necessary to distinguish between the activities that really do fall into a third sector which is genuinely different from the market, and those which, by contrast, will expand the area of the market or actually favour some of its worst forms. The aim and the internal structure of the organizations must be considered. For example, one need only think of the laws in Italy that have recently granted more "autonomy" to the state universities: this means, in practice, a reduction of public funding and the freedom to accept sponsorship from (non-profit) foundations belonging to private industrial groups. Another case to be considered is the ambiguous status of (non-profit?) organizations that set workers up in temporary jobs.

It is striking that the debate on the third sector in Italy does not sufficiently take into consideration many reports and proposals, which are really an alternative both to the market and the state sector (see for example Laville [ed.] 1994, Aymone 1996, and Shragge [ed.] 1997). As Shragge observes in *Community Economic Development*, we cannot but start from the "problems of unemployment, poverty and social decay," which our society seems incapable of solving, in spite of its increasing and "globalized" production of wealth. It is most important, however, to seek new forms of communitarian economic activity, characterized by fully democratic relations, and linked "to a wider political-social movement and an alternative vision for economic and social development" (Shragge 1997, p. ix).

In conclusion, the non-profit sector needs to be analyzed in all its complexity and contradictions. I must here cite two examples, two cases that represent two opposite poles. The term "non-profit" is applied to alternative savings associations that exist in many countries (in Italy there are the MAG, *Mutue autogestite*) (Davico 1992), which are now attempting, together with other organizations, to found a real "ethical bank"). Also the think tanks that have so successfully spread neo-liberalist market ideology (Smith 1991; Desai 1994)are "non-profit" organizations.

The debate on the third sector started in the 1970s, in the wake of the post-war 'golden age'. It drew inspiration, in those years, from different, sometimes contrasting, theoretical and political tendencies: the criticism of productivism and the intrusiveness of the market, the utopia of freedom which technological development seemed to bring within reach, the criticism of the century-long social-democratic model of the workers' movement, the "post-modern" lack of confidence in the grand vision of a rational organization of society. Later, in the years of the crisis of post-war development and the quest for a new model of capitalist accumulation, two opposing viewpoints have been put forth. On the one hand, the third sector is deemed the first step toward and even the model of an alternative to present society, to a kind of development which creates unemployment, inequality, and the decay of the natural and social environment. On the other hand, the third sector is considered simply as an opportunity to attenuate unemployment, the fiscal crisis of the state, social unease, and the insufficient demand of goods and services: or as an opportunity for private (and mostly Catholic) organizations to enter an enlarged welfare market.

This second viewpoint fits in with the hegemony of neo-liberal ideology. Not only is the crisis of the welfare state taken for granted, but there is also an acceptance of the failure of politics at the state level, and, a fortiori, of the impossibility of facing consciously and democratically the problems confronting society as a whole. The appeal to decentralization, social links and solidarity results, in this case, in the dissimulation of the gravity and the consequences of the crisis of politics. Society thus becomes more "irresponsible," as Richard Titmuss (1963) feared, owing to the hegemony of the market view and the interest of private corporations.

BIBLIOGRAPHY

VV. AA. *Le organizzazioni senza fini di lucro*. Milano: Giuffrè Editore, 1996.

Michel Albert, *Le pari français*. Paris: Seuil, 1982.

Achille Ardigò, "Volontariato, welfare state e terza dimensione," *La Ricerca Sociale*, No.25, 1981, pp. 7-22.

Lunaria Associazione, *Lavori scelti. Come creare occupazione nel Terzo Settore*. Roma: Edizioni Gruppo Abele, 1997.

Tullio Aymone, *Amazzonia. I popoli della foresta*. Torino: Bollati Boringhieri, 1996.

Guy Aznar, *Travailler moins pour travailler tous. 20 propositions*. Paris: Syros, 1993.

Gian Paolo Barbetta (ed.), *Senza scopo di lucro*. Bologna: Il Mulino, 1996.

Alain Bihr, *Du 'Grand soir' à 'l'alternative'. Le mouvement ouvrier européen en crise*. Paris: Les Éditions Ouvrières, 1991.

C. Borzaga, B. Gui, and M. Schenkel, "Disoccupazione e bisogni insoddisfatti: il ruolo delle organizzazioni non profit," *Quaderni dell'Economia del Lavoro*, No. 52, Milano: F. Angeli, 1995.

Federico Caffè, "Prefazione," in J. O'Connor, *La crisi dello stato fiscale*. Torino: Einaudi, 1979.

Michele Cangiani (ed.), *The Milano Papers. Essays in Societal Alternatives*. Montréal: Black Rose Books, 1997.

Charles T. Clotfelter, "Public Services Versus Private Philantropy. Are there Winners and Losers?," in VV. AA., *Le organizzazioni senza fini di lucro*. Milano: Giuffrè Editore, 1996.

Commissione Zamagni. "Relazione," *Non profit*, No. 3/95.

Luca Davico, *Solidarietà: il risparmio autogestito*. S. Martino di Sarsina (FO): Macro Edizioni, 1992.

R. Desai, "Second-Hand Dealers in Ideas: Think-Tanks and Thatcherite Hegemony," *New Left Review*, No 203, Jan-Feb, 1994. pp. 27-64.

Pierpaolo Donati, *Pubblico e privato: fine di un'alternativa?*. Bologna: Cappelli, 1978.

Pierpaolo Donati (ed.), *Sociologia del terzo settore*. Roma: La Nuova Italia Scientifica, 1996.

André Gorz, *Adieux au prolétariat*. Paris: Galilée, 1980.

André Gorz, *Métamorphose du travail. Quête de sens*. Paris: Galilée, 1988.

André Gorz, *Il lavoro debole. Oltre la società salariale*. Roma: Edizioni Lavoro, 1994.

André Gorz, and Jacques Robin, "Forger un autre avenir," *Le Monde*, Oct. 8, 1996, p. 1.

Benedetto Gui, "La rilevanza economica e sociale delle organizzazioni *non-profit* in Italia," in VV. AA., *Le organizzazioni senza fini di lucro*. Milano: Giuffrè Editore, 1996.

Friedrich Hayek, *The Road to Serfdom*. London: Routledge, 1944.

Ivan Illich, *Tools for Conviviality*. New York: Harper & Row, 1971.

John Maynard Keynes, "Possibilities for our Grand-children," *The Nation and Athenaeum*, Oct. 11 and 18, 1930; now in J. M.

Keynes, *Collected Writings*, vol. IX, *Essays in Persuasion*, London and Basingstoke: Macmillan & St. Martin's Press, 1972.

Jean-Louis Laville (ed.), *L'économie solidaire. Une perspective internationale*. Paris: Desclée de Brouwer, 1994.

Alain Lipietz, *Choisir l'audace. Une alternative pour le XXIè siècle*. Paris: La Découverte, 1989. English transl.: *Towards a New Economic Order. Postfordism, Ecology, Democracy*. Cambridge: Polity Press, 1992.

Alain Lipietz, "The Next Transformation," in Cangiani M. (ed.), *The Milano Papers. Essays in Societal Alternatives*. Montréal: Black Rose Books, 1997.

Giorgio Lunghini, *L'età dello spreco. Disoccupazione e bisogni sociali*. Torino: Bollati Boringhieri, 1995.

James O'Connor, *The Fiscal Crisis of the State*. New York: St. Martin Press, 1973.

James O'Connor, "La seconda contraddizione del capitalismo: cause e conseguenze," *Capitalismo Natura Socialismo*, II, No. 3, 1992.

Karl Polanyi, *The Great Transformation*. New York: Holt,

Rinehart & Winston Inc., 1944.

Robert Pollin, "Economics with a Human Face," *The Nation*, Sept. 30, 1996.

Marino Regini, *Confini mobili. La costruzione dell'economia fra politica e società*. Bologna: Il Mulino, 1991.

Robert B. Reich, *The Work of Nations. Preparing Ourselves for 21st Century Capitalism*. New York: Vintage Books, 1991.

Marco Revelli, "Il Terzo è dato," *Il manifesto*. 11 ottobre, 1996.

Jeremy Rifkin, *The End of Work. The Decline of the Global Labor force and the Dawn of the Post-Market Era*. New York: G. P. Putnam's Sons, 1995.

Pierre Rosanvallon, *La crise de l'État-Providence*. Paris: Seuil, 1981.

Giorgio Ruffolo, *La qualità sociale*. Bari: Laterza, 1985.

L. Salamon, H. Anheier, *The Emerging Sector. An Overview*. Baltimore: Institute for Social and Policy Studies, The Johns Hopkins University, 1994.

E. F. Schumacher, *Small is Beautiful*. London: Abacus, 1974.

Eric Shragge (ed.), *Community Economic Development. In Search of Empowerment*. Montréal: Black Rose Books, 1997.

James Allen Smith, *The Idea Brokers: Think-Tanks and the Rise of the New Policy Elites*. New York: The Free Press, 1991.

Richard Titmuss, *Essays on the Welfare State*. London, George Allen & Unwin, 1963.

Alvin Toffler, *The Third Wave*. New York: Batam, 1980.

Giorgio Vittadini (ed.), *Il non profit dimezzato*. Milano: Etas Libri, 1997.

Burton A. Weisbrod, "Toward a Theory of the Voluntary Non-profit Sector in a Three Sector Economy," in E. Phelps (ed.), *Altruism, Morality and Economic Theory*. New York: Russel Sage Foundation, 1975.

Burton A. Weisbrod, *The Voluntary Non-profit Sector*. Lexington (Mass.): Lexington Books, 1977.

Burton A. Weisbrod, "The Economic and Social Importance of Nonprofit Organizations," in VV. AA., *Le organizzazioni senza fini di lucro*, Milano: Giuffrè Editore, 1996.

Chapter 4

The Social Economy and the Neo-Conservative Agenda

Jack Quarter

Across Canada, governments are reducing the scale of their services and engaging in a process euphemistically referred to as "restructuring." The primary rationale for this process is deficit-reduction, but neo-conservative forces have also argued for downsizing government as part of a free-market philosophy. At least several Canadian governments have attempted a downsizing that goes far beyond what is needed to balance the budget. For example, the current Ontario government under Premier Mike Harris is boldly implementing a 30-per-cent income-tax cut at the same time as the province is running a deficit of $7.5 billion (1997), thereby necessitating about $6 billion of additional cuts to balance the budget by the year 2001. This strategy of reducing government involvement in society has been adopted by New Zealand, parts of the United States, and Britain; and with pressure from international bond agencies and the International Monetary Fund, it has become a worldwide trend.

Within Canada, the most prevalent strategy for expenditure reduction has been the withdrawal of government from direct service provision and its replacement by various forms of alternative service delivery (referred to by the acronym ASD). This includes sell-offs to the private sector (privatization), joint ventures, franchising and licensing arrangements between government and outside service providers. Under ASD, government's role is limited to formulating policies and regulating services rather than direct provision. In addition to ASD, governments are simply eliminating or greatly reducing the scale of services and, indeed, the scale of government. The philosophy behind this redefined role for government is set out in the book *Reinventing Government: How the Entrepreneurial Spirit Is Transforming the Public Sector* (Osborne and Gaebler, 1993). It is also described in various policy documents, for example, see the Ontario government's "Alternative Service Delivery Framework" (April 1997).

In the context of ASD, there is reference to organizations within the social economy, the assumption being that, because of their volunteer labour, these can provide services more cheaply. For example, in a presentation to a round-table looking at co-operatives as alternatives for public services, Dina Palozzi, the Deputy Minister of Finance in Ontario, states: "We are especially interested in hearing about cases where public service co-ops have succeeded in reducing the cost of service delivery and improving customer service, while preserving accountability" (June 23, 1997, p. 5). Such usage of the social economy has posed a challenge for its advocates.

This paper will deal with the following issues: first, a brief delineation of the social economy in Canada, including a typology for grouping the mosaic of organizations within the social economy; second, a discussion of Jeremy Rifkin's (1996) proposals to strengthen the social economy (as outlined in his book, *The End of Work*); and third, a discussion of the impact of both the neo-conservative agenda and Rifkin's proposals, broken down according to the typology outlined in the first part of the paper.

Canada's Social Economy

Because defining the precise characteristics of the social economy has proven problematic, one strategy has been to define it by default—that is, by those parts of the economy in neither the private nor the public sector. In general, the social economy includes co-operatives and non-profits, both incorporated and non-incorporated (DeFourney, 1988; Jeantet, 1991; Snaith, 1991; Quarter, 1992).[1]

Organizations in the social economy can also be juxtaposed in relation to the private and public sectors. Many forms of co-operatives (for example, in such areas as financial services and insurance, farm marketing, retailing and wholesaling) and some non-profits (for example, Blue Cross and Travel Cuts) compete in the market with private-sector firms. Some non-profits such as the Ys, Scouts, and Guides might not perceive themselves as competing; but they are financially self-reliant organizations that must also meet the measure of a market in which private-sector firms provide similar services. Other organizations in the social economy—non-profit agencies and co-operatives in housing, daycare and healthcare—depend in varying degrees on government programs for their revenues. Some non-profits (for example, publicly funded hospitals, zoos and museums) are so dependent upon government funding that they might be considered as part of the public sector, except that they have their own boards of directors and have some freedom in setting their policies. Financially dependent non-profits are also supported by private donors—through either central organizations such as the United Way or private fund-raising efforts. Historically, the responsibility for funding financially-dependent non-profits has shifted from private individuals and businesses to the government (Martin, 1985). Although the funding patterns vary according to the type of service, in Canada governments are the dominant source for financially-dependent non-profits. For that reason (as will be discussed in greater detail later), public-sector cutbacks also are having an impact on such non-profits.

The social economy then is not a homogenous entity but rather a mosaic of disparate organizations. For the purposes of this paper, three broad groupings will be used (see Table 1)—entrepreneurial organizations, mutual associations and financially dependent non-profits.

An accurate statistical profile of the social economy is hard to come by. In 1992 there were about 175,000 non-profits in Canada, including organizations

Table I

A Typology of Organizations in the Social Economy

	Entrepreneurial	*Mutual Associations*	*Financially Dependent*
Examples	Co-ops in farm marketing, financial services and retailing; entrepreneurial non-profits	Social clubs, religious and ethno-cultural associations; unions, managerial and business associations	Social service agencies; social housing, healthcare and childcare centres
Financing	Revenues and member investment	Membership fees	Government programs and grants; private donations; fund-raising
Labour	Paid employees; volunteer directors	Largely volunteer	Varies; both paid employees and volunteers
Market Dynamic	Competition with private sector	Serving a particular membership: semi-protected market	Serving the public i.e., those needing the service

with charitable status. A more recent estimate (Hirshhorn, 1997) suggests that the figure might be in excess of 200,000 organizations. The co-operative sector in Canada alone transacts more than $28 billion of business annually and has assets of over $114 billion (Co-operatives Canada 1995). If one extrapolates from the labour force of the co-operative sector, which averages about 13.3 employees per organization, then organizations in the social economy as a whole would embrace about 13 per cent of the labour force. Even if such an estimate is on the high side, it can be seen that the labour force of organizations in the social economy is not an insignificant part of the labour force. The range of services in which these organizations are involved is vast: from social service agencies (such as Children's Aid, homes for the aged, Meals on Wheels, rape crisis centres, the John Howard Society); health services (hospitals, community health centres, the Canadian Cancer Society and other related organizations); educational organizations; ethno-cultural and religious groups; the arts; organized sports and recreation; unions, professional and business associations; political parties; feminist and environmental groups; social housing and non-profit daycare; social clubs; and veterans groups.

Although some organizations with common objectives relate to each other through second- and third-tier organizations that they establish (for example, labour federations), it would be an exaggeration to refer to the organizations in the social economy as a movement or even embracing a common purpose. Some are at opposite ends of the political spectrum and others are in adversarial relationships. For example, what do the Saskatchewan Wheat Pool (a farm-marketing co-operative in the Fortune 100 list) or the caisse populaire Desjardins system (the sixth largest financial institution in Canada, with majority ownership of the Laurentian Bank) have in common with Meals on Wheels (a social service agency relying on volunteers to provide meals to dependent seniors) or LETS (an organization that promotes barter)? Or what do the members of a Baptist congregation have in common with Greenpeace?

But even though these organizations differ in their social objectives and organizational structure, they (like other organizations in the social economy) do have some common features. First, they do not function simply to earn money but rather to serve a social purpose. Second (and related to this point), there are no shareholders who, in the sense of a private-sector business, must be satisfied by business profits. These organizations either operate without shareholders or, in the case of co-operatives, have shares with a relatively constant value that are analogous to a membership fee. Rather, surplus earnings are applied to improving or broadening the availability of the service (the primary objective of the organization). Because of the absence of shareholders, it could be argued that organizations in the social economy are not owned by anyone. Rather they are forms of social property set up to serve a social purpose and under the control of a board of directors elected by a membership. (In the case of non-profit social service agencies, the board and the membership are often the same.)

Volunteer labour is an important aspect of organizations in the social economy. A survey done by Statistics Canada during the mid-1980s indicates that

27 per cent of Canadians are volunteers in formal organizations—mostly religious, recreational, educational, health and social services (Duchesne 1989). Ottawa consultant David Ross (1990) estimates this volunteer labour represents the equivalent of 615,000 full-time jobs (equivalent to the combined labour forces of Saskatchewan and New Brunswick). In 1987, if volunteer labour had been costed at $12 per hour, it would have been worth $12 billion (Ross and Shillington, 1990; Ross and Shillington, 1990a)—not taking into account out-of-pocket expenses of $841 million.

Although it is commonplace to refer to the social economy as the voluntary sector, this label is over-simplistic. As noted in Table 1, among organizations in the social economy there is a lot of variability in their dependence on volunteers. Some rely heavily on them; others use predominantly paid employees. Data on volunteers are based on formal organizations, either incorporated or duly constituted. Volunteers also make a valuable contribution through informal social arrangements. Such arrangements might be referred to as the "informal economy" (Ross and Usher, 1986) and also considered as part of the social economy.

Both the dependence upon volunteers and the importance of membership build strong ties between organizations in the social economy and the community—either a geographic community or a community of common social interest. Such ties exist for large market-based firms as well as the small groups relying upon volunteers.

The Social Economy and Public-Sector Restructuring

Although there are small networks of academics specializing in the study of co-operatives and non-profits and others (particularly in Western Europe) that deal more generally with the social economy, it was not until the publication of Jeremy Rifkin's best-seller book, *The End of Work* (Rifkin 1996) that the social economy received extensive currency in public discussions. Rifkin's advocacy of the social economy is premised upon a penetrating social analysis of the impact of the technological revolution upon the labour market and the social fabric. He argues that, unlike the past when technological developments also reduced the need for labour, there is no new market sector emerging to absorb the many people who are being displaced. In the past, the development of new technologies in agriculture was offset by the growth of manufacturing industries and technological developments related to manufacturing were offset by the growth of the service economy. Rifkin argues that revolution in information technologies is creating opportunities for an elite group of technocrats, and furthermore that the pace of technological development is accelerating and that the smart technologies being developed will increase the pace of labour displacement.

Citing largely US data, Rifkin argues that the technological revolution is accelerating the tendency in capitalism for inequitable distributions of wealth and income. This point is presented more forcibly by US economist Lester Thurow (1996) in his book *The Future of Capitalism*. Thurow points out that the real income of US male workers has been in decline since the early 1970s; and since

1989, family incomes have followed the same pattern. Income disparities have increased, with the top earners (senior executives, elite technocrats and other professionals) being the beneficiaries of almost all of the gains. The younger generation (that is, new entrants to the labour force) have suffered the sharpest decline in earnings, in part because the economy is not generating sufficient opportunities to absorb them.

The US pattern is not dissimilar to that of Canada and other countries in the OECD (Organisation for Economic Co-operation and Development) group. In Canada, where unemployment is substantially higher than the US, incomes have remained relatively flat since the mid-seventies (Betcherman and Lowe, 1997). Many of the Western European countries have succeeded in protecting the standard of living of existing members of the labour force, but at the price of unprecedented rates of unemployment.

Rifkin argues that hours of work have to be distributed more equitably within the formal economy. However, much of his analysis is devoted to advocating an enhanced role for the social economy. Interestingly, Rifkin does not dwell on what types of organization are included in the social economy, but he seems to suggest that they are organizations relying largely on volunteer labour. In other words, his analysis turns primarily on the non-market organizations in the social economy rather than market-based co-operatives and entrepreneurial non-profits. Unlike conservative proponents of the same scenario (President George Bush's "thousand points of light" in reference to the role of volunteer organizations), Rifkin recognizes that, although the strengthening of volunteer-based organizations could help to revitalize communities and improve the quality of life, income is a problem. Because of the informal assistance available, revitalized communities might reduce the amount of income that the average person requires. But Rifkin is not so naive as to ignore the increasing income disparities resulting from market forces. This then is the point of departure that separates Rifkin from the more conservative proponents of volunteer organizations.

Rifkin presents a series of proposals that bring together his concern about increasing income disparities with his goal of strengthening the social economy. None of these proposals is original to him, but the totality of the package in combination with his earlier analysis tenders his argument forceful. He begins by proposing a "shadow wage" for voluntary work, the wage to take the form of an income tax deduction. The idea behind this proposal is to put voluntary labour in a charitable organization on the same footing as financial donations. There are difficulties. First, only a minority of non-profits in Canada (including unincorporated associations) have a charitable status that allows donors a tax deduction, and generally these are the larger, better established non-profits (predominantly religious organizations) as well as those with social objectives that are not explicitly political. Second, the benefit of a tax deduction increases in proportion to income, and the benefit to those with very low incomes would be negligible. However, if the benefit were in the form of a tax credit, this problem could be overcome—because the credit would be the same for everyone regardless of income.

Rifkin appreciates that the community value of voluntary labour varies and furthermore that there might be a reaction against the financial cost of such a program. Therefore, he suggests that some types of activity be given priority over others in qualifying for a shadow wage. However, ranking organizational claims for shadow wages, whether it be according to social priorities or the needs of the organization, would open up a political mine-field and could lead to the same sort of policies that create income disparities: that is, powerful politically-connected organizations would receive priority over small community groups.

In addition to a tax deduction for volunteer work, Rifkin advocates a "social wage for community service" as an alternative to welfare payments for those permanently unemployed. Except for the proviso that the participants would be "willing to be retrained," this proposal is similar to the workfare programs that seem to proceed on the assumption that people on welfare are lazy and should be forced to work. However, Rifkin's intentions differ in that he argues "an adequate social wage would allow millions of unemployed Americans, working through thousands of neighborhood organizations, the opportunity to help themselves." (1997: 258) He argues that the social wage should be applied not just domestically but internationally as well. To enhance the effectiveness of such work, he proposes that the government should give grants to non-profit organizations to recruit and train those on welfare and suggests that such a program be extended also to unemployed skilled and professional workers.

As Rifkin recognizes, the social wage for community service, is a variation of a "guaranteed annual income," an idea that has been tossed about for at least three decades. The social wage proposal differs in that it ties the receipt of income to work in the social economy rather than guaranteeing it as a right. This is consistent with the direction of redefined welfare schemes (that is, workfare). Such a proposal could be viewed as progressive rather than punitive if it resulted in a larger income for the participants and training for useful jobs in community organizations—in other words, if it improved the standard of living of participants and enhanced the quality of life in their communities. That is Rifkin's intention.

But from where will the money come? This same problem exists at present without either the shadow or the social wage. Why will the beneficiaries of society's wealth be more willing to transfer some of it for the shadow and social wage programs than for welfare and grants to voluntary organizations? At present the political climate in Canada and the United States, as well as other OECD countries is in the direction of reducing taxes and (as noted) government programs, including those that involves grants to voluntary organizations. Governments are expecting volunteer organizations to reduce their costs not increase them and also seem willing to tolerate high levels of unemployment.

Rifkin proposes a series of measures to free up financing for these proposals. These include: a value-added tax on products and services related to the knowledge-based industries; discontinuing subsidies to those transnational corporations that are doing most of their business in other countries; and increasing the tax-deduction limit for corporations to donate money to volunteer organizations. The first two measures would lead to a financial transfer from those with wealth to those in need; at present, other measures of this sort are not receiving much political support, and it is not clear why these would be treated differently. With respect to the third measure, Rifkin notes that corporations are donating far less than the existing limit. Why then would increasing the limit lead to any sort of increase in corporate philanthropy?

Rifkin's proposals for a shadow and social wage require financing, much like government social programs. Although the idea of strengthening the organizations in the social economy is worthwhile, it is not clear why Rifkin's financing proposals are more likely to succeed than those that currently exist to support social programs. The problem is more political than conceptual; the neo-conservative agenda with its emphasis on the free market is working against the social fabric built up over several generations. It may be possible to mobilize political support to transfer more of the social fabric from the public sector to organizations within the social economy; but it is also necessary to bear in mind the distinct types of organizations within the social economy (see Table 1) and to recognize that these proposals might not affect each in the same way.

a) Entrepreneurial Organizations

The entrepreneurial firms in the social economy have a similar relationship to the market as private-sector businesses, but they differ in their ownership arrangements and governance. Rifkin's proposals do not bear directly on the entrepreneurial organizations in the social economy, but these organizations are being affected by the neo-conservative agenda in at least two different ways. First of all, they often find themselves under competitive pressure from large multi-nationals that threaten their markets, and as such they are forced to adopt strategies of their competitors in order to survive. Thus, Co-op Atlantic (the parent corporation for the retail co-operatives in the Atlantic provinces) is having to restructure because of competition from superstores and is closing outlets that aren't profitable. Credit unions (financial co-operatives) are consolidating rather than starting new organizations because they lack the stability to withstand economic downturns. Blue Cross sold its business operations in Ontario to Liberty Health because it was good business. This same motive also explains why Quebec's caisses populaires movement purchased a majority stake in the Laurentian Bank, which it apparently intends to sell.

The well-known Mondragon co-operatives consolidated into one corporation (referred to by Jesus Larranaga, a founder of the first co-operative in the system, as a "neo-co-operative" structure) because much of the control has been transferred from the individual in each co-operative to the central corporation (Larranaga, 1990). Moreover, Mondragon's expansion in recent years has been to set up subsidiaries in other countries because these are considered essential for exports. Therefore, competitive pressures are causing weaker co-operatives to close (much like weaker private businesses do), and they are also causing stronger co-operatives to consolidate and to converge towards the norms set by their competitors. They still maintain distinct characteristics, particularly in their ownership and control arrangements, but the difference is lessened.

Then, as a result of modern economic conditions, entrepreneurial organizations in the social economy have experienced a second effect. Globalization of business has opened up for them opportunities in smaller communities that lack a sufficient marketplace for multi-nationals. At the same time as multi-nationals have established dominant positions in the global marketplace, a community development movement has taken off to generate employment and to provide services in areas that do not interest the large corporations. Some communities such as Evangeline in the Acadian region of Prince Edward Island (Wilkinson and Quarter, 1996) have succeeded in creating an economic and social infrastructure based largely upon co-operatives, non-profits and small businesses. One might speculate that both of these trends—growth of social enterprises in small communities and downsizing in large metropolises—will continue to occur.

b) Mutual Associations
Globalization might also accelerate the growth of non-profit mutual associations—that is, self-financed organizations which provide a service to a membership. Originally, such associations were set up in rural communities for insurance against fire and other hazards, and in urban centres for such services as burial insurance and, among recent immigrant groups sharing their old-world culture. With modernization and the resultant weakening of community structures, these associations have tended to involve people who share a specific interest and who often are living in disparate locations. Mutual associations tend to be protected from market forces in that they provide a service to a group of members who are committed to supporting the organization through such mechanisms as a membership fee and volunteer labour. The members have a bond association related to such commonalties as religion, ethnicity, a social interest or political interest. Unions are part of this grouping as are business and managerial associations. Mutual associations are an important part of our social fabric and arguably have assumed even greater importance as communal bonds associated with geographical locations have weakened. Although there is not an exact count of such organizations in Canada, there is every reason to believe that they are increasing and will continue to do so as the processes of modernization both weaken ties based upon location and make it possible for people throughout the world to associate with each other.

The proposals that Rifkin makes would probably enhance the strength of these associations because, unlike entrepreneurial firms, they rely heavily on volunteers. However, Rifkin's proposals would bear most directly on non-market organizations in the social economy that are dependent on external finance.

c) Financially-Dependent Non-Profits

Financially-dependent non-profits (including some forms of co-operatives) serving the public (as opposed to a membership) are the organizations in the social economy that are chiefly being hurt by cutbacks in the government programs. For example, the entire social housing sector that was built up over the past three decades finds itself in a precarious position as a result of downloading to the provinces and cuts by the provinces. In Ontario, the government even went so far as to cancel contracts for new developments, not just in housing but also in healthcare. Childcare, too, finds itself in a precarious situation, and cutbacks are also affecting arts groups, social service agencies, hospitals, universities and virtually every form of non-profit dependent upon government funding. Introducing a shadow and social wage would, in essence, be trading off one type of expenditure against another. Why would governments that are attempting to reduce their expenditures finance people to participate in the very organizations whose budgets they are cutting? The argument has it that by doing so, governments would create opportunities and incentives for those who have lost out in the private and public sectors and would help to rebuild the social fabric that is being torn apart by a reduction of services. Moreover, by making this investment in voluntary organizations, there would be a synergy that would enhance volunteerism and presumably make it possible to have these services at a reduced cost.

But for the people transferring their labour from the private and public sectors to volunteer associations, there would also be a loss of benefits including pension plans. For such a transfer to be financially equitable, there would have to be an enhanced investment in public pensions and benefits.

Concluding Comments

The proposal to create incentives for the transfer of surplus labour from the private and public sectors to the social economy is potentially constructive. However, as noted, for such a proposal to be effective, there would be a cost involved and that would entail a political struggle. At one level, the issue becomes what is the most sensible way to deploy society's resources; at another level, the issue is creating a more equitable distribution of income and wealth—or, at least, reducing the tendency in the market to accentuate inequalities. Perhaps, if it were done in the name of the social economy or some variant of it such as community development, there might be a way to create a coalition that would lead to a more egalitarian distribution of wealth. Having livable communities is a concern that crosses social class boundaries. However, this optimistic note must be offset by the recognition that over the past decade the neo-conservative agenda has eroded our social fabric and weakened, not strengthened, the organizations in the social economy that depend upon government programs.

Moreover, it should be noted that even though a political strategy to redeploy surplus labour from the private and public sectors to the social economy might have beneficial consequences both for the individuals involved and for their communities, such a proposal is unlikely to affect the tendency in the market towards an increasingly inequitable distribution of both income and wealth. Addressing that issue requires policies that allow a broader array of people to benefit from the wealth being created and, inevitably, effective taxation policies to redistribute wealth.

NOTES

1. Quarter (1992) uses a finer classification by subdividing the non-profit sector into mutual associations that serve a membership and other organizations (non-profits in public service) that serve either the entire public or a subset of it who either desire or need a service.

BIBLIOGRAPHY

Gordon Betcherman and Graham Lowe, "The Future of Work in Canada," Canadian Policy Research Networks, 1997.

Jacques DeFourney, "De La Coopération à L'Économie Sociale," in Proceedings of the Congreso de Co-opertivisimo, University of Duesto and the World Basque Congress, 1988, pp.72-88.

Doreen Duchesne, "Giving Freely: Volunteers in Canada." Ottawa: Statistics Canada, 1989.

Government of Canada, "Co-operatives Canada." Co-operatives Secretariat, 1995.

Government of Ontario, "Guiding Principles for Alternative Service Delivery," Corporate Policy Branch, Management Board Secretariat, 1997.

Ronald Hirshhorn, (ed.), "The Emerging Sector: In Search of a Framework," Ottawa: Renouf.

Thierry Jeantet, "Economie Sociale et Coopératives," Unpublished paper, 1991.

Jesus Larranaga, "Neoco-operativism: Mondragon Prepares for a Global Economy," Worker Co-op, Vol. 10, 1, 1990, pp. 30-33.

Samuel Martin, An Essential Grace. Toronto: McClelland & Stewart, 1985.

Noble, "Alternative Service Delivery Framework," Government of Ontario Management Board Secretariat, April 12, 1996.

David Osborne and Ted Gaebler, Reinventing Government: How the Entrepreneurial Spirit Is Transforming the Public Sector. New York: Plume, 1993.

Dina Palozzi, Speech to Roundtable on Co-ops as Alternatives for Public Services, June 23, 1997.

Jack Quarter, Canada's Social Economy: Co-operatives, Non-Profits and Other Community Enterprises. Toronto: Lorimer, 1992.

Jeremy Rifkin, The End of Work. New York: Tarcher/Putnam, 1996.

David Ross, "How Valuable Is Volunteering?," Perception, Vol. 4, 1990, pp. 17-18.

David Ross and Peter Usher, From the Roots Up. Toronto: Lorimer, 1986.

David Ross and Richard Shillington, "A Profile of the Canadian Volunteer," Ottawa: National Voluntary Organizations, 1990.

David Ross and Richard Shillington, "Economic Dimensions of Volunteer Work in Canada," Ottawa: Secretary of State, 1990a.

Ian Snaith, "The Economie Sociale in the New Europe," Yearbook of Co-operative Enterprise. 1991, pp. 61-75.

Lester Thurow, The Future of Capitalism. New York: William Morrow and Co., 1996.

Paul Wilkinson and Jack Quarter, Building a Community-Controlled Economy: The Evangeline Co-operative Experience. Toronto: University of Toronto Press, 1996.

Chapter 5

The Neo-Liberal Uses of the Social Economy: Non-Profit Organizations and Workfare in Ontario

Paul Leduc Browne

The Debate About the Social Economy in Canada

In Quebec, the October 1996 Employment Summit has given renewed salience to the notion of the "social economy." Forgotten by all but a handful of academics and policy analysts, this 19th-century concept[1] has suddenly sprung forth as a ubiquitous topic of newspaper articles and politicians' speeches, promising to lend greater impetus to a dynamic third sector.

In English Canada, with rare exceptions, the term "social economy" is scarcely used at all.[2] But if the term social economy is still uncommon, there is certainly much talk of the *third sector, civil society, civic community, volunteering* and *charitable giving*. Although the non-profit sector is not being promoted quite as much as a vehicle for job creation in the rest of Canada as it is in Quebec,[3] it figures prominently in the discourse of "reinventing government" and "improving social security."

The tradition of volunteering is deeply rooted in Canada.[4] According to Statistics Canada, it is even more widespread in the rest of Canada than in Quebec.[5] The co-operative movement has had a long, varied and very strong presence throughout the country.[6] Canadians give generously of their time and money to charities.[7]

Public debate about the role in society of the third sector has become more salient in the 1990s. Today, neo-liberals dominate discussion and policy-making around these themes. The neo-liberal uses of the social economy are illustrated by Mike Harris's "Common Sense Revolution" and workfare policies in Ontario. Neo-liberal policies are not without contradictory outcomes, however, not the least of which is to provoke a response within the social economy itself.

Neo-Liberalism and the Welfare State

What with the development over the past twenty years of *Thatcherism on a global scale* (in its various guises of structural adjustment, Rogernomics, the Common Sense Revolution, or the Contract with America), the neo-liberal approach is all too familiar. Neo-liberalism holds that (1) a strictly capitalist society provides greater individual freedom than any other form of social order; (2) it frees individuals from the tyranny of the state and dependency on others; (3) it subjects them all equally to the forces of the market, and (4) it allows them

to succeed or fail on the basis of their own abilities, initiative, risk-taking and hard
work.

Dismantling alternatives to the market and strengthening the freedom of
action of private business are the central goals of neo-liberal governments.
Neo-liberalism rejects the three pillars of the social-democratic welfare state: full
employment, the social wage, and political pluralism—whereby the state
nurtured a dense network of "interest groups," as a way of managing conflict
within society and the state. As such, neo-liberalism reveals itself as a strategy of
unabashed and outspoken class war by business against labour (which is not to
say that it does not also, in its specific incarnations, target women, people of
colour, immigrants, gays and lesbians).[8]

In this scenario there needs to be a strong state to ensure that the rules of
the marketplace and the sanctity of private property are respected by all. Beyond
this, however, the state must not interfere with the workings of the market. All
forms of government regulation of the economy are viewed with suspicion
(whether of financial markets through regulations on banks, or of labour markets
through minimum wage legislation, laws guaranteeing trade union rights,
unemployment insurance, etc.). It follows from these principles that the welfare
state with its large public sector must be unproductive and parasitical, leeching
wealth away from those sectors of society that create it (i.e. business) and giving it
to those that do not (the poor, public servants).[9] Broadly speaking, this is the
same agenda that the Harris Government has announced and begun to
implement in Ontario since 1995.[10]

Neo-Liberalism and the Social Economy

Within the framework of dismantling the welfare state, there is a multi-faceted
neo-liberal strategy for the social economy. It is common on the Right to claim
that the growth of the welfare state stifled voluntary and charitable work.[11] In
launching great waves of cuts to the public sector in 1981, Ronald Reagan
declared: "We have let government take away those things that were once ours to
do voluntarily."[12] Reaganites accused the welfare state of crushing the voluntary
and community organizations that had buffered the individual from remote,
impersonal state bureaucracies. Rolling back the welfare state, in this view, can
only lead to a tremendous upsurge of voluntary action, empowering and
reinvigorating communities and individuals.

In reality, the rise of the welfare state and the pluralistic nature of
liberal-democratic politics in the 1960s, 1970s and 1980s, gave a considerable
impetus to the expansion of the third sector.[13] Over the last thirty years, the
number of registered charities has, for example, more than tripled. In general,
they are very reliant on public funding.[14] The social economy is in fact very
much, to use the title of an influential book from the 1980s, "in and against the
state."[15] Historically, the nature, structure and evolution of the social economy
has been a function of state formation.[16] Simply rolling back the welfare state can
only harm the voluntary sector.

However, the neo-liberal attack on the welfare state does not in fact reduce state power as such; rather, it reconfigures and redirects it. As a set of individuals and organizations operating "in and against the state," the voluntary sector is also struck by the tidal wave of restructuring. Public social spending is reduced as financial responsibility for social programs is offloaded to lower levels of government, or to the private sector and the family. In some cases, voluntary organizations may receive less money from government; in other cases, they may receive more, but in conditions that erode their autonomy and distinctive culture. Finally, the decision on *how* to spend public monies is partly privatized, for example by the replacement of direct grants by tax expenditures for charitable donations.[17]

The federal government has already made changes to the rules governing tax deductions and credits for charitable giving, e.g., allowing individuals to claim 50% of their net income in their tax return, as opposed to 20% as they have up till now. The federal finance department and House of Commons finance committee are studying further changes. The 1996 Ontario budget extended crown foundation status to a much broader group of public sector institutions, including hospitals, public libraries, the Ontario Arts Council, museums and galleries.[18] It also announced that it would use gambling revenues to fund community groups (i.e. tax the poor), raising $180 million via casinos and video lottery terminals.[19]

Another facet of neo-liberal social policy is privatization of the management of poverty. This can take several forms.[20] The entire social assistance system can be handed over to the private sector, as the State of Texas in the United States has been planning on doing.[21] Alternatively, parts of the system can be contracted out to private corporations, for example case management functions or financial administration.[22] The Ontario Government has retained Andersen Consulting, "the world's largest management-consulting firm," to advise it on how to save money in running the social assistance system.[23] As yet, Andersen Consulting is not supposed to be involved in formulating policy, delivering programs, determining recipients' eligibility or managing the caseload. But the government has floated the idea of privatizing social assistance.[24]

Public-private partnerships and contracting out are essential aspects of the privatization agenda. British, American and Canadian researchers have charted the rise of a new contracting regime,[25] in which the voluntary sector has been enrolled as a "shadow civil service"[26] and agent of labour market policy, and non-profit agencies have been subjected to much tighter state control.[27]

As sub-contractors, non-profit organizations often offer neo-liberal governments a cheap substitute for the unionized, better-paid public service. A survey commissioned by the Canadian Centre for Policy Alternatives and conducted by Ekos Research Associates in May and June of 1995 revealed that average pay levels in the third sector are considerable lower than those in the public sector.[28] With the exception of top management, most full-time paid staff in third sector organizations are paid less than the average industrial wage (which was just under $30,000 in 1995). By contrast, the average yearly wage in public administration was about $39,000 in that year.[29] Furthermore, non-profit organizations often receive the benefit of volunteer, i.e., free, labour and can raise money through charitable donations (although it must be said that many public sector institutions, such as libraries, hospitals and museums, have been using volunteers and receiving charitable donations for years).

Establishing a clear contractual framework can be beneficial for both parties,[30] but it is also a way for governments to exercise far more control over their non-profit partners. Obtaining public financing under such a regime requires that organizations meet strict performance criteria imposed by government. In the process, they get drawn more and more in the direction of professionalization and bureaucratization, adopting managerial structures and organizational cultures more and more similar to those in other sectors.[31] Invoking tough economic times, governments pit service delivery against advocacy, increasingly stating that only the former will receive funding, while the latter will not. In a sense, they seek to weed out the "unworthy" in the voluntary sector, just as they separate out the "worthy poor" from the "sturdy rogues" when it comes to social assistance. Both the federal and provincial governments have stressed the need to help the needy in opposition to "wasting resources" on "interest groups" that are deemed unrepresentative.

For a neo-liberal government there is much to be gained in placing the delivery of social services within a market or quasi-market framework, and injecting private-sector principles, values and objectives into the management of the agencies providing the services,[32] while at the same time claiming that bureaucracy is being eliminated, altruism being promoted and the local community acquiring control over the process. The ideological gains are all the greater if the appearance can be created that service delivery has been decentralized, while the government has in reality retained—or in some cases increased—its effective central control. This is illustrated by the Harris government's workfare initiative.

"Ontario Works": The Harris Government's Workfare Program

In its first Throne Speech, the Harris government undertook to fulfill its key election campaign promise to introduce a new workfare program for social assistance recipients, warning that all those who refused to participate would lose their benefits.[33] It also announced a new initiative to promote volunteering and charity. Volunteering was referred to as the "spirit of Ontario" at the same time as cuts to the public sector were promised. The Parliamentary Assistant to the Premier, Julia Munro (MPP for Durham-York) was put in charge of promoting the voluntary sector and civic community in Ontario. An Advisory Board on the Voluntary Sector was set up. Its report was made published in January 1997.

The link between charity and workfare was hinted at by Premier Harris in comments to reporters: "We invite the churches to help people. That's what they're there for, to help their neighbours, to help their communities. We want to break [the welfare] dependency, and we invite churches and the public and members of Parliament to help those who have become accustomed to something that has become a lifestyle, to assist them in getting out to become productive members of society."[34]

Ontario Works, the Harris government's workfare plan unveiled on June 12, 1996, was presented as a reform whereby "people receiving social assistance who are able to work will be required to work on community projects to earn their welfare cheques."[35] Community and Social Services Minister David Tsubouchi announced that work-for-welfare programs would initially be launched in twenty municipalities, before being put in place throughout the province at a later date.

In July 1996, the Ministry of Community and Social Services issued guidelines for *Ontario Works*. They stipulated that all recipients of the municipally-administered general welfare assistance who had been on the rolls for more than four months would be placed in one of three mandatory programs: employment support, community participation, and employment placement. The first "includes activities that support participants in their efforts to become job-ready and access their shortest route to paid employment, such as structured job search activities, basic education, and job-specific skills training."

The second consisted of "any unpaid community service activity under the direction of officials within communities and/or public or non-profit organizations." Such community placements would involve a maximum of seventy hours per month (on average seventeen hours per week) of work for a maximum normally of six months.[36] As examples of the type of community work social assistance recipients could do, the Minister suggested cleaning up rivers and lakes, planting trees, maintaining snowmobile trails, helping out at a seniors' drop-in program.

Finally, "employment support" is a scheme whereby the government would pay job placement agencies or self-employment development agencies (which could be in the private or non-profit sectors) to place social assistance recipients in paid employment. The agencies would be paid "on a performance basis using a share of the funds that would otherwise be paid out in social assistance to the participant."[37] Social assistance recipients refusing to participate in mandatory training or work placements would be denied benefits for three months, or six months for a second offence.

Community placements, the actual mandatory work-for-welfare component of *Ontario Works*, are to be restricted to municipalities and non-profit organizations. For now at least, social assistance recipients can not be placed in for-profit businesses. The role of the non-profit organizations participating will be to "develop and administer on-site placements, where appropriate; develop and administer proposals for financial or in-kind support for placements; [and supervise] participants in placements and report non-compliance to the service delivery agent [i.e., the municipality]."[38]

One can see how such a subcontractual role fails to coincide with the main mission of organizations which, after all, were set up to help people with disabilities, to offer child care services, or to bring aid to the poor, to mention just a few of the many services they provide to the community. And indeed, community groups of all sorts did not fail to point this out at the various fora on Ontario Works organized throughout Ontario during the autumn of 1996.[39]

Some pointed out an additional dilemma. Many organizations enjoy the help of numerous volunteers, some of whom are social assistance recipients. Under Ontario Works, they could potentially use that volunteer activity to make up their 17-hour weekly workfare placement. Just keeping on those volunteers, it was felt, would be tantamount to an organization "passively" supporting, or participating in, Ontario Works.

Turning away all social assistance recipients "eligible" for workfare who wanted to do volunteer work, and who might indeed have been doing volunteer work for some time, would go against many of the practices and principles of the agencies, who combat discrimination against social assistance recipients. One person at an Ottawa community forum said she had already had some 30 volunteers who are on welfare telephone her to ask to be kept on by her organization, should they be forced into workfare placements.

Could voluntary agencies get around this dilemma by refusing "active" participation in Ontario Works (for example by refusing to receive money for placements), but still participating "passively" by accepting social assistance recipients as volunteers, so they could fulfil their mandatory work placements? This would be impossible. An agency could not in fact participate "passively" in Ontario Works. Part of what the government is doing with its workfare plan is devolving responsibilities on to lower levels of government, from the ministry to the municipalities. They, in turn, will be expected to enrol voluntary organizations in the social control of social assistance recipients.

One of the jobs of a voluntary organization will be to "police" workfare, by reporting the attendance and work habits of workfare participants to the local authority in charge of the scheme ("to supervise recipients in placements and report non-compliance to the municipality"). Volunteer work could then only count officially as a workfare placement if the agency filed reports to the government. Surely that qualifies as "active" participation, even if the agency receives no money from the government to help defray the extra administrative costs of taking part in the workfare program.

Representatives of voluntary organizations are angry about workfare. They know that it would certainly increase the workloads of already overworked staff. It raises difficult ethical and practical issues, such as screening workfare participants, checking for police records (e.g. in the case of anybody called upon to work with children), and so on. The agencies feel caught between a rock and a hard place: on one hand, government pressure to participate; on the other, their own lack of resources to do so (where, they all asked, are the money and staff going to come from to manage all these new "volunteers?").[40] They do not want to exploit people on social assistance forced into work placements; but they also do not wish to turn away people they may know personally, who have become part of their community of volunteers. And indeed, the Harris government has found community groups not only reluctant to participate in *Ontario Works*, but on the whole actively hostile to doing so.[41]

Bill 142, the Social Assistance Reform Act, was presented to the Ontario Legislature in June 1997. It will expand *Ontario Works* to include 380,000 people across Ontario, encompassing not only recipients of general welfare assistance, but also single-parents of school-age children, hitherto the recipients of family benefits and exempt from workfare. The Family Benefits Act and the General Welfare Assistance Act are to be combined in the new law. People with disabilities would be removed from social assistance altogether and placed under another income support plan defined by the new Ontario Disability Support Program Act. All social assistance would be delivered at the municipal level. Municipalities would pay 20 per cent of the total cost of benefits and 50 per cent of the administrative costs, while the provincial government would bear the rest of the costs. (In 1995-96, the province's share was eleven times that of the municipalities.) Social assistance recipients would be fingerprinted (using "finger-imaging" technology). The entire caseload is 582,000, or 1.16 million people, including 400,000 children.[42]

As of late August 1997, only 36,000 people in 36 communities were participating in *Ontario Works*.[43] Only people on social assistance for over four months have been channeled into the program and the vast majority of them are enrolled in training or counselling programs. Only a few are in community placements.

Janet Ecker, who succeeded David Tsubouchi in late 1996, claims that her government's workfare plan was never meant to be draconian, but merely to stipulate that all social assistance recipients must participate in some constructive activity likely to help them find work.[44] Yet there is no doubt that her words are at odds with the much harsher statement of her Ministry under her predecessor that "people receiving social assistance who are able to work will be required to work on community projects to earn their welfare cheques." It may be that such statements were misunderstood; or it may be that the Ontario government used harsh rhetoric to intimidate social assistance recipients, and workers and the poor more generally (clearly a key aim of any workfare program), while being "softer" in actual practice in order not to alienate the municipalities. Actually finding and paying for work placements for the tens of thousands of people targeted seemed from the start an exorbitantly expensive and unmanageable task.[45] Doing so in the teeth of resistance on the part of the municipal social service departments and community non-profit organizations expected to implement the plan was surely impossible. Time will tell to what extent the Harris government goes beyond the very modest steps towards work placements it has so far taken. What seems clear is that most of the people in community placements so far are doing work that could otherwise be done by municipal workers.[46] If Ontario follows the American example (notably that of New York City), the temptation to use the unpaid labour of those on workfare as a substitute for paid municipal workers may become irresistible, especially in an era of huge budget cuts.

The "Advisory Board on the Voluntary Sector"

Non-profit organizations' resistance to *Ontario Works* is symptomatic of a broader phenomenon. The neo-liberal goal of restructuring the state typically involves a restructuring of the non-profit sector. Service delivery is hived off from the public sector, while the alternative service providers face restrictions on their advocacy role, as well as new contractual and bureaucratic controls. This scenario only seemingly establishes *partnerships*, i.e. relationships *between free and equal parties with congruent interests*. To be sure, there is a formal air of equality in the contractual nature of the relationship. But the substantive conditions of the relationship rule out any true equality. "Partnerships" between the state and non-profit organizations are characterized by conflict and coercion as much as by cooperation and collaboration.

Conflict is only compounded by the fact that many alternative service providers begin their lives as organizations set up by social assistance recipients, users of social services, or other disadvantaged groups, to defend their interests against the often impersonal or even oppressive government bureaucracies to which they were subjected. It is clear that transforming such organizations into contractors run by professionalized managers and staffed by technocratic experts can only provoke a backlash from the organizations' members and constituencies. The same is true of attempting to enrol such groups as junior partners in coercive programs such as workfare.

Echoes of the concerns aroused by *Ontario Works* can be found in the report of the Ontario government's Advisory Board on the Voluntary Sector,[47] which held consultations between July and October 1996—the period between David Tsubouchi's initial launch of *Ontario Works* pilot projects in June 1996 and Janet Ecker's November 1996 announcement that only participation in the overall program, not work placements per se, would be mandatory.

The Advisory Board on the Voluntary Sector proposes a set of "first principles of voluntary action" to guide the public, private and voluntary sectors. These principles state that "voluntary action is willing and non-salaried," and that: "Volunteering needs to be clearly distinguished from those actions required as part of government or other programs, e.g., community service orders, workfare."[48] Furthermore: "Voluntary action should not actively seek to replace employment or jobs, and should be taken by individuals of their own choice to augment but not compete with paid activity."[49] In other words, volunteers should not, for example, be used as substitutes for public servants.

The principles also say that: "Government should continue to be accountable and responsible for the provision of essential services to meet basic needs, although voluntary organizations may choose to participate in the provision of services."[50] Finally, they also assert that: "Advocating at all levels within society is a legitimate mechanism by which voluntary organizations represent and promote the interests of those they serve (e.g., representing the rights of people in institutions, or encouraging wheelchair accessibility)."[51] The report calls for the government "to act as an enabler of voluntary action rather than as a director or controller."[52]

The Advisory Board's list of principles clearly reflect the widespread concern in the Ontario voluntary sector to counter, or at least limit, the conflation of workfare and volunteering, privatization, the erosion of publicly funded services, and the suppression of advocacy as a key function of voluntary organizations. The contents of the report suggest that there is a growing self-consciousness in the voluntary sector fuelled by a sense of having been left out, of having been the mere object of government policies. In keeping with this, the report presents "three overarching themes": the demand to be consulted by government ("a place at the table" as a "partner"); the project of forming alliances within the voluntary sector to develop a cohesive, common front; and the search for new partnerships in the public and private sectors to promote the voluntary sector's capacity to act.[53]

The report of the Advisory Board on the Voluntary Sector provides an index of the type of dialogue currently under way between the Ontario government and civil society. While it betrays no hint of the fear, anger and frustration aroused by *Ontario Works*, it nevertheless affirms the minimum conditions for the survival and development of an independent voluntary sector: the difference between voluntary action and forced labour; the political independence of the voluntary sector (the affirmation of the essential character of advocacy); the economic sustainability of the voluntary sector (the necessary role of government in providing the financial, legislative and logistical support for voluntary action).

This, however, is only a minimum. It is instructive to contrast the report of the Advisory Board on the Voluntary Sector with its counterpart in Quebec, the report of the Orientation Committee on the Social Economy.[54] Struck in the wake of the Quebec Women's March Against Poverty, the Committee gave voice to a feminist analysis of the inadequacy of the neo-liberal model of economic development, while affirming the central place of a progressive, democratic social economy as a way of joining social and economic development, fighting poverty (especially among women), recognizing the value of unpaid work, and generating meaningful, well-paid employment in partnership with a reinvigorated welfare state.

The Ontario Advisory Board was essentially concerned with volunteer work, the Quebec Orientation Committee with paid employment. The Ontario Advisory Board provided no analysis of the Ontario economy or the voluntary sector's role in it; the Quebec Orientation Committee analyzed the Quebec economy quite critically, and discussed the social economy's past and future role in detail. The Quebec report is pervaded by the spirit of the Women's March Against Poverty; it is full of references to inequalities and other systemic social problems to be fought against and conquered.

The Quebec report's definition of the social economy coincides with the Ontario report's definition of the voluntary sector in evoking the role of volunteering, as well as the autonomy and not-for-profit nature of third-sector organizations. But it differs in one crucial point: for an organization to be considered part of the social economy, according to the Orientation Committee, its employees, volunteers, members, and those who use its services, must be involved in managing it, establishing its policies, and making its executive decisions. This element of participatory democracy is absent from the Ontario report. In itself this does not signify that the non-profit sector is more progressive, more politically aware or better organized in Quebec than in Ontario.[55] Rather, it reflects the very different relations between social movements and the government in power in the two provinces.

Conclusion

There is no doubt that the promotion of charity is the flip side of the neo-liberal downsizing of public social services and social security. The return to the political economy of the Victorian era only too naturally leads to a return to 19th-century philanthropic ideals and practices. Is there any doubt that Mother Teresa's missionary work only received the accolades that it did because she resolutely refused to question the social and political causes of poverty and disease, preferring instead to bind the wounds, while offering the consolations of the hereafter?

Similarly, the charity work of the late Diana, Princess of Wales no doubt enabled many charitable organizations to raise considerable sums of money. But surely such saintly activities are all in a day's work for members of the British Royal Family? Surely the promotion of altruistic, non-"political,"private philanthropy is necessary to shore up the social cohesion of a society that unbridled capitalism threatens to tear apart.[56] For a thousand years, under the principle of *noblesse oblige*, it has been the aristocracy's role to bring relief to the poor in order to preserve an oppressive social order.[57] Charitable activities are not just touted as a good way to preserve "social cohesion"; creating "social capital"[58] is also a great help in building networks to facilitate the accumulation of economic capital.[59]

And yet, the 1990s are not the 1830s, nor is today's social economy the same as the last century's friendly societies or philanthropic organizations. The level of resistance to the Harris government's policies in the non-profit sector is highly encouraging. While many in the English-Canadian charitable community are imbued with a communitarian ideology that elides fundamental divisions of class, gender and ethnicity, many others are not. And while many favour partnerships with the very forces of big business that are driving the processes of exclusion and polarization, many others are far more sceptical. Behind the ever more prominent discourse about civil society, civic community and social capital, there is a fundamental split between those who would be content to bandage the wounds, and the democratic social movements who seek real social change to prevent those wounds from occurring.[60]

The question is: will the trend to co-optation ultimately be successful, transforming large parts of the non-profit sector into often unwitting agents of a neo-liberal order, and marginalizing the more radical groups? Or will resistance grow and alliances develop between the social economy, the labour movement and other social movements opposed to neo-liberalism?

NOTES

1. See Robert Castel, *Les Métamorphoses de la question sociale. Une chronique du salariat*, Paris: Fayard, 1995, for an outline of some of the uses of the concept in the 19th-century; see also Jacques Defourny's contribution in Jacques Defourny & Jose-Luis Monzon (eds.), *Économie sociale. Entre économie capitaliste et économie publique/The Third Sector. Cooperative, Mutual and Nonprofit Organizations*. Brussels: Centre international de recherches et d'information sur l'économie publique, social et coopérative, De Boeck Université, 1992.

2. Jack Quarter uses it in the title of his excellent book, *Canada's Social Economy*, but indicates that it is borrowed from European authors (Toronto, Lorimer, 1992). The 1997 *Alternative Federal Budget* (a collective project co-ordinated by the Canadian Centre for Policy Alternatives and CHO!CES, involving popular sector groups across Canada) contains a section on the social economy. The concept is also central to my paper, "Post-social-democracy, or the Dialectic of the Social Economy," delivered at the Eighth Conference on Canadian Social Welfare Policy in Regina, June 28, 1997.

3. See *Un parcours vers l'insertion, la formation et l'emploi. Document de consultation.* Québec, Ministère de la Sécurité du revenu, 1996; *Osons la solidarité! Rapport du groupe de travail sur l'économie sociale.* Chantier de l'économie et de l'emploi, Sommet sur l'économie et l'emploi, 1996; *Entre l'espoir et le doute. Rapport du comité d'orientation et de concertation sur l'économie sociale*, 1996; Camil Bouchard, Vivian Labrie, Alain Noël, *Chacun sa part. Rapport de trois membres du comité externe de réforme de la sécurité du revenu.* Montréal, 1996; Louis Favreau, "Les expériences d'insertion sociale par l'activité économique: éléments de bilan," and Louis Gill, "L'économie solidaire comme stratégie d'emploi?" in *Correspondances. Bulletin syndical et populaire*, Vol. 5, No. 2/3, Spring/Summer 1997; *Économie et solidarités*, special issue on "L'insertion sociale par l'économique," Vol. 28, No. 2, 1997; François Aubry, Jean Charest, *Développer l'économie solidaire. Éléments d'orientation*. Montréal, CSN, 1995.

4. See Janet Lautenschlager, *Volunteering. A Traditional Canadian Value.* Ottawa, Multiculturalism and Citizenship Canada, Voluntary Action Directorate, 1992; Samuel A. Martin, *An Essential Grace. Funding Canada's Health Care, Education, Welfare, Religion and Culture.* Toronto: McClelland and Stewart, 1985.

5. See the exhaustive, although now somewhat dated, data on volunteering in Doreen Duchesne, *Giving Freely: Volunteers in Canada.* Ottawa: Statistics Canada, Labour Analytic Report No. 4, Cat. 71-535, 1989.

6. See Jack Quarter, *op. cit.*; the report of the Co-operative Future Directions Project, *Patterns & Trends of Canadian Co-operative Development*, Saskatoon, the Co-operative College of Canada, 1982; Sylvie Jean, *Histoire du mouvement coopératif en Ontario français*. Ottawa: Conseil de la coopération d'Ontario, 1986; Paul Bélanger, Jacques Boucher & Benoît Lévesque, "L'économie solidaire au Québec: la question du modèle de développement," in Jean-Louis Laville (ed.), *L'économie solidaire. Une perspective internationale.* Paris: Desclée de Brouwer, 1994; Benoît Lévesque & Marie-Claire Malo, "L'économie sociale au Québec: une notion méconnue, une réalité économique importante," in Jacques Defourny & Jose-Luis Monzon (eds.), *op. cit.*

7. For recent statistical profiles of the charitable sector in Canada, see Paul Leduc Browne, *Love in a Cold World? The Voluntary Sector in an Age of Cuts.* Ottawa: Canadian Centre for Policy Alternatives, 1996; David Sharpe, *A Portrait of Canada's Charities. The Size, Scope and Financing of Registered Charities.* Toronto: Canadian Centre for Philanthropy, 1994.

8. See J. Smith, "Class-War Conservatism: Housing Policy, Homelessness and the 'Underclass'," in Leo Panitch (ed.), *Socialist Register 1995: Why Not Capitalism.* London: Merlin Press, 1995, pp. 188-206.

9. The central issues in the New Right attack on the welfare state are discussed by Ramesh Mishra, *The Welfare State in Capitalist Society. Policies of Retrenchment and Maintenance*

in Europe, North America and Australia. Toronto: University of Toronto, 1990; Fred Block, Richard Cloward, Barbara Ehrenreich and Frances Fox Piven, *The Mean Season. The Attack on the Welfare State.* New York: Pantheon Books, 1987; Stuart Hall & Martin Jacques (eds.), *The Politics of Thatcherism.* London: Lawrence & Wishart, 1983; and Frédéric Lesemann, *La politique sociale américaine. Les années Reagan.* Montréal: Éditions Saint-Martin/Paris, Syros-Alternatives, 1988.

10. These elements are summed up in Paul Leduc Browne, "Déjà Vu: Thatcherism in Ontario," and André Régimbald, "The Ontario Branch of American Conservatism," in Diana Ralph, André Régimbald & Nérée St-Amand (eds.), *Open for Business, Closed to People: Mike Harris's Ontario.* Halifax: Fernwood Publishing, 1997. See too Jane Kelsey, *Economic Fundamentalism.* London: Pluto Press, 1995.

11. According to Lester Salamon, the prevailing view in the United States is that the welfare state is "a gigantic enlargement of the apparatus of government—particularly the national government—at the expense of other social institutions, among them private non-profit groups. The central image has been that of a large bureaucratic state, hierarchic in structure and monolithic in form, taking on social functions previously performed by other social institutios." "Of Market Failure, Voluntary Failure, and Third-Party Government: Toward a Theory of Government-Nonprofit Relations in the Modern Welfare State," in Susan Ostrander and Stuart Langton (eds.), *Shifting the Debate: Public/Private Sector Relations in the Modern Welfare State.* New Brunswick, N.J.: Transaction Books, 1987, pp. 33-34.) In fact, there is an elaborate network of partnerships between the two "sectors" in the United States. In health and social services, non-profit organizations "actually deliver a larger share of the services government finances than do government agencies themselves."(*Ibid.*, pp. 29-30.) This is explored in detail by Steven Rathgeb Smith and Michael Lipsky, *Non-profits for Hire. The Welfare State in the Age of Contracting.* Cambridge, Mass.: Harvard University Press, 1993.

12. Quoted in B. Gidron, R. Kramer & L. Salamon, "Government and the Third Sector in Comparative Perspective: Allies or Adversaries?," in *Government and the Third Sector: Emerging Relationships in Welfare States.* San Francisco: Jossey-Bass, 1992. See also Peter Dobkin Hall, "Abandoning the Rhetoric of Independence: Reflections on the Non-Profit Sector in the Post-Liberal Era," in Susan Ostrander & Stuart Langton (eds.), *op. cit.*; as well as Lester Salamon & A.J. Abramson, "The Nonprofit Sector," in *The Reagan Experiment*, ed. by J.L. Palmer & I.V. Sawhill, Washington, D.C.: Urban Institute, 1982, pp. 219-243.

13. See Paul Leduc Browne, *Love in a Cold World?* pp. 14-15, 74ff.; Josephine Rekart, *Public Funds, Private Provision. The Role of the Voluntary Sector.* Vancouver: UBC Press, 1993; Leslie A. Pal, *Interests of State. The Politics of Language, Multiculturalism and Feminism in Canada.* Montreal/Kingston: McGill-Queen's University Press, 1993.

14. See Paul Leduc Browne, *Love in a Cold World?* and David Sharpe, *A portrait of Canada's Charities.*

15. London Edinburgh Weekend Return Group, *In and Against the State: Discussion Notes for Socialists.* London: Pluto Press, 1980.

16. This idea is developed in chapter 1 of Paul Leduc Browne, *Love in a Cold World?* Pete Alcock and Lars Christensen come to strikingly similar conclusions for Britain and Denmark in their article "In and Against the State: Community-Based Organizations in Britain and Denmark in the 1990s," *Community Development Journal*, Vol. 30, No. 2, April 1995, p. 110: "Our conclusion was that community-based organizations in both countries had developed as a result of *top-down* state support as well as *bottom-up* community activity, and that their focus of concern was often with the interface between state and citizen. They thus operated *in and against the state* (to resurrect a phrase from the 1970s) rather than as an alternative to it; and consequently the temporary nature of state support for many of these organizations, and recent policy development which had led to reductions in this support, threatened rather than encouraged the future

development of the community base in social policy in both countries, at a time when governments in both were extolling the virtues of such third sector agencies."

17. When it gives tax credits and deductions to those who give money to registered charities, the federal government gives up a portion of tax revenue as a way of encouraging taxpayers to donate an even larger sum to a registered charity of their choice. Revenue Canada decides which types of activity will receive charitable status and which organizations will be registered. But it is not in a position to decree how much will be donated to each category or each organization. That is left up to the donors. In effect, Revenue Canada has conferred on individual donors the power to decide how to spend millions of dollars that would otherwise have been collected in taxes. That is why such foregone tax revenue is referred to as a "tax expenditure."

18. Crown foundations differ from other charities in that donors may claim up to 100% of their net income in their tax returns.

19. The Hounourable Ernie Eves, Q.C., *1996 Ontario Budget: Budget Speech.* Toronto, Queen's Printer for Ontario, May 7, 1996, pp. 13, 26. See also Margaret Philp, "Video lotteries coming to bars," *The Globe and Mail,* May 8, 1996, p. A4B. According to a more recent report, the $180 million "marks a major windfall for charities, which now receive only about $10 million a year through gambling at roving monte carlos. But it is expected to be an even greater new revenue source for the province, which could reap up to $740 million a year from installing as many as 13,200 video lottery terminals in the 44 planned charity casinos and racetracks. Charities would receive $100 million from the VLTs and perhaps as much as $80 million from the gaming tables. As much as $140 million would go to the operators of the casinos and the racetracks, while up to $20 million would be allocated to help problem gamblers, according to the government's projections." (Richard Mackie, "Government to reap millions from new charity system," *The Globe and Mail,* August 26, 1997, p. A7.)

20. See the special issue of *Studies in Political Economy* on privatization (No. 53, Summer 1997).

21. See Kathleen Kenna, "Profits in the misery business," *The Toronto Star,* May 23, 1997.

22. For example: "The defense contractor BDM International Inc. won a contract to automate New Mexico's welfare system as early as 1988; Lockheed was in the business of collecting child support and fingerprinting (or "finger-imaging," as the euphemism goes) recipients in various states; Curtis & Associates and the job-brokerage firm America Works were propelling recipients into the workforce in Buffalo, San Francisco, and other cities." (Barbara Ehrenreich, "Spinning the poor into gold: How corporations seek to profit from welfare reform," *Harper's,* August 1997, p. 47.)

23. James Rusk, "Ontario signs pact to manage welfare: U.S.-based firm promises savings," *The Globe and Mail,* February 18, 1997.

24. James Wallace, "Private welfare on way?," *The Toronto Star,* October 12, 1996. In Bill 142, the Social Assistance Reform Act introduced in June 1997, the Ontario government confers on cabinet the power to privatize any part of the social assistance system simply by way of creating new regulations. See *Social Safety News. The Newsletter of the Ontario Social Safety Network,* Issue 17, July 1997, p. 6.

25. See in particular Michael Lipsky and Steven Rathgeb Smith, *Non-profits for Hire. The Welfare State in the Age of Contracting*; Susan Ostrander and Stuart Langton (eds.), *Shifting the Debate: Public/Private Sector Relations in the Modern Welfare State*; Benjamin Gidron, Ralph Kramer and Lester Salamon (eds.), *Government and the Third Sector: Emerging Relationships in Welfare States*; Paul Reading, *Community Care and the Voluntary Sector. The Role of Voluntary Organizations in a Changing World.* Birmingham: Venture Press/British Association of Social Workers, 1994; Eric Shragge, "Community-based Practice: Political Alternatives or New State Forms?," in Linda Davies and Eric Shragge (eds.), *Bureaucracy and Community. Essays on the Politics of Social Work Practice.*

Montreal: Black Rose Books, 1990; Josephine Rekart, *Public Funds, Private Provision: The Role of the Voluntary Sector*; Paul Leduc Browne, *Love in a Cold World? The Voluntary Sector in an Age of Cuts*; *Merchants of Care? The Non-Profit Sector in a Competitive Social Services Marketplace*. Toronto: The Social Planning Council of Metropolitan Toronto, April 1997.

26. See Josephine Rekart, *op. cit.*

27. Yves Vaillancourt has written of the need to make a clear distinction between privatization (shifting services from the public to the private sector) and "communitarization" (*communautarisation*), by which he means shifting services to the social economy or third sector. See his report, *Vers un nouveau partage des responsabilités dans les services sociaux et de santé: rôles de l'État, du marché, de l'économie sociale et du secteur informel*. Montreal: UQAM-LAREPPS, 1997. Vaillancourt regards his welfare pluralist position as a way of creating a new progressive—I would say "post-social-democratic," to use Pierre Rosanvallon's term—social development strategy opposed both to traditional social democracy and to neo-liberalism.

28. See Paul Leduc Browne and Pierrette Landry, *The "Third Sector" and Employment*. Ottawa: Canadian Centre for Policy Alternatives, 1996, pp. 14-15.

29. A similar finding is reported in a study of the non-profit sector in four neighbourhoods of Montreal. There the average yearly wage of non-profit-sector employees is $20,590 (without benefits) or $22,855 including benefits. See Réjean Mathieu (ed.), *L'impact économique et social du secteur communautaire dans quatre arrondissements de la Ville de Montréal*. Montreal: UQAM-LAREPPS, 1996, pp. 43, 46.

30. See Paul Reading, *op. cit.*, pp. 27-28.

31. See Eric Shragge, *op. cit.*, p. 142.

32. A further symptom of the neo-liberal colonization of the third sector is the proliferation of university-based courses and centres, as well as expensive conferences sponsored by governments and big business, that are designed to instill the principles of sound administration and fund-raising in the executives and managers of non-profit associations.

33. A discussion of the early history of the Harris government's workfare policy can be found in Ernie Lightman, "'It's Not a Walk in the Park': Workfare in Ontario," in Eric Shragge (ed.), *Workfare: Ideology for a New Under-Class*. Toronto: Garamond Press, 1997, pp. 85-107.

34. Quoted in Margaret Philp, "Tories make it official: Ontario first province to impose workfare," *The Globe and Mail*, September 28, 1995.

35. "People will work for their welfare cheques starting this September," Ontario Ministry of Community and Social Services, News Release 96-24, June 12, 1996.

36. The figure of seventy hours was arrived at by dividing the maximum monthly benefits on general welfare assistance, $520.00, by the minimum wage, $6.85. The aim was to perpetuate the confusion between workfare (unremunerated forced labour) and a job (freely chosen waged labour). At the same time, the government wanted to forestall the accusation that workfare would pay less than minimum wage.

37. *Program Guidelines for Early Implementation of Ontario Works. Companion document to MCSS Guidelines for the Development of Business Plans for Early Implementation of Ontario Works*. Ontario: Ministry of Community and Social Services, July 18, 1996, pp. 10-17.

38. *Ibid.*, pp. 31-32.

39. In Ottawa, for example, a forum on workfare for community organizations was organized by the Social Planning Council of Ottawa-Carleton on September 10, 1996, with sponsorship from Labour Community Services, the Ottawa District Labour Council and the Volunteer Centre of Ottawa-Carleton. A similar event was held in Toronto on October 11-12, 1996. Thanks to pressure from community organizations and activists, many

municipalities, such as Toronto, Kingston and Windsor, passed motions stating their opposition to participation in workfare schemes.

40. Moreover, they faced pressure on another front: the Canadian Union of Public Employees announced that it would—quite understandably—refuse to support United Way organizations that funded non-profits participating in *Ontario Works*. See Paul Leduc Browne, "Why the United Way should take sides on workfare," *Kitchener-Waterloo Record*, 17 September 1996.

41. And, as Ian Morrison and Melodie Mayson point out: "Most municipalities have been unable to identify community participation placements to send people to. They project that only a small number of people will ever participate in a workfare placement, in part because of a lack of interest from voluntary sector agencies. The few placements generated will end up costing about $27 per hour." ("From the Steering Committee: Workfare and the Not-for-profit Sector," *Workfare Watch*, Volume 1, Issue 3, November 1996, p. 1.)

42. Caroline Mallan, "Sweeping welfare reforms introduced," *The Toronto Star*, June 13, 1997; Richard Mackie and Margaret Philp, "Ontario introduces welfare reform," *The Globe and Mail*, June 13, 1997.

43. Caroline Mallan, "Debate begins on workfare plan included in welfare bill," *The Toronto Star*, August 20, 1997.

44. "Notes for Remarks by the Honourable Janet Ecker, Minister of Community and Social Services, to the Ontario Municipal Social Services Association," November 18, 1996; Margaret Philp, "Workfare begins with a whimper," *The Globe and Mail*, June 4, 1997.

45. "Workfare requirements will apply to about 100,000 people in Metropolitan Toronto when the program is fully mature. For the past two years Metro's Job Incentive Program (JIP), a *voluntary* program, placed people in community agencies to gain training and work experience. JIP placed about 2,000 people in community agencies over 2 years simply because such programs are extraordinarily expensive and the voluntary sector has limited capacity to absorb placements of any kind—voluntary or forced. Metro officials admit that JIP was the largest program of its kind possible in Metro. (...) Metro Toronto probably has the largest infrastructure of voluntary sector organizations in the province. Smaller municipalities will not be able to generate more than a few placements in the non-profit sector." ("From the Steering Committee: Workfare and the Not-for-profit Sector," *Workfare Watch*, Volume 1, Issue 3, November 1996, p. 1.) Officials from the Regional Municipality of Ottawa-Carleton have confirmed this in conversation with the author. Even at the best of times, there are not enough placements for social assistance recipients wishing to volunteer or enough places in training programs for those wishing to enrol in them.

46. The guidelines for *Ontario Works* do state that "community or paid employment placements must not displace any paid employment position in the participating organization (including any associated or related organization) currently held by an employee or previously held by an employee within a minimum of two years of the organization offering an Ontario Works placement." (*Program Guidelines for Early Implementation of Ontario Works*, p. 34.) However it must also be noted that the initial community placements involved tasks such as painting municipal buildings and building wheelchair ramps into them—work that would otherwise typically done by a public servant or the employee of an "associated or related organization," i.e., a contractor.

47. *Sustaining a Civic Society: Voluntary Action in Ontario*. Report of the Advisory Board on the Voluntary Sector, Toronto, Queen's Printer for Ontario, 1997.

48. *Ibid.*, pp. 7-8.

49. *Ibid.*, p. 8.

50. *Ibid.*, p. 8. "Notwithstanding government rationalization at all levels, governments have a responsibility to provide a policy, legislative and regulatory environment that facilitates and supports voluntary organizations and voluntary action. Inadequacies exist, particularly in

organizational and supervisory law, and the various levels of government should work with the voluntary sector to determine appropriate reforms." (*Ibid.*, p. iii.)

51. *Ibid.*, p. 7.

52. *Ibid.*, p. 9.

53. *Ibid.*, p. ii.

54. *Entre l'espoir et le doute. Rapport du Comité d'orientation et de concertation sur l'économie sociale*, May 1996.

55. For a highly progressive vision of democratic economic planning for Ontario, involving the third sector, see the Ontario Alternative Budget Papers 1997, especially Paper 4, "Working Down Our Debts: Creating 600,000 Jobs to Rebuild Our Communities." (The Ontario Alternative Budget is an exercise co-ordinated by the Ontario Federation of Labour.)

56. It has been suggested that members of the British Royal Family are patrons of some 3,000 charities, and that this is one of its main functions in post-Thatcherite Britain. (W.M. Dick, letter to the editor, *The Globe and Mail*, September 9, 1997.) To be fair, the late Diana, Princess of Wales, did go beyond the bounds of Victorian philanthropy in at least two areas: working with AIDS sufferers was in itself a political statement because of widespread prejudices within the Conservative Party; and this is even truer of her participation in the campaign for the banning of land mines.

57. "The tradition that big property-owners should dispense hospitality and relieve the poor goes back a very long way. It is at once ostentation and a form of social insurance: it is the tribute which members of a ruling class pay to surviving ideals of a more equal society, memories of which haunt so many mediaeval movements of social protest. The tradition remained that hospitality was a duty incumbent upon the very wealthy. The derivation of our word 'generous' from the Latin word meaning 'well-born,' 'noble,' is suggestive. In mediaeval society this duty may not have been regularly observed; its observation was no doubt restricted and selective; but the acceptance of it, at least as a theoretical concept, helped to smooth the workings of that brutal society, to blunt the edge of class hostility on each side. Even in the seventeenth century manorial lords were by the customs of many parishes still deemed to have a special duty to maintain the poor of those parishes." (Christopher Hill, *Society and Puritanism in Pre-Revolutionary England*. London: Mercury Books, 1966, pp. 259-260.)

58. See Robert Putnam, *Making Democracy Work: Civic Traditions in Modern Italy*. Princeton: Princeton University Press, 1994; "Bowling Alone: America's Declining Social Capital," *Journal of Democracy*, January 1995; and "The Strange Disappearance of Civic America," *The American Prospect*, No. 24, Winter 1996. For an interesting commentary, see Nicholas Lemann, "Kicking in Groups," *The Atlantic Monthly*, April 1996.

59. There is nothing terribly new about this. See Robert Castel, *op. cit.*, on the promotion of private philanthropy in 19th century France. On the United States, see Peter Dobkin Hall. "A Historical View of the Private Nonprofit Sector," in Walter W. Powell. *The Nonprofit Sector. A Research Handbook*. New Haven: Yale University Press, 1987. On Britain, see Geoffrey Finlayson, *Citizen, State and Social Welfare in Britain, 1830-1990*. Oxford: Clarendon Press, 1994.

60. These two trends are discussed in my book *Love in a Cold World?* as well as in my paper, "Post-social-democracy, or The Dialectic of the Social Economy," *op. cit.*

Chapter 6

Reflections on Work, the Social Economy and the Dangers of 'Carefare'

Andrea Levy

We should not expect to achieve anything by treating the symptoms of "the crisis" because there is no crisis: a new system has been established which abolishes work on a massive scale. It is reviving the worst forms of domination, servitude and exploitation by compelling everyone to fight a war of each against all to obtain the "work" that it is eliminating.[1]

—*André Gorz*

There is no problem more fundamental to the task of fashioning a political alternative in today's global cities than the problem of work—or rather the lack of it for a growing segment of the urban population. The global city is itself a creature of the global mobility of capital, which in turn has given rise to a global workforce. The problem of work cannot be viewed any longer in a local or even a national context: even the most highly skilled, highly paid workers in the major urban centres of North America and Europe are competing with lower wage counterparts throughout the developing world. As Richard Barnet and John Cavanagh amply document in their book *Global Dreams*, the reserve labour army has assumed staggering global proportions, placing downward pressure on wages and working conditions in the advanced industrial nations.[2] And population growth in the developing world ensures that this vast surplus labour force will continue to grow. In the OECD countries alone there are roughly 35 million unemployed, up from ten million a quarter of a century ago.

What is more, the international labour contest is going to be fought out over continuously diminishing spoils. Repetitive tasks, which form the basis of many menial and lower level jobs, are being eliminated through mechanization. And this process is taking place globally, displacing workers from Boston to Bangladesh. For instance, there has been a recent breakthrough in automating the sewing process—a previously labour intensive industry employing a legion of labourers in the developing world. Of course, manual labour is not the only target. The service sector, touted just decades earlier as the great hope for generating jobs in the post-industrial economies of advanced capitalism, is rapidly being automated, with few apparent limits to the process. Automated tellers replace live ones, voice recognition technology takes over from telephone operators and robot cashiers will soon tally our purchases at supermarket checkout counters. With the advance of technology, the competition for McJobs will intensify.

Nor is it only low-skill, low-wage jobs that are being decimated, as countless former middle managers downsized by their corporate employers can attest. The unemployed and the underemployed are no longer synonymous with the undereducated and the underskilled. Far from it. According to the Canadian Council on Social Development, for example, nearly a third of poor adults possess post-secondary education. Certainly, some can retrain and find a gateway into the elite knowledge-based sector, becoming the manipulators of data and consciousness in the brave new economy. But the ranks of the symbolic analysts are not infinitely elastic.

If social critics such as André Gorz in France, Jeremy Rifkin in the U.S. and Peter Glotz in Germany are correct, as I believe they are, this is not a temporary disjuncture that will resolve itself as the microchip millennium matures. The capacity of industrialized societies to eliminate work in both the industrial and service sectors through automation and mechanization has permanently outstripped the pace of job creation. Technology has allowed the volume of production of goods and services to be disengaged from the size of the labour force. William Greider points out that during the twenty years from the 70s to the 90s the world's 500 largest multinational corporations grew sevenfold in sales, yet their worldwide employment scarcely increased, hovering at roughly 26 million people.[3] Growth in employment is no longer an effect of increasing productivity and increasing wealth. And even if new sectors of economic activity emerge, as growth junkies on both sides of the political spectrum believe must happen, these are bound to deploy the latest technology and are thus unlikely to be labour intensive.

> All the appeals to work more and harder, and all the arguments in favour of investing in new technologies in the hope of fighting unemployment will increase the dilemma [of the drastic reduction in the need for human work]. After all, where will industrialists invest? They will invest in productivity enhancing, work-saving technologies in order to become more competitive internationally.[4]

As it turns out, the great emancipatory movement of the twentieth century has been the liberation of capital from labour rather than the other way around.

While it is undoubtedly true that an agglomeration of command and control functions in the global cities creates significant new opportunities for small decentralized firms to service the needs of global corporations, such opportunities are not likely to offset the trend in the advanced capitalist countries towards polarization. Global cities, such as New York and London, are also what German social democratic theorist and former SPD leader Peter Glotz has called "two-thirds societies"[5] in which a relatively privileged group of professionals and skilled workers coexists with a growing minority of the unemployed, underemployed and precariously employed—the detritus of the information age.

With an official unemployment rate of roughly 9.5 per cent, and a youth unemployment rate of 15.5 per cent, Montreal, while above the Canadian average, is about on a par with many of the major European cities. Even these official figures on joblessness are remarkable, considering that in the 1950s and 1960s economists generally pegged the upper limit of unemployment that a society could tolerate at between three and five per cent.[6] And when one begins looking beyond the official statistics to estimates of a phenomenon of combined unemployment, underemployment and temporary employment affecting as much as half the adult population, it becomes hard to imagine a situation of enduring social stability.[7] The social fabric is far more likely to unravel where people feel they have no stake in society, and when they are excluded from the social benefits traditionally attached to stable, full-time employment.

In the absence of viable responses to this problem, notions such as equity, democracy and citizenship, which are the *sine qua non* of humanistic politics become hollow concepts. Moreover, the looming problem of mass unemployment threatens whatever fragile gains have been made by the ecological movement in promoting awareness of the limits to economic growth. During the last 30 years some probing questions began to be asked about the nature, purposes and consequences of economic growth. Now, once again, economic and social well being is being predicated on the constant expansion of the production of goods and services. Political and philosophical challenges to the conventional economic model of limitless growth driven by technological innovation and by the perpetual proliferation of new consumer needs are more and more muted. And fuelling the renewal of the cult of growth is, above all, anxiety over the disappearance of jobs, with the result that any obstacles to investment, production and profit as perceived by the global corporations and national business elites—whether these take the form of environmental regulations or job security—must be attenuated or eliminated in the name of progress and prosperity. This position is being espoused, or at least tolerated, despite evidence that increases in production and productivity no longer necessarily generate jobs—and certainly not the stable full-time jobs typical of the post-war boom years.[8]

The declaration signed by business and labour at the socio-economic summit held in Quebec in the fall of 1996 is an instructive example. Apparently neither side felt compelled even to pay lip service to the idea of sustainable development. Global warming, vanishing fish stocks, industrial accidents with long-term toxic consequences…the environmental price of growth was passed over in silence as, amid a plethora of platitudes, the unsustainable premises of productivism were enshrined as gospel: the virtues of competition, flexibility, profitability. In their public pronouncements, at least, the representatives of the labour movement appeared to concur with the neo-liberal line that a resumption of growth will revive the glory days of full employment and full consumerism. But even if growth rates were to return to 1960s levels and even if this were not environmentally hazardous, it is arguable that such growth rates would not curtail unemployment but only contain it at existing levels,[9] especially given that new "growth industries" such as biotechnology are based on advanced, labour-minimizing technology and tend to grow profits more than they grow jobs. Although the summit presented a golden opportunity to rally public opinion around creative solutions to the employment problem, the unions ultimately failed to present any far-reaching proposals for public discussion.

One potentially consequential outcome of the summit, however, was a commitment to help promote job creation in the social economy by injecting into it $250 million to be raised through a dedicated tax. While proposals to recognize and strengthen the role of the social economy as a generator of employment—an alternative to welfare and shrinking unemployment insurance benefits—have been put forward in various forms in many countries, this discussion at the summit inaugurated the first real public debate in Quebec about the role of the social economy.

There is, of course, an extensive debate in the academic literature about what precisely constitutes the social economy.[10] The term has had relatively little currency in the English language until recently; but it is perhaps a more precise categorization than the "third sector," which has been more commonly used in North America in reference to not-for-profit and volunteer organizations. The social economy appellation originated in France in the mid-nineteenth century to designate co-operative and mutualist associations operating outside and in opposition to the dominant market economy. The term has shifted in meaning a number of times in its history, but it is now generally understood as the intermediary sector between the public and the private sector, which is not subordinated to the profit-maximizing imperatives of the market, but remains in a close and complex relation with the market economy. A wide variety of co-operative, mutual, and not-for-profit projects, enterprises and organizations are seen to fall into this category, from daycare centres to agricultural co-operatives to libraries. While in some respects the social economy is in fact an ancient phenomenon, it has received renewed attention since the 1970s with the crisis of the welfare state that fuelled its growth.[11] What is seen to distinguish the activities and organizations that constitute the social economy is that they are governed primarily by an ethic of service to the community rather than the profit motive, without however being wholly dependent on government funding; social economy activities and organizations differ as well in being managed democratically and in deploying volunteer workers in addition to paid staff.

The social economy has been estimated to make up between four and seven percent of the total economy in Europe, employing as many as five million people;[12] in the U.S. it has been estimated to contribute more than six per cent to the economy and to account for as much as nine per cent of total national employment;[13] and here in Quebec it accounts for nearly 100,000 jobs.[14]

One of the most comprehensive proposals for developing the social economy, or at least the voluntary/community service segment of it, as a means to combat unemployment has been put forward by Jeremy Rifkin in his book *The End of Work*. Rifkin combines an eloquent expression of the human and humanistic dimensions of the third sector with a practical approach to it as the only remaining potential source of gainful employment in face of technological displacement and the contraction of government. Blending the descriptive and the prescriptive, he writes:

> Unlike the market economy, which is based solely on productivity and therefore amenable to the substitution of machines for human input, the social economy is centered on human relationships, on feelings of intimacy, on companionship, fraternal bonds and stewardship—qualities not easily reducible to or replaceable by machines. Because it is the one realm that machines cannot fully penetrate or subsume, it will be by necessity the refuge where the displaced workers of the Third Industrial Revolution will go to find renewed meaning and purpose in life after the commodity value of their labor in the formal marketplace has become marginal or worthless.[15]

Rifkin is one of many social commentators who see the social economy as an indispensable means to revitalize civil society while harnessing the time, energies and talents of the growing segment of the population excluded from the labour market. He proposes that a social wage be awarded to those skilled and unskilled individuals rendered economically redundant who are willing to work in the domain of community services, and he advances a variety of means to finance this employment program, including a value-added tax on high-tech goods and services, a government grant program and the termination of corporate welfare for transnational corporations that have no allegiance to the localities in which they are based. In Rifkin's view, governments will have few options but to help finance the third sector if they want to inhibit the spread of a criminal underclass and preserve social peace.

A project such as Rifkin's has much to recommend it. However, if the social economy is to be cast as the new employer of last resort, taking up where the state is increasingly leaving off, there are a number of arguments about the inherent problems and dangers of such an approach that deserve serious consideration. First, there is an element of making a virtue of necessity in the emerging progressive vision of the social economy. There is no inexorable step leading from the acknowledgment that the retreat of the welfare state has thrown people onto their own resources, resulting in new forms of mutual aid and social organizing, or that cutbacks are leaving it to community organizations to provide more and more services, to the incorporation of these developments into a socio-political program. In making the case for the social economy there is an implicit concession to the interment of the welfare state by the neo-liberal pallbearers. This is rather more understandable from the perspective of someone like Rifkin who lives in a country where the state has traditionally been viewed with a jaundiced eye and where charity is preferred to social democratic programs. The promotion of the social economy may have a somewhat more defeatist ring in the mouths of Canadians and Quebecers, who have more to lose from the unraveling of the post-war social democratic compromise.

None of this is to say that the Keynesian welfare state is an institution beyond question or innocent of the assorted defects (bureaucratic impersonality, insensitivity to individual and cultural differences, inculcation of passivity and dependency...) for which, in its halcyon days, it was indicted by segments of the left as well as the right. It does, however, suggest a more substantive concern. As well trodden as the ground is, it bears repeating the caveat that promoting the expansion of social services at the community level specifically as a stimulus to employing the excluded represents a tacit invitation for the government to further minimize its social role by continuing to cut well paying jobs from the public sector as it downloads a burgeoning share of its responsibilities onto community organizations with inadequate resources.[16] The danger here lies in creating a low-wage parapublic sector where, moreover, working conditions are not as well defined and regulated. As the authors of one study observe, to the extent that the social economy is, in its very essence, less structured, less codified and less regulated, it constitutes a double-edged sword; its intrinsic openness and flexibility create opportunities for new forms of exploitation.[17]

This concern is not new by any means. It recalls an earlier controversy over the development of the social economy as a response to an economic crisis resulting in mounting unemployment, and the attendant risk of enshrining a two-tier society. The debate in question took place in France in the late 70s and early 80s against the background of the initial deployment of a comprehensive neo-liberal strategy in all the western countries in the 1970s: decentralization and globalization of production (relocation to sources of cheaper, less organized labour both within and outside the advanced industrial economies), a new international division of labour, "flexibilization" (increased use of temporary and contractual labour, lower wages, irregular hours), a retreat from expenditures on social benefits and social welfare.

In this context, under the guise of "industrial redeployment," the administration of Prime Minister Raymond Barre abandoned the *dirigiste* policy that had been keeping many ailing industries afloat. With industry laying off workers, the crisis of unemployment that had already impressed itself on the French public as the most serious concern of the day grew more dire. France began to wrestle with the phenomenon of growing numbers of workers who would be left behind by the internationally competitive high-tech economy the ruling elite wanted to nurture. By 1980 there were nearly a million and a half unemployed in France (a problem which might seem altogether manageable from the vantage point of the more than three million jobless in France today).

The dualism debate revolved around two very different conceptions of the desirable response to the economic crisis in France.[18] On one side of the divide figured an official report by two advisors to the government, C. Stoffaes and J. Amado, on technology and employment in French society, produced with a view to shaping public policy. In it the authors envisaged a social and economic dualism whereby one sector of society would be tied into the global economy, adapted to new technologies and highly competitive, while the other sector would remain more traditional, convivial and less competitive, peopled by less technologically savvy individuals earning lower incomes. Dominique Michaud explains the proposal for the dual society as a system that depends on an articulation between a highly productive global economy providing high income and job security for workers and an informal economy engaged in sub-contracting, allowing the preservation or revival of certain traditional crafts and offering greater conviviality, although less social protection, to those who are voluntarily or involuntarily excluded from the other sector.[19] Commenting on the plan, Guy Roustang observed that the scheme's proponents couched support for a flourishing a low-wage informal sector in the recognition that some citizens were seeking fulfilment and creativity in their work and rejected hierarchy and the parcellization of tasks; in other words they used the rhetoric of conviviality in a bid to institutionalize the marginalization of growing numbers of people.[20]

André Gorz was one of a number of critics to challenge this proposal, branding it as a plan for the South-Africanization of society.[21] The counter-argument rejected this division of society into two distinct and unequal segments in favour of a dualist arrangement of a different kind, a temporal rather than a social dualism[22] whereby each individual would partake of both the high-tech productive and convivial spheres. This is an idea to which we will return.

In the debate about the virtues of the social economy for those employed in it, it is possible in some instances to make a case for conviviality as a compensation for lower wages, but caution is in order. Despite arguments about the democratic management and bonds of solidarity that characterize associations in the social economy, the quality of the working environment does not necessarily offset other privations. And without collective agreements governing wages and the organization of work, the quality of the working environment can also vary greatly from one organization to another. Unfortunately, the socially meaningful vocation of non-profit organizations does not do away with hierarchies of authority and does not guarantee that the people in charge are committed to treating subordinates with consideration, respect and dignity. There is a danger, I think, of romanticizing the nature of interpersonal relations in community organizations.

It is also useful to remember that although the jobs likely to be created in this sector are by definition socially useful, they are not necessarily intellectually or personally rewarding. One of the notable projects presented by the social economy workshop during the 1996 summit was the expansion of the co-operatively run funeral homes in Quebec. Indisputably, preparing corpses for burial and cremation is a socially necessary function and it is far preferable to remove it from the profit-maximizing domain of the private sector, but it would strain credulity to contend that it is an enriching way for anyone to spend the better part of their waking hours.

But the more fundamental point about the embrace of the social economy as a response to the advent of post-Fordism which emerges in the critique of the dual society by Gorz and others is that it sidesteps the need for more far-reaching structural measures to bring about a more equitable distribution of work and wealth. The 1980s saw an increase in inequality of income in the majority of OECD countries, and that gap has continued to grow in the 90s.[23] In Canada, in 1989, the richest fifth of the population had a (pre-tax and pre-transfer payment) income 17 times higher than that of the poorest fifth; by 1995 it was 22 times higher.[24] From 1995 to 1996, there was an average loss in pre-tax income of $500 for the poorest fifth of Canadian families and an average gain of $2000 for the richest fifth.[25] The social economy can be developed as a resort for the marginalized without even beginning to remedy this fundamental social and moral problem. Indeed, in the absence of other redistributive mechanisms, the social economy, and particularly that segment of it which involves ministering to "new needs" (a phrase that often implies various forms of personal care—healthcare, childcare, eldercare) might well perpetuate and exacerbate a dualism whereby one part of the population with more disposable income relies on a more economically depressed and insecure segment to see to the needs of the community, as well as providing personal care and other services to the now relatively "privileged" strata occupying full-time, stable, well-paid unionized positions in the anti-social economy. In short, we must take care that the social economy does not spell the rise of "carefare."

In my estimation, Jeremy Rifkin's proposals for supporting and promoting the third sector are more cogent and equitable than some because he explicitly ties the construction of the social economy to the reduction of working hours for all. "Regardless of the particular approaches used to shorten the workweek," he writes, "the nations of the world will have no choice but to downshift the number of hours worked in coming decades to accommodate the spectacular productivity gains resulting from new labor-and-time-saving technologies."[26]

If society can produce more goods and services with less labour it is a fairly obvious conclusion that existing work should be spread among more people by introducing shorter hours, benefitting both those without sufficient work and those without sufficient time. This was, of course, the original aim of the labour movement everywhere,[27] and is once again high up on the agenda of many unions and social movements in Europe.

In France, the various associations of the unemployed such as AC! (Agir contre le chômage) and the Mouvement national des chômeurs et précaires (MNCP) call for a 32-hour week tied to job creation and without loss of purchasing power for workers. And under the impetus of the Parti Socialiste led by Prime Minister Lionel Jospin, the French parliament passed a law making the reduction of the work week to 35 hours without loss of pay legally obligatory in all workplaces of more than 10 as of January 1, 2000—a move that aroused the ire of French employers.[28]

Linking the development of the social economy to the reduction of working time is fundamental to the approach of the 35 prominent French intellectuals who were signatory to an appeal calling on Europeans to support measures to combat the adverse effects on social life of neo-liberal policies.[29] The appeal was presented as a first step in an endeavour to forge a European-wide network of resistance on the part of intellectuals, union leaders and community leaders to the rise of unemployment and the dogmatism of the free market. Signatories came together around two fundamental premises: first, that it is illusory to expect a return to growth to solve the problem of massive unemployment, and second, that strict neo-liberal approaches to the crisis are catastrophic for Europe. Setting aside potentially divisive analytical and prescriptive differences, they agreed on three main policy directions: 1) the reduction of working time and redistribution of work; 2) development of projects in the *économie solidaire*—specifically the appeal calls for state financial support for socially useful activities that fall outside the market economy; and 3) opposition to all forms of workfare and support for the introduction of an unconditional minimum income granted to those people falling below the social minimum and which may be combined with income from other sources. The three prongs are presented as indissociably related and each is integral to a coherent social project. As several signatories of the appeal underscore in a subsequent contribution to the discussion: "Today, it is no longer a question of being for or against the reduction of working time, but of choosing how to manage it."[30] If there is no active intervention to direct and manage the reduction of working time it will happen in the most "insidious and unegalitarian" way by leaving a growing number of people without work or with insecure poorly paid unstable work. The same authors also emphasize, very much in the spirit of the writings of André Gorz for the last two decades, that the reduction of working time does not have to be merely a defensive measure to combat unemployment; it can serve as the basis of a new social project—one that is more ecologically viable because less growth oriented. It aims to allow people to work less *and* to live better by being freed to partake of a multiplicity of activities, within and outside the realm of the production of goods and services.

A great variety of practical strategies and schemes for achieving this goal have been put forward in France in the last two decades, with arguments revolving around the scale and form of the reduction in hours, about whether there should be a legislative framework, about whether and how to preserve worker purchasing power intact and about how to maintain business's competitive ability, among other questions. Most proposals have in common the development of various means by which to share the wealth that is now being created without direct human labour, to redistribute some of the fruits of the information revolution, itself regarded as a common heritage, the result of accumulated collective knowledge and investment.[31]

For Rifkin, as for a significant number of European left social critics, the end of mass labour represents a potentially unique opportunity in human history. If the productivity gains realized through ongoing technological advances are shared more democratically among the population we can all conceivably work less and spend more time occupied at socially useful community-oriented and autonomous projects outside the realm of the market economy. Linking the social economy to work time reduction can help to guard against the danger of transforming the social economy into a workfare program with a human face, liable to reproduce in the third sector the low-wage, precarious jobs proliferating in the private sector. It combats dualism by creating the conditions for a redistribution of socially necessary labour within the market economy.

In keeping with this aim, the creation of jobs in the social economy must be presented as inseparable from redistributing work in the market economy and the public sector. In addition to being more equitable, this is what would genuinely create the conditions of possibility for the flourishing of the social economy precisely as a realm beyond and outside market relations, where people give willingly of their time, rather than being compelled to sell themselves in exchange for a wage. In principle, community and neighbourhood development is an area to which every citizen should freely and willingly contribute; not simply those who can't find a job. Vibrant communities cannot be built by a marginalized segment of the population alone. Everyone should have time to pitch in, and under those conditions people who decline to participate should be given incentives to do so, such as Rifkin's proposed tax breaks for volunteering.

This argument can be advanced a step further, and although the radical critique is open to debate, it is certainly worthwhile to consider the warnings of critics such as André Gorz and Ivan Illich against the monetarization and professionalization of activities previously outside the realm of contractual exchange. In the conception of some proponents of the social economy, community services are seen as an infinitely elastic arena of economic activity, with the prospect of continually identifying new needs in the domain of social and personal care. However, it can be argued that just as industry has limits to growth in the finite resources of the earth, the service sector finds its limits to growth in the danger of an overweening dependency of individuals upon professional or paid providers of personal care and domestic services, whether these be provided through the state or by an expanding cadre of employees of community organizations.

André Gorz distinguishes between those activities that can be pursued for economic ends without losing their meaning and those that cannot.[32] In a word, not every socially useful human activity should be performed for an exchange value and reduced to an abstract equivalent in money. Gorz elaborated this critique precisely at a time when various French government officials began to put forward proposals to create jobs for unemployed young people in the sector of convivial activities, namely, provision of home care for the handicapped, the aged, the sick, and so on.

For instance, Gorz has denounced the professionalization of domestic work through the development of housekeeping services, which, in his view, relieves a privileged minority of work that each person ought to perform for themselves, in addition to creating a new caste of servants.[33] More pertinent to the topic at hand, he also maintains that caring activities from healthcare to education should be performed out of a sense of vocation on a voluntary basis, rather than out of economic necessity. Is it right, he asks, to hand over to paid professionals activities which each of us could just as easily perform ourselves if we had the time? Where does this process end? With the professionalization of reproduction, parenting and filial duty?[34]

Interestingly Rifkin himself refers to community service as an activity outside fiduciary arrangements, which is performed willingly and often without expectation of material gain and akin to the economics of gift-giving. He remarks that "[t]he nurturing commitment of volunteers often leads to better results in the providing of care services than the more detached care of salaried professionals."[35] What Rifkin oddly fails to consider in his subsequent proposal to develop the third sector as a basin of new employment is that the nurturing commitment may derive precisely from the strictly voluntary character of the work, and that once people perform this work to secure their subsistence there may be little to prevent it becoming, in Stephen Leacock's phrase "a task done consciously for a wage, one eye on the clock."[36] When Rifkin proposes that community organizations implement job classification schemes, grading systems and salary scales similar to the public sector it is easy to appreciate the motivation, which is to avoid the potential for exploitation. But it may be asked whether this will subvert the very qualities the social economy is held to possess in contrast to the market economy. Don't job classification schemes and grading systems potentially reproduce the hierarchies and bureaucracies of the pubic sector? And will the quantitative criteria of number of jobs generated come to predominate in the assessment of the work carried out by the organizations of the social economy itself?

Furthermore, to what extent will community organizations perceived as motors of employment become increasingly subordinated to the imperatives of economic rationality? As Gabriel Gagnon warned ten years ago: "It seems to be the bosses and the unions who are talking about participatory management and the quality of working life while the alternative sector is focusing all its efforts on job creation, often at the risk of forgetting its own sense of purpose, not to mention a possible broadening of its horizons in the direction of cultural and social emancipation."[37] In this respect again, various schemes for work reduction—such as the four-day week or the generalization of the practice, dear to academics, of sabbatical years—offer the possibility of eliminating a considerable amount of unemployment while making it possible for more people do things for themselves and their families and neighbours outside the bounds of economic rationality. They can enable society to begin measuring wealth in qualitative terms, such as the available free time for individual, family and community development and the health of the planet that sustains human and other life.

There are questions to be raised about the merit of assimilating every type of human activity to work, in the principal meaning of the word today as an activity performed in exchange for remuneration. As French philosopher

Dominique Méda argues, there is a tendency, particularly in face of the critical problem of unemployment and its ill effects, to overvalue work as the supreme human activity, the sole activity that makes us genuinely human and forges social bonds among human beings.[38] But this conception overlooks other types of activity distinct from productive activity but equally important to human life, which Méda, following Hannah Arendt, groups into three categories: cultural activities (including education), individual human and family relations, and collective activities (such as political debate). Instead of expanding the realm of work, we have an historic opportunity to extend the time each individual has to engage in these other vital but non-work activities.

While there appears to be a fair amount of sympathy for proposals to strengthen the social economy, work time reduction is more often greeted dismissively and with resistance—and not only by business, which has, since the first movements to abolish child labour and shorten the working day, protested that shorter hours would ruin their competitiveness. Unlike its European counterpart, the labour movement in North America has not rallied around the goal of shorter hours, even with the proviso of no loss of purchasing power. In Quebec, there have been scattered struggles by local unions, and some cautious but encouraging positions have been taken by the CSN,[39] but there has been no concerted mobilization around this issue.

The so-called shorter work week that was portrayed in the press as a concession to labour at the 1996 economic summit was something of a smokescreen. What was actually reduced from 44 to 40 hours was the standard of the normal week that is used as a frame of reference to determine when overtime payment should apply, and the adjustment brought Quebec in line with four other Canadian provinces, as well as with the Canadian labour code. However, in practice, during the 1990s both Canadian and Quebec adult males worked, on average, a 40-hour week, while women worked an average of 34 hours.[40] So if there are any actual reductions resulting from this disincentive for businesses to exact overtime they are likely to be negligible. It has been clearly established that work reduction must be substantial to have the desired effect of generating employment.[41] A small reduction in working time tends to result in higher productivity, offsetting the intended effect of requiring the hiring of additional labour. Nevertheless, the business community expressed its discontent with the prospect of calculating overtime based on a 40-hour standard; but employers typically prefer to pay overtime rather than train and hire new workers.

Judging from the relative immobility on the reduction of working hours, there appears to be a puzzling attachment by many even on the social democratic left in North America to the 40-hour week, as if there can be no other definition of full employment. It has been established that the reduction of working time, from 80 to 60 hours and from 60 to 40 hours, has played a vital role historically in absorbing the growth of the employable population.[42] Even John Maynard Keynes, whose ideas remain the touchstone for many social democrats, expected that by the year 2000 the work week would be reduced to 18 hours![43] Consequently, a four-day week or a 30-hour week or any other arrangement for a diminution of working time appears as a natural evolution, the logical next step after the five-day week. Because it offers so many possible benefits, this type of demand could unify a variety of currently fragmented groups around a common program uniting unions, the unorganized and the unemployed within cities and regions, and even internationally via transnational networks. It is perhaps due to ingrained attitudes to work (the work performed in exchange for a wage), which are part and parcel of the productivist paradigm of the industrial age shared by the political right and a large part of the left as well that a massive public works program or its post-industrial equivalent, a massive public service employment program, is preferred by some over the option of reducing working time and thereby creating opportunities for more people to partake of remunerative work, in addition to spending more time and energy working on a voluntary basis in their communities. It is no accident that it is ecologists who have widely campaigned for work reduction as the key to a more sustainable pattern of development and consumption and a better quality of life.

Of course, both business and labour appear open in principle to voluntary work time reduction, based on arrangements between individual employers and employees. However, without a massive educational and promotional campaign, and in the absence of some sort of legislative framework, a voluntary program is unlikely to produce the scale of work time reduction necessary to effect any significant redistribution of work. While studies show that some individuals, and especially women, would prefer to work less, even at the price of earning less, the climate of economic insecurity along with the tendency to define ourselves and our sense of self-worth through work will pose impediments to significant work time reduction on a purely voluntary basis, and this of course is even truer among middle class professionals who tend to perform the more interesting and stimulating work in our society.

But there are many rewarding activities that people can engage in once they dispose of more time. And a movement to bring about a society where secure and well paid work is not the privilege of a minority and free time is not an unhappy monopoly of the excluded is the precondition not only for rebuilding the infrastructure and the soul of local communities but for any kind of vibrant democratic political life. There can be no democracy in the absence of an engaged and informed citizenry, which in turn requires leisure as its condition of possibility. This principle was recognized in ancient Greece and remains true in our time.

NOTES

1. André Gorz, *Misères du présent, richesse du possible*. Paris: Éditions Galilée, 1997, p. 11 (My translation).

2. Richard Barnet and John Cavanagh, *Global Dreams: Imperial Corporations and the New World Order*. New York: Simon & Schuster, 1994, part III, "The Global Workplace."

3. William Greider, *One World Ready or Not: The Manic Logic of Global Capitalism*. New York: Simon & Schuster, 1997, p. 21.

4. Bernhard Wilpert, "Cultural Meanings in Transition: A Crisis at Work," in *Work of the Future*, ed. Paul James, Walter F. Veit and Steve Wright, St. Leonards NSW: Allen & Unwin, 1997, p. 85.

5. Glotz uses and explains the term, among other places, in a conversation with Eric Hobsbawm, published under the title "The Emancipation of Mankind," and included in Hobsbawm's *Politics for a Rational Left*. London: Verso, 1989, p. 190.

6. See the discussion in John A. Garraty, *Unemployment in History*. New York: Harper Torchbooks, 1986, pp. 242-245.

7. The point that official statistics on unemployment grossly underestimate the problem by failing to count important categories, such as those persons who have ceased to look for work or involuntary part-time workers, has been made over and over by social commentators. [For a critique of the Canadian count see, for instance, Bruce O'Hara, *Working Harder Isn't Working*. Vancouver: New Star Books, 1993, "The true scope of unemployment," pp. 34-41.] Moreover some countries underreport more than others. French journalist Bernard Cassen points out that if the same criteria for what constitutes joblessness were applied across the board in all the industrialized countries the much vaunted low unemployment rates in the United States and Japan would be considerably higher. ["Imperative transition vers une société du temps libéré," *Le Monde Diplomatique*. November 1994, pp. 24-25.] And French journalist and academic Jean-Paul Maréchal points out that at the beginning of the 90s the U.S. underemployment toll exceeded its official unemployment rate by four points, while at mid-decade 30 million Americans working full time also lived below the poverty line. ["Le capitalisme, l'emploi et l'environnement," *Transversales Science Culture*, 44, available online]:

    http://www.globenet.org/transversales44/marechal.html [accessed May 21, 1998].

8. As a document issued by the Confédération des Syndicats Nationaux (CSN) notes, half a decade of economic recovery did little to improve the employment situation in Quebec (CSN, "Portrait de la situation sociale et économique," March 1998, p. 25). Temporary and part-time employment has been a significant proportion of what job growth there has been in Quebec and in the rest of Canada. There were fewer full-time jobs in Quebec in 1997 than in 1989 (*Ibid.*, p. 33). In Canada as a whole, between 1975 and 1994 the proportion of part-time employment in the labour force increased from 11 to 17 per cent, and the number of individuals seeking a full time job but unable to find one increased from 11 to 35 per cent. (Grant Schellenberg, "Involuntary Part-time Workers," *Perception* 18 available [journal on-line]: http://www.ccsd.ca/part-time.html). Schellenberg has estimated that one in ten working Canadians occupy what would be classified as temporary positions. While the jury may still be deliberating on the future of work, a fateful verdict on the fate of the secure job, even in a growth economy, appears to have been rendered.

9. The point that moderate growth rates of around three per cent would do no more than maintain current unemployment rates is made by Bernard Cassen, among others. See his "Imperative transition vers une société du temps libéré," p. 24.

10. For an overview, see the introduction to *L'Autre économie: une économie alternative?* Proceedings of the 8th annual colloquium of the Association d'économie politique, ed. Benôit Lévesque, André Lojal and Omer Chouinard, Sillery: Presses de l'université du Québec, 1988. See also Jacques Defourny, "The Origins, Forms and Roles of a Third Major Sector," in *Économie sociale: entre économie capitaliste et économie publique/The Third Sector: Cooperative, Mutual and Non-Profit Organizations*, ed. Jacques Defourny and José L. Monzón Campos, Brussels: De Boeck-Wesmael, 1992.

11. For a survey of institutions and activities making up the social economy in Canada, see Jacques Quarter, *Canada's Social Economy: Co-operatives, Non-Profits and Other Community Enterprises*. Toronto: James Lorimer & Company, 1992.

12. "The Social Economy," ARIES homepage, available [online]:

   http://www.poptel.org.uk/aries/socioecon.html [accessed December 5, 1996].

13. Jeremy Rifkin, *The End of Work*. New York: G.P. Putnam's Sons, 1995, pp. 240-241.

14. This figure is cited in the "Appel en faveur d'une économie sociale et solidaire," issued by the Centre Interdisciplinaire de Recherche et d'Information sur les Entreprises Collectives (CIRIEC), available [online]: http://www.unites.uqam.ca/ciriec/appel.html [accessed June 10, 1998].

15. Rifkin, *The End of Work*, pp. 291-292.

16. For a forceful discussion of this danger, see Paul Leduc Browne "The Two Faces of the Social Economy," paper presented at the Eighth Conference on Canadian Social Welfare Policy in Regina, Saskatchewan, June 1997, available [online]:

   http://www.policyalternatives.ca/regina.html.

17. Benoît Lévesque, André Joyal and Omer Chouinard, Introduction to *L'Autre économie: une économie alternative?*, p. 9.

18. On this debate see for instance Guy Roustang, *Le travail autrement*. Paris: Bordas, 1982, pp. 131-138, and Michel Schiray, "D'un dualisme à l'autre," *Autogestions*, Spring 1982, pp. 36-37.

19. Dominique Allan Michaud, *L'avenir de la société alternative: Les idées 1968-1990*. Paris: L'Harmattan, 1989, p. 47.

20. Guy Roustang, *Le travail autrement*. Paris: Bordas, 1982, p. 134.

21. Gorz uses this term to characterize the Stoffaes and Amado proposal in an article translated into English as "The American Model and the Future of the French Left," trans. Carl Hathwell, *Socialist Review* 15, November-December 1985, p. 106.

22. This helpful terminological contrast originates with O. Corpet, J. Gaudin and M. Schiray. See Michel Schiray, "D'un dualisme à l'autre," p. 38 and p. 39 n. 14. For another presentation of a similar idea see Joseph Huber, "Autogestion et économie duale," *Futuribles*, 24, June 1979.

23. For a comparison of some OECD countries, see Guy Herzlich, "Les inégalités de revenus s'accentuent," *Le Monde, Dossiers & Documents*. October 1996, p. 2.

24. CSN, "Portrait de la situation sociale et économique," March 1998, pp. 11-12.

25. The National Anti-Poverty Organization, "Poverty in Canada: Some Facts and Figures," January 1998, available [online]: http://www.napo.onap.ca/nf-figur.html.

26. Rifkin, *End of Work*, p. 233.

27. A fascinating book in this regard is Benjamin Hunnicutt's *Work Without End* (Philadelphia: Temple University Press, 1988), which traces and analyzes the cessation of the struggle for shorter hours by the American labour movement. Hunnicutt shows how in the 1920s during a period of high labour demand the historic demand for shorter hours suffered an initial blow as the labour movement began to partake of the "economic gospel of consumption" in which an increasingly commercialized conception of leisure was itself enlisted as a spur to work more in order to finance leisure activities. The death knell sounded after the Depression, when, following a temporary resurgence of militancy in pursuit of a reduction of work time as a measure to combat unemployment, the labour movement embraced the idea of incessant economic growth as the sole route to social progress.

28. The then president of the powerful Conseil national du patronat français, Jean Gandois, resigned over the issue and the organization declared war on the initiative. Greg Oxley, "The French 35-hour Workweek," *Timework Web*, October 26, 1997, [online]:

   http://www.vcn.bc.ca/timework/html.

29. The appeal was signed by such luminaries as Guy Aznar, Yoland Bresson, Alain Caillé, Chantal Euzéby, Jean-Marc Ferry, André Gorz, Alain Lipietz, Antonio Negri, René Passet, among many others. "Appel Européen pour une Citoyenneté et une Économie Plurielles," June 1996, available [online]: http://www.globenet.org/aecep/appel.html. A version of the text appeared in translation as "European Call for a Pluralistic Citizenship and Economy" in *Dissent*, Summer 1997, pp. 26-27.

30. Guy Aznar, Alain Caillé, Jean-Louis Laville, Jacques Robin and Roger Sue, "Vers une économie plurielle: un travail, une activité, un revenu pour tous," *Transversales Science Culture*, 47 September-October 1997, p. 24 (my translation).

31. The French literature is vast. An excellent starting point is the journal *Transversales Science Culture* which has published extensively on the topic of work time reduction, especially in the last five years. The books and essays of André Gorz, most of which are available in English translation, and of Guy Aznar, among others, are also indispensable. See for instance Gorz's *Paths to Paradise: On the Liberation from Work*, trans. Malcolm Imrie, Boston: South End Press, 1985, and his *Capitalism, Socialism, Ecology*, trans. Chris Turner, London: Verso, 1994, and Guy Aznar, *Travailler Moins Pour Travailler Tous*, Paris: Syros, 1993. For a good discussion dealing with the Quebec context see Stéphane Chalifour, "La question sociale et la réduction du temps de travail," *Possibles*, 21, Spring 1997. The relevant literature in English is scant by comparison, but two worthwhile contributions are American economist Juliet Schor's *The Overworked American*, New York: Basic Books, 1993, and Canadian Bruce O'Hara's *Working Harder Isn't Working*, Vancouver: New Star Books, 1993.

32. Gorz makes this argument in a number of books and articles; see, for instance, his *Critique of Economic Reason*, translated by Gillian Handyside and Chris Turner, London: Verso, 1989.

33. On this point see Gorz,"Making Space for Everyone," *New Statesman and Society*, November 25, 1988.

34. See his essay "The New Servants" in Gorz, *Capitalism, Socialism, Ecology*, especially pp. 51-52.

35. Rifkin, *End of Work*, p. 255.

36. Stephen Leacock, *The Unsolved Riddle of Social Justice* (1920), cited in Jamie Swift, *Wheel of Fortune*, Toronto: Between the Lines, 1995, p. 209.

37. Gabriel Gagnon, "Dualisme, partage du travail et autogestion," in *L'Autre économie: Une économie alternative?* Proceedings of the 8th annual colloquium of the Association d'économie politique, ed. Benoît Lévesque, André Joyal and Omer Chouinard (Sillery: Presses de l'université du Québec, 1989), p. 157 (my translation).

38. Dominique Méda, "Plein emploi, pleine activité et multi-activité," *Transversales Science Culture*, 35, September-October 1995.

39. CSN researcher François Aubry produced an important series of documents on the subject, including an overview entitled "Le temps de travail autrement" (May 1994).

40. Data cited by François Aubry in the Confédération des syndicats nationaux (CSN) document "Les heures et les horaires de travail." Montreal: CSN, 1994.

41. On this point see, for example, Alain Lipietz, *Vert espérance*. Paris: La Découverte, 1993, pp. 54-55.

42. On the importance of reductions in work time for keeping unemployment in check see, for instance, Jean-Paul Maréchal, "Demain, l'économie solidaire," *Le Monde Diplomatique*, April 1998, p. 19 and René Passet, "Saisir le moment où tout peut basculer," *Le Monde Diplomatique*, September 1997, p. 23.

43. Bernard Cassen points this out in "Imperative transition vers une société du temps libéré," p. 25.

Chapter 7

Strange Bedfellows: Seduction of a Social Movement

Kathryn Church

It's your eyes I want to see
Looking into mine
Got you live on my mind
All the time...   *Bruce Cockburn*

Introduction

My contribution to debates on the social economy begins with practice. It is concerned with the hopes and uncertainties that are lived out by members of the psychiatric survivor movement in Ontario as they attempt to create and organize survivor communities using processes of economic development.[1] With an unemployment rate estimated at 85%, psychiatric survivors are painfully familiar with the "crisis of work." For them it is both an historical and a contemporary reality. They are also familiar with an array of barriers to their participation as full and equal members of a democratic society. The more subtle of these barriers come cloaked as "treatment" and "help." Long-term unemployment and social stigma are the collective wounds that motivate survivor engagement in the third sector.

My vantage point on this situation requires some elaboration. As an intellectual entrepreneur, I make my living in the same shifting community sector about which I raise questions. I am paid by community organizations to think, speak, write and organize around issues of work and learning among people who are excluded from the labour market. My office is located in a community action centre on Queen Street West in an area of Toronto known as Parkdale. Slowly becoming trendy, it hosts "the largest psychiatric institution in Ontario, in the midst of what is reputedly the largest psychiatric survivor ghetto in North America" (Chambers, 1997).

My association with the psychiatric survivor movement is substantial. Ten years of collaborative work on issues of survivor representation in the mental health system resulted in a life-altering deconstruction of my professional identity. (Church, 1995) Over the past five years, I have watched both the momentum and the leadership of the survivor movement shift to community economic development. As this happened I made a sustained effort to keep my scholarship accessible and useful to this community. Survivors reciprocated by continuing to allow me access to their culture, organizations and daily practices. Writing these words, I am grounded in this relationship—both personally and politically. At the same time, I stand back from it in order to analyze psychiatric survivor economic development within a broader context.

The focus of this chapter is the Ontario Council of Alternative Businesses (OCAB), and how OCAB has responded to dramatic changes in provincial health and social policy over the past four years. Established in 1994, OCAB is a provincial organization run by and for psychiatric survivors for the purpose of doing economic development. The election of the Tory government in September 1995 created enormous uncertainty within OCAB about its own future and the future of survivor-run businesses in Ontario. The organization feared serious threats to the social fabric of their communities and to the Council's work with fledgling groups across the province. It faced the possibility of retrenching in order to defend its workers. Now, towards the end of the Tory's mandate, two things are clear. First, there has been tremendous support for survivor-controlled community businesses. Secondly, there has been a multi-faceted attack on the rights and entitlements of people who have experienced psychiatric treatment and services. In ways that I hope to demonstrate, OCAB and its leaders inhabit the tension between these conflicting developments.

Playing the Field

The psychiatric survivor movement in Ontario has had three incarnations.[2] The first was its anti-psychiatry phase, a time during the 1960's and 70's of profound challenge to psychiatric hegemony—not just from people who had been diagnosed and labeled but also from allied intellectuals. The anti-psychiatry movement was a separatist movement; its dominant form was the self-help group (Weitz, 1984). The second phase of the movement was "consumerist" in nature. A feature of the 1980's, it was characterized more by activist attempts to infiltrate and control the mental health system than by attempts to overturn it. "Consumer participation" was the buzzword of the times. A tremendous amount of labour was expended by "consumers" and their professional "partners" on attempts to ensure that users of services had a voice in decision-making at all levels of the service system (Pape, 1988; Church, 1996b). By contrast, the survivor movement of the 1990's is (becoming) entrepreneurial. Its leaders use the language and processes of community economic development (CED) to organize their members. The emerging form is the "alternative business" (Church, 1996a; 1997).

Although muted, earlier phases of the survivor movement still exist; previous forms of activism continue to find expression. There is, for example, a network of some fifty state-funded psychiatric survivor groups across the province controlled by survivor boards of directors (Consumer/Survivor Development Initiative, undated; Trainor, Shepherd et al, 1996; Shepherd, 1997). A legacy of movement activities in the 1980's, these groups feed current developments. Survivor CED itself reproduces features of the movement from the past three decades. Founded on strong notions of self-help and a separatist sensibility, alternative businesses can be considered a form of anti-psychiatry. At the same time, their leaders sometimes partner with the mental health system in the tradition of "consumer participation." Thus, there are continuities and discontinuities. This is true even within the movement of the 90's. In response to economic restructuring, psychiatric survivors have taken up employment as an issue for which they themselves are responsible. However, they are approaching it in three different ways: through intensified competition for mainstream jobs, through self-employment and through community economic development.

Self-Management

Some 'consumers' of mental health services are attempting to enter the existing labour market by honing their job search and interview skills. A recent document produced by the Canadian Mental Health Association (National) with consumer input characterizes this approach (Lindsay, 1997). Presented as a workbook for people who have experienced mental health problems, it encourages readers to do a skills inventory, network their way into information about jobs, polish their resumes, and study the do's and don'ts of job interviews. This approach is useful in a very limited way. It makes some sense for those consumers who have skills and experience that they can market through such techniques. It does not make sense for those who have experienced long-term poverty and unemployment. The CMHA approach is to link consumers who possess a relatively high quality of survival with mainstream employers. The focus is on whipping the unemployed individual into shape for the labour market. What remains unexamined is the labour market itself. The changing shape of that market in response to the forces of globalization and the ensuing crisis of work are not identified. There are only faint hints that most of the jobs for which consumers are being encouraged to ready themselves are either low paid and precarious or completely non-existent. "Work can be found," declares the workbook, "and might in the long run even be an enriching experience. Looking for work is never easy. But it is a manageable process, and learning to manage it is a useful skill." In the face of massive economic restructuring, the CMHA calls consumers to self-management.

Self-Employment

Some 'consumers' of mental health services are attempting to start and run their own businesses. A recent request for proposals from the National Network for Mental Health (NNMH) characterizes this approach. NNMH is a national organization managed by and for "people who have directly experienced the treatment and services of the mental health system (consumers/survivors)." Anti-psychiatry in its mental health politics, the organization is taking a right wing approach to employment. It recently pulled itself out of its own ashes using a million dollar grant from the Human Resources Development Canada Opportunities Fund. In return for its continued existence, the NNMH will co-ordinate the establishment of four pilot programs across Canada that will be evaluated against the broad criteria applied to all HRDC initiatives:

• jobs created (increased earnings by participants through paid employment or self-employment);

- costs reduced (reduction of reliance by participants on income support including CPP, disability, welfare and similar programs).

Applicants are requested to specify the results expected each year and how they intend to measure their success. However, program goals already established by NNMH include:

- increased financial self-reliance among project participants, which will be measured by the growth of additional income directly from business revenues or self-employment;

- decreased reliance on social assistance which will be measured by total amount of reduction in monthly benefits cheques and by the number of participants who leave social benefits rolls altogether.

In contrast to the CMHA, the NNMH has abandoned the mainstream labour market as a source of jobs for people who have experienced psychiatric treatment. Better by far, it concludes, to strike out on your own. This is probably a better read of the context. However, the organization completely embraces entrepreneurial culture right down to imposing a quantitative standard for "success" that will be almost impossible to meet. The new director of the NNMH is a consultant with a university education proving therein that since she has made herself anew, everyone else can too. Again, this is a strategy that makes sense only for a thin slice of the survivor population, for consumers with skills, business experience and some resources of their own to invest in projects. It does not make sense for people who have experienced long-term poverty and unemployment, who have few internal or external resources from which to launch into small business development. Once again, employment is understood as an individual responsibility. Taking up a corporate, neo-liberal discourse, NNMH hopes that its four pilot sites will "aid in the development of best practices to help us learn which strategies work best to help consumers/survivors become more self-reliant from the social benefits system." In the face of massive economic restructuring, the NNMH calls consumers/survivors to self-employment.

Community Economic Development

Some consumers of mental health services, most of whom identify as psychiatric survivors, are engaging in community economic development. Survivor CED is characterized by an ongoing concern for process. Businesses are started very simply, by getting a few people together to learn about each other's skills and ideas. Development proceeds through practical problem-solving; organizational structures are sufficiently flexible to accommodate employee needs. Survivor-run businesses make use of peer rather than professional training and skills development. They operate with the expectation that participants will make mistakes and "fail forward." Participatory management is a key feature, accomplished through board membership and affirmative hiring. Both give survivor employees experience in decision-making, a critical necessity for leadership development. Survivor-run businesses sometimes partner with other organizations or agencies but they do so cautiously, with a close eye to future independence. As most operate with a creative blend of public dollars and employee generated revenues, they value persistent funding partners.

Psychiatric survivors involved in community business development have ceased to look to the mainstream economy for solutions to the severe unemployment problems that affect their members. Excluded from the labour market for decades, they have decided to make it a virtue and create a parallel market of their own. To that extent, they too have embraced entrepreneurial culture. They have not, however, accepted the dominant notion of what being a successful entrepreneur means. Survivor run businesses maintain a commitment to employing the most poor and vulnerable members of their community, people who have been classified as "permanently unemployable" as well as "mentally ill." The businesses do not screen for the most skilled and experienced; they do not take the cream of their applicants. Most take applications on a first come, first served basis. The major implication of working with these folks is a reliance on government grants for some portion of business revenue. Thus, financial self-sufficiency is not the key criteria for success in these initiatives; profit is not the bottom line.

Survivors doing CED have begun to evolve a qualitative standard for success to balance the demands for quantitative data made by most funding bodies. It includes understanding survivor run businesses as sites for learning, participation and the establishment of community (Church and Creal, 1995). Beyond job skills, survivor employees learn to become decisions-makers in the businesses through membership on boards and committees. These roles enable democratic participation, something which was stripped away from many through psychiatric treatment and service provision. Survivor CED is a recent development that takes in a thin slice of the population. Significantly, it is the slice that no one else wants. For these folks, employment becomes a real possibility when it is a collective process and responsibility. "The goal of survivor-controlled businesses," argues OCAB, "is not improvement in the skills, behaviors and general functioning of employees. Rather, it is empowerment" (Church, 1997: 36). Success is a sense of ownership, a voice in making decisions. Thus, in the face of massive economic restructuring, OCAB calls psychiatric survivors to empowered community.

Flowers and Candy

In the early days of the Harris government, psychiatric survivors were most concerned about cuts to subsidized housing, and social assistance reform. A key feature of the latter was the replacement of the General Welfare Assistance Act (GWA) and the Family Benefits Act (FBA) with the Ontario Works Act. It established mandatory workfare in the province. This change had direct implications for the survivor community—even for those members already working in economic development initiatives. Psychiatric survivors employed by alternative businesses support themselves through a combination of earned income and social assistance. While they work they continue to receive benefits either provincially through GWA/FBA or federally through the Canada Pension

Plan (CPP). Program regulations cap their income; their own life circumstances prevent most from working full-time. Thus, their jobs are best described as permanent part-time. Ontario Works threatened to destabilize this arrangement.

As the lead organization for survivor-run businesses, the Ontario Council of Alternative Businesses (OCAB) is firmly opposed to workfare. Highly sensitive to coercive authority, its members reacted to the powers of control and surveillance that the government granted itself with this Act (Beatty, 1997; Social Planning Council of Metro Toronto, 1997). Primary examples:

- Eligibility criteria have been tightened and it is easier to remove people from assistance.

- Welfare case workers have been given access to recipients' personal records.

- If they believe that a recipient is squandering his/her cheque, program officials may pay that recipient's rent directly to his/her landlord.

- The Act permits the government to place liens on homes owned by people who have collected welfare for more than 12 months.

- Whether welfare recipients will be given the right to appeal judgments made against them in these matters is uncertain.

All of this concerns survivors but their most fundamental criticism is pragmatic. Survivor business leaders do not believe that workfare actually works for their folks. They do not believe that community groups and agencies have the skill or the sensitivity necessary to support "permanently unemployable" survivors in work placements. Nor do they believe that such placements will lead to jobs for members of the survivor community—many of whom struggle daily with "proper" self-presentation.

Ontario Works set the stage for confrontation between the Harris government and psychiatric survivor run businesses over the issue of work. Few in number and already significantly challenged on a number of fronts, survivor business leaders faced tough questions. How should they respond to the choices given? Should they strategize around workfare as a whole or just a piece of it? Should they work on behalf of all social service recipients or focus primarily on psychiatric survivors? These questions forced the OCAB board of directors to make a blunt assessment of the organization's resources (limited) and to recognize a profound feeling of responsibility for its own constituency (generally neglected). After much deliberation, members decided to use both formal and informal consultation to influence the government's treatment of people labeled disabled within the workfare scenario.

Income and Employment Supports

In the June 4, 1997 edition of the Toronto Star there was an op ed column entitled "Psychiatric survivors need flexible supports." Written by Diana Capponi, OCAB's coordinator, the column was a thinly veiled survivor directive to Janet Ecker, Minister of Community and Social Services, on the issue of income and employment supports. It requested:

- a definition of disability that reflects its cyclical nature;

- an income support system that does not label people "permanently unemployable";

- an income support system that does not remove other kinds of benefits (e.g. prescription drug card);

- voluntary rather than mandatory employment services.

In November 1997, following a series of community consultations that were organized for MCSS by consultant David Reville, (significantly, a psychiatric survivor and former politician) Minister Ecker gave the key note address at OCAB's annual general meeting. Speaking to a large crowd gathered at the Raging Spoon Cafe, a survivor-run restaurant, she introduced the community to the Ontario Disability Support Program Act (ODSPA). A replacement for the Vocational Rehabilitation Services Act and a companion to Ontario Works, it delivered almost precisely what OCAB had asked for, including:

- a definition of disability structured around substantial restriction in the person's ability for personal care, in his/her ability to function in the community, or his/her ability to function in the workplace;

- removal of the phase "permanently unemployable" in the program's eligibility criteria;

- rapid reinstatement so that people who go off benefits for employment can come right back onto the program if the job doesn't work out;

- no mandatory counselling in order to receive benefits.

The ODSP Act effectively removed "the disabled" from the workfare scenario and placed them in a separate income support plan.

Survivors doing economic development publicly supported the Act on this basis. Particularly crucial was the government's agreement to 'grandfather' existing FBA recipients into the program, and to ensure rapid reinstatement of benefits for anyone who attempts to work. OCAB believes that these provisions will stabilize its expanding survivor workforce, as well as enable other disabled people to gain access to work opportunities. With this decision, they came under fire, both in and outside of their community, from critics who felt that they were "selling out." The issues, however, are far more complex than the accusation implies. Playing a game that was not of their own choosing, survivor business leaders were forced to weigh significant potential gains from ODSP against the risk of being silenced on broader issues of social assistance reform. Rather than oppose the government unilaterally, they made the best deal they could for their folks within the emerging policy frameworks. They did so conscious that it was a partial and temporary convergence of interests.

Anti-Professionalism

Each month by email I receive something called the Consumer/Survivor Information Bulletin. Produced by the Consumer/Survivor Information Centre of

Toronto, it is a compilation of relevant newspaper clippings, job ads and announcements. The Centre's clippings over the past couple of years are revealing.[3] They document the restructuring of mental health services including a significant number of hospital closures (both general and psychiatric), cutbacks in community services of all kinds alongside bottlenecks in the criminal justice system, threats to subsidized housing and tenant rights, and significant increases in homelessness.

Psychiatric survivors read this list in a very particular way. They are generally more concerned about housing and tenant rights than they are about hospital closures and service cutbacks. For many survivors, hospitals have been places of constraint and containment rather than care. While less openly coercive, community services are often dominated by professionals who have resisted the inclusion of survivor representatives in decision-making roles. Actively opposed to or alienated from these institutions/organizations, survivors have wasted few tears over their recent troubles. Those involved in economic development have openly celebrated the impending demise of vocational rehabilitation services and service provider jobs.

Deeply historical, the reasons are sketched out in a document that I wrote several years ago in collaboration with the OCAB board:

> In the process of diagnosis, the individual ceases to play a central role in his/her own destiny and becomes subject to the opinions and decisions of a wide range of professional intervenors: psychiatrists, social workers, case workers, behavioral therapists, occupational therapists, life skills trainers, vocational rehabilitation workers, etc., etc. OCAB knows that many mental health professionals genuinely feel that they are helping consumers/survivors to reach their full potential. Regardless of good intentions, the work performed by professionals has the effect of controlling, containing and limiting the ways in which psychiatric survivors live. The programs and services which have been developed, including vocational rehabilitation and case management, entrench consumers/survivors in a system which not only fails to meet their real needs but leaves them alienated and angry (1995:4).

This is a rather careful expression of the anti-professional (anti-psychiatry) sentiment that permeates the survivor community. Survivors feel that they have been serviced nearly to death by a system that not only does not meet their needs but routinely strips them of rights and entitlements.

For different reasons, the Tories, too, are anti-professional. The Harris government is opposed to state social service provision because it costs money; members believe that service provision breeds debilitating dependency. They mirror the survivor community on the issue of self-reliance. The government and the survivor community share the belief that people can and should take care of themselves, that people must take responsibility for their own lives. Thus, we hear an echo of survivor activist Diana Capponi in MCSS minister Janet Ecker.

Capponi: *We got tired of professionals telling us what was good for us. We decided we knew what was good for us. Today there are more than 400 of us working in survivor businesses across Ontario. With the right kind of support, we can do it ourselves. In fact, we are doing it ourselves.* (Speaking at OCAB'S 1997 annual general meeting.)

Ecker: *I am very pleased to be here today and see how survivors have been able to fight so hard for what they believe in and to prove that people can contribute, that people can take control of their lives and that people can do wonderful things if government or the system can just get out of the way or provide the support that they need.* (Speaking at OCAB's 1997 annual general meeting.)

No wonder the Harris government has been so taken with OCAB and the whole notion of survivor-run businesses. The appeal is obvious. If a bunch of poor broken-down 'crazies' can put their lives back together again by becoming entrepreneurs, anyone can! Corporate ideology must be correct. Survivor businesses prove its benefits, its general applicability, beyond a doubt. There is no need, as critics suggest, to maintain costly service systems or develop fancy social policies in support of the marginalized. One size fits all.

Balls and Chains

The new Ontario Disability Support Plan took effect June 1, 1998. Regulations covering specific details were released just two weeks earlier to "cautious approval" from voices typically raised in anger against the Harris government. The Tories continue to seek the politically popular role of providing assistance to disabled people—at least where employment is concerned. Outside of that single area, their actions have persistently eaten away at services and support structures that enable disabled people to become economically viable. This has been systematically orchestrated through government departments of health, community and social services, housing, and justice.

Hospital restructuring means massive loss of psychiatric beds. Government plans include closing half of Ontario's 10 psychiatric hospitals—up to 1800 provincial psychiatric hospital beds—by 2003 (Toronto Star, June 4, 1998). Other institutions will be amalgamated. The most prominent example of this is in Toronto where The Clarke Institute of Psychiatry, Queen Street Mental Health Centre, the Addiction Research Foundation and the Donwoods have merged to form the new Addictions and Mental Health Services Corporation. (Survivors quickly dubbed it the "Megamental.") Psychiatric survivor leaders have been fighting a long while for closures of this magnitude to occur; deinstitutionalization is a basic tenet of the movement. At the same time, they recognize that the resources which kept these institutions going have not been reallocated to hospital alternatives in the community. Priority has been given, for example, to "Assertive Community Treatment Teams" comprised of psychiatrists, nurses, social workers, occupational therapists and other health care workers which will provide wrap-around care for people considered to be at risk. Priority has not been given to non-medical crisis alternatives or survivor-run initiatives. Where institutions amalgamate, survivors are having to fight all over again for basic representation and a voice at the board table (Capponi, 1997).

One of the first actions of the Harris government was the cancellation of new subsidized housing projects. It then instigated the downloading and privatization of existing housing projects across the province. More recently, the Tories have attacked tenant protections with a Bill that eases rent controls and gives landlords the right to refuse to rent to people below certain income levels. In conjunction with cuts and changes to social assistance, these actions profoundly affect the lives of psychiatric survivors. Homelessness has visibly increased in the City of Toronto; hostels are bulging at the seams. Mayor Mel Lastman's task force on homelessness is studying the matter while City Council contemplates a by-law that would crack down on panhandling—also clearly on the increase. The changes affecting hospitals and housing put pressure on the criminal justice system. Jails are fast becoming a substitute for more appropriate shelter and care in a society where the latter are being systematically deconstructed. Criminalization of social problems is an especially sensitive topic for psychiatric survivors. Amongst a host of issues, it is here that they have chosen to organize resistance.

Outpatient Committal

Several months ago, several disturbing incidents occurred on the Toronto subway system in which one patron was pushed under an oncoming train by another patron who was later identified as "mentally ill." They were followed by a high profile feature on "Madness" in the Toronto Star. According to the journalist, Theresa Boyle, this seven part series looked at the illegal jailing of mental patients, the criminalization of the mentally ill, the increasing number of homeless with psychiatric disorders, the shortage of hospital beds for individuals in crisis and the shortage of forensic beds. Reading the articles differently, members of the survivor community argued that it "took entirely isolated incidents completely out of their proper context" (Bacque, 1997) and "demonized the shit out of us" (Weitz, 1997).

Shortly after the "Madness" series appeared, under pressure from the Schizophrenia Society of Ontario and Canadians Against Violence Everywhere Advocating Its Termination (CAVEAT), the Minister of Health announced a five week long review of mental health reform. She appointed her legislative assistant, Member of Parliament, Dan Newman, to consult with stakeholder groups. His task was to test the waters around proposed changes to the Mental Health Act that would introduce community treatment orders (outpatient committal) into the mental health system. From the survivor perspective, such orders "could result in persons with a diagnosis being subjected to mandatory psychiatric treatment in the community on pain of incarceration in a mental institution or general hospital psychiatric unit for failure to comply" (Bacque, 1997). Across their ideological fractures, members of the psychiatric survivor movement agree that any such provision in legislation is a profound step backwards.

Psychiatric survivors doing economic development responded to the threat of outpatient committal by spearheading the formation of the Care Nòt Cuffs Coalition. Said spokesperson, David Reville, "We define care to include measures that remove barriers to participation. We define care to include a home, a job and a friend. We do not define care to include enforced treatment and we do not define care to include cuffs." As members of Care Not Cuffs, survivor business leaders were quoted in newspaper accounts speaking in opposition to community treatment orders. Cornered publicly by OCAB coordinator, Diana Capponi, Dan Newman agreed to consult with the psychiatric survivor community about mental health reform. OCAB staff organized the event by faxing a fast invitation to survivor organizations across the province, creating a speaker's list and running an orderly meeting. Shadowed by two provincial police officers, a cautious Mr. Newman attended the survivor "speak-out" held at the Raging Spoon Cafe in February, 1998. The audience numbered over one hundred survivors. Also present were two TV crews and several members of the press. Twenty-four people spoke over a period of two hours. Their message was clear: opposition to community treatment orders; education for mental health professionals with respect to the existing provisions of the Mental Health Act; a plea for jobs, housing and friendship as the basic elements of community life.

The 'speak out' at the Raging Spoon was a successful event for psychiatric survivors in what promises to be a longer battle over outpatient committal. Many forces are at work; the outcome is uncertain. While they watch and wait, survivor leaders take heart from the cohesiveness of the message that their community delivered to the government in spite of the fact that speakers ranged from moderate consumers of service to anti-psychiatry radicals. This is a recent development building on but in sharp contrast to the 1990 provincial consultation on community mental health services legislation (Church 1995). Back then, the survivor voice was often a sharp cry of despair that expressed beyond words the poverty of body and soul that they live in Ontario communities. Eight years later, the angst (and the poverty) remain but survivors and survivor groups have become much clearer about their agenda.

Media Magnification

I want to look briefly at the role the media is playing in the dance between psychiatric survivors and the Harris government. Over the past year, media interest in OCAB and its member businesses has been high. Television crews arrived from CBC's "It's a Living," then from "W5." A long newspaper column entitled "Jobs that are making people sane" appeared in *The Globe and Mail* (December 31, 1997). *The Toronto Star* ran a prominent spread entitled "Businesses for healing" (December 28, 1997) followed later by a profile of the Raging Spoon (March 4, 1998). The survivor business community celebrated each of these stories, and in particular its promotion from the Life to the Business and Food Sections of the paper. Then the "Madness" series appeared linking psychiatric survivors once again to a discourse of pathology, deviance and dangerousness. Collective delight turned to outrage. I share the sentiment but would argue that all of the media accounts produced during this time were problematic. The following is a particularly good illustration of what I mean.

As an impromptu social marketing strategy, employees from one Toronto business nominated two survivor business leaders for the "Women on the Move" contest sponsored by the Toronto Sun in the fall of 1997. Reporters converged and two full page profiles appeared in the paper. The first, entitled "She's getting on with her future" featured Laurie Hall, executive director of A-Way Express, a survivor-run courier company. It describes a woman who spent years in and out of hospitals "battling" mental illness, a woman whose arms are scarred by suicide attempts, who became incompetent at her work and ended up homeless on the street. Having successfully portrayed her as deviant, the article then crafts another description of Laurie, this time as a public speaker, a rights advocate and nurturing boss. This woman smiles constantly, wears an air of peaceful calm and likes to spend time puttering in the garden with her three cats. A-Way Express, the courier company that Laurie worked for and now directs, is positioned at the heart of the transformation. However, beyond a few basic facts of its operation, we learn little about it. In particular, we learn nothing about broad-based survivor decision-making within the company and the building of collective solidarity that happens as a result of the work.

The second profile demonstrates the same split. Entitled "Back from the brink of madness,' it features Diana Capponi, OCAB's coordinator. It highlights her emergence from an abusive childhood as a self-destructive young woman who was in and out of hospitals in delusional and paranoid states. A former heroin addict jailed for theft, vagrancy and narcotics, she claims her own street smarts as the basis of her current skills. The article pivots on this "amazing turnaround," moving to describe Diana's return to college and her career as a shelter worker. As we read, she becomes a passionate advocate for her community before committees at City Hall and Queen's Park. She becomes a tough woman who has made sacrifices in order to cope with her life. Like Laurie, the "miracle" of Diana's transformation is intimately linked with business development but neither of their stories illuminate that process. We are fed titillating pieces of Diana's past (topless dancing?!!) but learn very little of her work in the present, work which is highly oppositional to the right wing ideology of the Toronto Sun.

Laurie and Diana are, indeed, amazing women. Both have integrated difficult histories into leadership roles within the survivor community. The Toronto Sun presented them in an appropriately positive light: women who have overcome through the power of work. As such, their nomination to "Women on the Move" was a successful public relations gambit, one that both women approved. But there were costs, and the costs are instructive. The gala luncheon for the contest was held in the glittering ballroom at the Harbor Castle Hilton to the tasteful tunes of a three piece string ensemble. A full course meal was served by waitresses who were almost exclusively women of color. Clutching gift bags of corporate donations, we sat through a long procession of "winners:" a black high school student who exhorted us to find some tiny way to become useful to the unfortunate of our community; a scientist in full uniform who extolled the virtues of the Canadian military; a social work professor who hoped that more young black women would choose the University of Toronto; an expensively turned out banker who encouraged us all to take the risks she had and open investment firms. Laurie and Diana were not selected. The depth and nature of their risks unrecognized, they were never really in the running. Instead, both were served to Sun readers as individuals who have pulled themselves up by their bootstraps. We were allowed to consume their personal courage only after swallowing their "deviance," and without learning the social/political context in which that courage became possible.

Conclusion

Many observers, government funders in particular, position psychiatric survivor community economic development as a new form of mental health programming (Trainor and Tremblay, 1992). In this chapter I have resisted such a conventional interpretation primarily because it obscures the radical roots of the process in the survivor movement. Alternative businesses are more adequately understood as an example of burgeoning practices within the social economy. More than that, the survivor vision of the social economy presumes an attack on the existing social order. At their best, alternative businesses are grounded in a critique of psychiatric discourse as a form of power that systematically defines people out of productive social roles. Explicit in its attempts to empower participants, individually and collectively, survivor CED is a utopian project.

The Ontario Council of Alternative Businesses demonstrates some of the contradictions characteristic of organizations located 'between' the private and public sectors. Complexities arise in practice as it attempts to do economic development with legislative and funding support from a government that reads the project as merely job creation. The government's liberalizing efforts are clearly confined to questions of employment and do not extend to matters of broader citizenship. Its task is to manage the disabled, and to be seen to manage them fairly, while simultaneously cutting away the services and supports of the welfare state upon which most are dependent. In part, OCAB helps resolve this dilemma by proposing entrepreneurial solutions. As the organization is taken seriously, its challenge is to continue animating the advocacy, knowledge, leadership and community building strategies that it claims to be "the business behind the business" of survivor CED.

Thus, there is an ongoing tension between the state and the psychiatric survivor movement around the definition and enactment of a new form: the alternative business. I have characterized this relationship as a seduction, a breathless courtship in which, for survivors at least, the government is "live on their minds/all the time." The metaphor is only partly tongue in cheek. As Fontan and Shragge point out in their introduction to this volume, " Practitioners face growing poverty, limited funding choices, and a wider environment which is not sympathetic to the type of broad social reform that is necessary to ameliorate deteriorating social and economic conditions faced by the poor." Under these circumstances, the sense of legitimacy that OCAB gains from significant budgetary increases and warm ministerial invitations can be heady indeed. Still, its leaders have kept their virtue. Funded by government and on record in support of some policy directions, they are also vocal critics, organizing against the government on others. As someone who shares their hope and fears their co-optation, I can only conclude that maintaining the balance is a difficult exercise.

NOTES

I am indebted to Eric Shragge for his assistance in the development of this chapter. Thank you to my survivor colleagues, Diana Capponi, Laurie Hall and David Reville, for their feedback, and to members of alternative businesses for the example of their practice.

1. In 1983, when I first started to work in the community mental health field, it was still fairly common to hear people talking about the "mentally ill" or the "psychiatrically disabled." Several years later, the term "consumer" of services was being used to challenge those terms. In 1990, I used the term "consumer/survivor" in a brief to government. It was intended to reflect the language disputes that were going on; its use has since become prevalent. The term "psychiatric survivor" was introduced to Canada in 1989 by British survivors who attended the first independent national conference of mental health service users in this country. It caught on and is now widely used. All of these terms are in use to some degree depending on the politics of the people involved. Because it is the term of choice for most of the people with whom I work, I use the term "psychiatric survivor" or just "survivor" even though it continues to be controversial among mental health professionals.

2. In 1993, when I was writing my doctoral dissertation, I wrote a short history of the psychiatric survivor movement in Canada. Because of the virtual absence of academic work on the subject, I had to rely on my own limited observations and on psychiatric survivor writings (primarily about treatment and/or hospitalization experiences). The best examples of the latter at the time were done by Burstow and Weitz, (1988) and Pat Capponi (1992). A couple of years ago, Irit Shimrat published an welcome volume, part auto/biography, part history that documents people and events in and around the short-lived Ontario Psychiatric Survivor Alliance. Today, more research is being done by progressive researchers both with survivors and about their initiatives but as far as I know we still do not have a definitive history of the survivor movement in this country. The best resource I know from Britain is an old one, a detailed overview of anti-psychiatry by Peter Sedgwick (1982). He reviews the work of Erving Goffman, R.D. Laing, Michel Foucault and Thomas Szasz, the major intellectual allies of the anti-psychiatry movement. Another useful and slightly more recent British paper is Rogers and Pilgrim (1991). I also recommend a paper by Norman Dain (1989) on the movement in the States.

3. The profile of changes to health and social services affecting psychiatric survivors was constructed from many newspaper accounts reproduced in the Consumer/Survivor Information Bulletin on the following dates: June 12, 1997; October 9, 1997; January 15, 1998; February 12, 1998; April 30, 1998; June 11, 1998; June 25, 1998. The Consumer/Survivor Information Resource Centre which publishes the Bulletin is located at 71 King Street East, 2nd Floor, Toronto Ontario M5C 1G3. Visit the centre on the web at http://www.iComm.ca/csinfo

BIBLIOGRAPHY

G. Bacque. Quoted from a verbatim transcript of the 'survivor speak out' with Dan Newman, 1997.

H. Beatty, Social Assistance Reform Act 1997: An analysis. *Archtype 35*, September, 1997.

B. Burstow and D. Weitz (eds.), *Shrink resistant: The struggle against psychiatry in Canada.* Vancouver: New Star, 1988.

P. Capponi, *Upstairs in the crazy house: The life of a psychiatric survivor.* Toronto: Penguin, 1992.

P. Capponi, "Psychiatric squeezeplay," *NOW Magazine,* August 1997, pp. 14-20.

J. Chambers. Quoted from a verbatim transcript of the 'survivor speak out' with Dan Newman, 1997.

K. Church, *Forbidden narratives: Critical autobiography as social science.* New York: Gordon and Breach, 1995.

K. Church, "Business (not quite) as usual: Psychiatric survivors and community economic development in Ontario," in Shragge, E. (ed.) *Community economic development: In search of empowerment* (2nd edition), Montreal: Black Rose, 1996a.

K. Church, "Beyond 'bad manners': The power relations of "consumer participation" in Ontario's community mental health system," *Canadian Journal of Community Mental Health, 15* (12), 1996b, pp. 27-44.

K. Church, *Because of where we've been: The business behind the business of psychiatric survivor economic development.* Toronto: Ontario Council of Alternative Businesses, 1997.

K. Church and L. Creal. *Working the margins: Qualitative dimensions of community economic development among people who experience serious barriers to employment.* 1995. Available from the author.

"Consumer/Survivor Development Initiative." (undated) Project descriptions: The 42 CSDI projects described in their own words. Toronto.

N. Dain, "Critics and dissenters: Reflections on 'anti-psychiatry' in the United States," *Journal of the History of the Behavioral Sciences, 25,* 1989, pp. 3-24.

Ontario Council of Alternative Businesses, *Yes we can! promote economic opportunity and choice through community business.* Toronto: Available from the Council, 1995.

J.D. Lindsay, *Steps to employment: A workbook for people who have experienced mental health problems.* Toronto: Canadian Mental Health Association (National), 1997.

B. Pape, *Consumer participation: From concept to reality.* Toronto: Canadian Mental Health Association (National), 1988.

D. Reville, Quoted from a verbatim transcript of the 'survivor speak out' with Dan Newman. 1997.

A. Rogers and D. Pilgrim, 'Pulling down churches': Accounting for the British mental health users' movement," *Sociology of Health and Illness, 13* (2), 1991, pp. 129-148.

P. Sedgwick, *PsychoPolitics.* London: Pluto Press, 1982.

M. Shepherd. Quoted from a verbatim transcript of the 'survivor speak out' with Dan Newman. 1997.

I. Shimrat, *Call me crazy: Stories from the mad movement.* Vancouver: Press Gang, 1997.

J. Trainor and J. Tremblay, "Consumer/survivor businesses in Ontario: Challenging the rehabilitation model," *Canadian Journal of Community Mental Health, 11* (2), 1992, pp. 56-71.

J. Trainor, M. Shepherd, et al., *Consumer/Survivor Development Initiative: Evaluation Report.* Toronto: CSDI, 1996.

D. Weitz, "On our own: A self-help model," in D.P. Lumsden, (ed.) *Community Mental Health Action.* Ottawa: Canadian Public Health Association, 1984.

D. Weitz. Quoted from a verbatim transcript of the 'survivor speak out' with Dan Newman. 1997.

Chapter 8

The Social Economy in Canada: The Quebec Experience

Benoît Lévesque and William A. Ninacs

Introduction

The position occupied by the social economy in Quebec, in the production of goods and services as well as collective services, is important enough for some to claim that a "*Quebec* model" exists. Be that as it may, use of the term "social economy" by other than a handful of academics influenced by European studies is relatively recent. Other expressions, such as "community economic development,"(CED) are more commonly used in Quebec and elsewhere in Canada (Ninacs, 1997) to identify social innovation in the field of economics. From this point of view, even if social economy enterprises are first and foremost local or, in a broader sense, civil society initiatives, they generally call upon a broad range of government programs related to local development, job creation, employability or community services. According to a sample of community groups that provide collective services (i.e., services associated with the social economy), Employment and Immigration Canada's Employment Development Program (EDP) and the community organization support service of the Ministère de la santé et des services sociaux[1] have been the two major government sources of funding (Bissonnette, 1990). The various programs provided by the two levels of government suggest a new compromise between governments and community groups and local associations, with the former discovering new ways of supporting local development and delivering services to the community (Economic Council of Canada, 1990) and the latter perceiving government aid as an opportunity for empowerment (Lévesque, 1984).

From this perspective, the originality of the Quebec experience rests in large part on a social dynamic open to co-operation and partnership. Two recent events have brought the social economy concept to the forefront of public debates in the media and within various organizations. The first event, the Women's March against Poverty, organized by women's groups in June, 1995, sparked renewed interest in the social economy as an alternative in the struggle against the unemployment and social exclusion that have victimized many people, especially women. Following the March, a steering committee on the social economy was struck, made up of representatives of women's groups and three Quebec government departments (Employment and Solidarity, Status of Women, and Income Security; Natural Resources and Regional Development; Health and Social Services), to advise the Government on its actions regarding the social economy.

The second event, a Socio-Economic Summit organized by this same government at the end of March 1996 to establish a plan of action in light of the economic and social crises facing Quebec, invited women's groups and other community groups, for the first time, to participate on an equal footing with the more traditional sectors (private sector, labour, state). Against all expectations, these new players introduced a ray of hope into the difficult discussions on reduction of unemployment and job creation by suggesting approaches that blend economic and social development within specific sectors of the economy. At the end of the Summit, a Task Force on the social economy was set up to draft recommendations for a fall 1996 meeting. Following that meeting, it was decided to assist the Task Force's work by creating a follow-up committee which, for all intents and purposes, has become an interim social economy secretariat.

In Quebec, these events stimulated a wide-ranging discussion on the social economy and revealed significant differences in substance regarding its definition and role in a context of budget cutbacks in the public service. The goal of this paper is to uncover this vibrant reality, rich in lessons to be learned, by an overview of the social economy in Quebec. We begin with a presentation of the definitions most commonly used in Quebec, followed by a look at the Quebec social economy model and related issues and challenges.

Definitions and Related Problems

If the debate on the social economy evokes a great deal of interest and passion, it is because it opens the door to discussion of much more fundamental issues concerning current changes in the various production systems and reconfiguration of the Welfare State. The possibility that jobs created by social economy enterprises will simply entail a shifting of jobs traditionally found in the public sector has led to a number of objections from the labour movement, even though it is relatively favourable to these initiatives and has participated in some of them. Moreover, the term "social economy" does not depict the same reality for everyone. Perspectives on the social economy are usually influenced, in whole or in part, by four definitions found in European works: 1) a descriptive legal definition; 2) a formal definition that focuses on the rules that link its associative and entrepreneurial components and address the twofold relationship of membership and economic activity; 3) a normative definition based on the values found within this type of enterprise; and 4) a substantive definition that sees the social economy as "pluralistic" and an intrinsic part of a new socio-economic regulatory mechanism.

A Descriptive Definition

This definition, conceived by Henri Desroches (1984), is based on the legal status of cooperative, mutual, and non-profit organizations. This status, based on the principle of "people before capital," is implemented within a democratic decision-making framework using a "one person, one vote" formula, and a particular form of funding that disallows individual benefit in either decision-making or distribution of surpluses. Moreover, should the enterprise cease to exist, accumulated reserves cannot generally be distributed to individual members. Under this definition, cooperatives, mutual, and non-profit enterprises are obviously components of the social economy. Certain private sector businesses, public sector agencies, and other mixed organizations may be part of the social economy. However, only by analysing each enterprise individually is it possible to ascertain if it shares certain traits with cooperative, mutual, or non-profit enterprises. For example, a capitalist business favouring worker participation in its share capital and on its board of directors could be part of the social economy, if its procedures for balancing maximum profitability and social objectives are put into practice.

This definition has the advantage of allowing rapid evaluation of the size of the social economy in any given society. Applied to Quebec, the definition indicates that the Quebec social economy is made up of two major groups of enterprises and organizations—on the one hand, cooperatives and, on the other, non-profit organizations and businesses—as well as some "undefined" components (e.g., in the public sector and the labour movement), that have close ties to the major groups. Unfortunately, characteristics are insufficiently defined in the legal status, especially those regarding non-profit organizations. This produces a situation where some only recognize organizations that produce goods and services as being part of the social economy, while others include all non-profit groups simply because of their legal status.

A Formal Definition

This definition, developed primarily by Claude Vienney (1994), is grounded in the idea that a social economy enterprise is an organization of a group of individuals on the one hand, and a business on the other, bound together in a framework of economic and partnership activities. This type of enterprise is characterized by at least four rules: 1) those related to membership: democratic operation; 2) those related to the relationship between members and the business: definition of the enterprise's activities by the individuals; 3) those related to the relationship between the business and the members: the distribution of profits; and 4) those related to the business: the sustainable community ownership of the reinvested surpluses.

This definition specifies that people involved in the social economy are usually "relatively dominated" individuals, whose economic activities or way of life have been disrupted. "Dominant" persons usually tend towards a capitalist business while "completely dominated" individuals do not have the resources (financial or human) required to start up a business. Although, in the past, traditional members of the social economy were small farmers and craftsmen and women, higher education and a better quality of life have made it possible for a larger number of people than ever before to develop the skills needed to start up a collective venture. Moreover, the support of professionals has made it possible to form groups of disadvantaged individuals on many fronts.

Because of the rules, the social economy challenges the belief that the market is the exclusive means of regulating the economy, but does not repudiate the market per se. The social economy should not, however, be confused with an informal or unregulated economy. The economic activities that are reorganized are, at the outset, essential activities that have been ignored or cast aside by both the private and public sectors. Capital-intensive fields are generally excluded, as are those controlled by large corporations or having significant entry barriers. The personal services sector, insofar as it can be rendered profitable, offers interesting potential markets, an idea that raises the possibility that the social economy could easily handle privatization of some public services. It is important here to distinguish between the old social economy—which operated in strongly competitive sectors—and the new, wherein a group of individuals tends to play a more determining role in enterprise viability.

A Normative Definition

This definition was developed by Jacques Defourny (1991) for the Walloon Council for the Social Economy. It is based on the premise that the social economy is made up of association—based economic initiatives founded on solidarity, autonomy, and citizenship, as embodied in the following principles: a)a primary goal of service to members or the community rather than accumulating profit; b)autonomous management (as distinguished from public programs); c)democratic decision making process; and d)primacy of persons and work over capital and redistribution of profits. These were adopted by the Quebec Task Force on the Social Economy, who added a fifth precept: operations based on the principles of participation, empowerment, and individual and collective accountability.

This definition's advantage is that it identifies the values that can be used to mobilize individuals engaged in development of the social economy. It argues that the social economy is not primarily a question of legal status, but rather of practices tending towards economic democracy and empowerment of disenfranchised individuals and communities in decline (Favreau and Lévesque, 1996; Favreau and Ninacs, 1993). On the other hand, it isn't easy to use this definition to take an inventory. How can it distinguish a true cooperative from a false one, a true mutual association from a false one, a true social economy enterprise from a false one? The problem becomes more difficult considering that values are often controversial, and democracy can take many forms. While it is possible to achieve consensus on such permanent, perhaps immutable, values of the social economy as equality, equity and solidarity, it is not really easy to establish a similar consensus on rules and practices (Lévesque and Côté, 1995).

A Substantive Definition

This definition, developed primarily by Jean-Louis Laville (1992) to discuss the new social economy in the field of collective services, has three basic elements: a) the birth of the new social economy (that he calls the economy of solidarity); b) the forms of its economic activities; and c) its role within a regulatory socioeconomic framework. Social economy enterprises stem from a reciprocal impulse that brings individuals together in a group composed of potential users and professionals (eventual staff) who together construct the supply and demand of services. This operation, wherein ongoing reciprocity is essential, transforms individual needs into collective needs through discussion and exchange. Meetings around a kitchen table and study groups become "incubators" for enterprises that produce goods and services. This pre-start-up phase enables the social economy enterprise to detect new needs and respond to them by mobilizing resources that neither capitalist business nor public service could enlist. It is not a phase to be ignored, although highly standardized government programs have a tendency to do so.

Secondly, the social economy enterprise calls upon both market and government redistribution forces, notably when it operates in the neighbourhood service sector. It is characterized by a hybrid economic mix of commercial activities (self-financing through sales), non-commercial but monetary activities (public funding, donations from churches and foundations), and non-monetary activities (voluntary work of members and others). The social economy, when seen through this lens, fits the Polanyi (1957) substantive definition. It also demonstrates that government funding is only one aspect of the financial resources mobilized by social economy enterprises.

Finally, regarding socioeconomic regulation, with the decline of both Keynesian and Welfare State models, the new social economy will be called upon to play an important role in labour-intensive activities, such as the provision of personal services. This will happen for two reasons: first, because of its ability to bring together, within an enterprise, the various forms of economic activity and its capacity to engage various players (e.g., users and professionals) in collective services through a broader democracy; second, because it gives new value to reciprocal (non-commercial and non-monetary) transactions by recognizing them as economic activities in their own right.

The Quebec Social Economy Model: The Quebec Model of Development

The preceding definitions coexist remarkably well in the Quebec social economy of today. This originates, in large part because of the type of development that has characterized Quebec society since the end of the XIXth century and the rise in an economic nationalism that is non-partisan—in that it is espoused by both federalist and sovereignist Quebec political parties, although of course with some differences. Whereas large natural resource manufacturing companies used to be controlled by foreign and English-Canadian capital, Francophone Quebeckers controlled only family businesses in industry and agriculture (Hamel et Forgues, 1995). The co-operation and corporatism of the 1920s and 1930s appeared as a method of strengthening the presence of Francophones in this economy, making Quebec a relatively traditional, economically different society. In line with the social doctrine of the Catholic Church and the corporate ideology then prevalent, this model was based on cooperation, as well as being anti-state and anti-socialist.

Over the years, this situation fostered the development of cooperatives in agriculture and in savings and credit.

At the end of the 1950s, the model based on corporatism and social Catholicism was set aside and replaced by state intervention, deemed necessary to modernize Quebec society. The Quiet Revolution added a number of crown corporations to the large cooperatives in strategic sectors (in terms of self-reliant economic development) such as the steel industry, mining and exploration, business funding, hydroelectric power, forestry, cultural industries, and pension fund management. This produced an economic structure made up of a complex network of cooperative, state, and private institutions and businesses. Compared to other provinces of Canada, Quebec boasts the largest concentration of co-operative businesses and Crown corporations. The federal government's regional development initiatives and industrial policy have also contributed greatly to modernization, especially the modernization of infrastructures and manufacturing. This broad range of initiatives has enabled the emergence of myriad small businesses, and a few giant companies, such as Bombardier (transportation), Cascades (pulp and paper) and Québécor (the media).

If some people talk about "Québec Inc." (Fraser, 1987) and even a "Quebec development model," (Dupuis, 1995) it is mainly because of a tradition of co-operation relatively unique in North America, although it does exist in Rhenish capitalism (Albert, 1991). In the 1960s, modernization of both the economy and society, supported by management and labour, was proposed to both the Quebec and federal governments, specifically with regard to regional development (e.g., Bureau de l'Aménagement de l'Est du Québec). After a period of labour radicalization characterized by confrontation in the 1970's, a new spirit of cooperation in the early eighties and the introduction of economic summits brought the various social players together as partners seeking solutions to the widespread economic crisis. The trend is also evident in the 1989 private sector Job Forum, which brought together management, unions and other non-government sectors with the aim of improving cooperation of all partners in the employment sector (Payette, 1992). The most recent Summit on the Economy and Employment, organized in 1996 by the Quebec government, is rooted in a thirty-year old tradition of tripartite—state, labour, private sector (including cooperatives)—cooperation, to which have been added women's groups and other community-based movements. For reasons apparently arising from the distinctiveness of Quebec society, co-operation among the various social players goes further and appears easier than in other provinces of Canada.[2]

The participation of community-based groups is the result of a cohesion and a maturity that have their origins in the mid 1960s. At that time, a large number of rural social animation activities and urban community development initiatives emerged (Côté and Harnois, 1978; Lesemann and Thiénot, 1972; Lévesque, 1979) that today would be considered part of the social economy. In the following decade, social policies in Quebec in conjunction with, for example, Employment and Immigration Canada employment development programs, fostered the development of community-based service organizations in fields relating to living conditions while a variety of federal job creation programs (e.g. local initiative projects (LIP) saw the number of relatively similar local initiatives soar (Bélanger and Lévesque, 1992). During the 1980s, new organizations in poor Montreal neighbourhoods, and in some semi-rural regions, re-ignited interest in community development and encouraged the rise of new community-based economic projects (Gareau, 1990; Ninacs, 1991). Recently, the many thousands of community organizations in Quebec have adopted new multi-sector structures for concerted action. These include the Corporations de développement économique communautaire (CDÉC) in Montreal, and Community Futures Development Corporations (CFDC) principally funded by the Federal Office of Regional Development—Quebec (FORD-Q) (Proulx, 1994). Quebec community groups have long been involved in working with and empowering marginalized and disadvantaged populations. It is therefore not surprising that a large number of leaders in Quebec's social economy have their roots in these movements, and bring with them an experience based on commitment and innovation to offset their meager financial and material resources.

The Quebec Model of the Social Economy

Because of the weak capitalist structures in French-speaking Quebec and, on the plus side, its social climate of consensus and commitment, collective enterprises (cooperatives and government bodies) have developed here much more than elsewhere in Canada. The largest of these are concentrated in the finance, agriculture, and natural resource sectors. If there is such a thing as a Quebec model of social economy, it is not an ideal or standard but a model having a set of characteristics that give it a relatively unique and legitimate shape, even if any one of its elements can be found in most OECD member countries. In this perspective, we can identify five elements typical of the configuration: (1) recognition by all social players in the new social economy of its potential for local development and job creation; (2) adoption of a relatively consistent development strategy, at least for some sectors, a strategy that combines government financial and technical assistance with continued autonomy of these businesses and organizations; (3) importance of sectoral consolidation and local government of the CDÉC or CFDC type; (4) replacement of a dual model by a social economy that is a full member of the economy as a whole, and of collective services; (5) a diversity of forms of institutionalization based on pilot projects.

We will not discuss recognition of the social economy by the various social players at any length here as we have already done so. However, we would like to point out that the job creation potential of these enterprises is also supported by the impressive development of specific enterprises in the old social economy. As a case in point, the success of the Mouvement Desjardins in the savings and credit co-op field is a source of inspiration and grounds for imitation. The Mouvement Desjardins, with 5 million members (out of a total Quebec population of about 7 million) and assets exceeding $82.9 billion ($CAN) in

1996, is the largest financial enterprise in Quebec (Lévesque and Malo, 1992). With its 1,300 local Caisses populaires and its 18,600 volunteer directors, the Mouvement Desjardins is present in most large urban neighbourhoods and rural communities; credit unions are primarily found in the workplace. In the mid-1980s, the labour movement became directly involved in job creation and local development. With the support of the federal and provincial governments, the two largest trade unions in Quebec established business investment funds that also promote local and social development.[3]

In some sectors, notably housing co-operatives, worker co-operatives and non-profit child-care centres, the development strategy adopted has given results that many consider exemplary. The strategy rests primarily on recognition of the specific nature of a social economy enterprise, i.e., the combination of an association of individuals and a company. As a result, the investment of financial and human resources essential to the pre-startup and startup phases is stressed. If the association is to emerge and the business project come to life, sponsorship or technical support in conjunction with financial assistance from one of the two levels of government, depending on specific jurisdiction, is essential. The conjunction of government financial assistance and technical resources, in this case the Technical Resource Groups (TRG), has resulted in housing co-operatives rapidly multiplying throughout Canada while worker co-operatives are largely concentrated in Quebec because of stronger support by Quebec for this type of enterprise (Quarter, 1989; Fédération québécoise des coopératives de travail, 1996).

Non-profit child-care centres, like housing and worker co-operatives, are sectoral groups that play a relatively determining role in defining the development conditions specific to the sector. Intersectoral groups also exist. A key characteristic of the new social economy is local commitment, ie. local management that ensures intersector co-ordination and a meshing of experiences at the local and regional levels (Favreau and Lévesque, 1996). This factor is even more important than community economic development, as local development cannot be reduced to a sum of small businesses. Local management promotes inter-project synergy and allows for preparation of a local development plan, which supposes a number of options. By so doing, it enables action to be constantly focused on the social and economic objectives (Lévesque, Klein and Fontan, 1996). Finally, it gives the local communities a way of being represented to outside governments, while ensuring support for local development initiatives and social economy enterprises.

The federal government, through the 1986 Community Futures Development Program (CFDP), has promoted the establishment of Community Futures Development Corporations (CFDC) to support development of the most disadvantaged Canadian communities. Fifty-five CFDCs have been established in Quebec. They carry out local management in a variety of ways, with the most decisive being those that involve major players and leaders in the community and are supported by an investment fund of approximately two million dollars (Canadian) per community, a fund supplied by the FORD-Q. In large cities the Corporations de développement économique communautaire (CDÉC) play a similar role, although the community groups are primarily responsible for their creation. At present, there are eight CDÉCs in Montreal, made up of representatives of unions, businesses and community groups, and funded by all three levels of government. At the same time, in various Regional County Municipalities (RCM), about thirty Corporations de développement communautaire (CDC) play a similar role, although they focus more on social than economic development. With the new wave of social economy, these organizations are, as it were, challenged by the Comités régionaux d'économie sociale (CRES) and the Coopératives de développement régional (CDR), which are attempting to establish a synergy between the various components of the social economy within a territory. In short, it is less local management as such that defines the Quebec experience than the widespread mobilization of resources that produces this situation.

Another characteristic of the Quebec configuration of the social economy is the refusal of a two-fold development that downplays a social economy that wants to be a full partner in the social and economic dynamic. In other words, for promoters of the social economy in Quebec, social economy is not synonymous with "starvation economy" from the point of view of either working conditions or quality of goods and services provided. Furthermore, for the jobs created by this sector, two parameters are generally agreed upon. The first is that job creation in the social economy sector must not he simply replacement of public sector jobs. Second, the hourly wage of workers in the social economy must be decent, i.e., a minimum of $8.50/hour. At the same time, the public services provided must be of equal quality whatever the purchasing power of users, as it is in the child-care centres. Finally, the Quebec social economy wishes to be integrated into the entire social and economic dynamic through partnerships that enable the transfer of innovations from one sector to another.

Issues and Challenges: For the Social Economy in General

These examples drawn from the Quebec experience illustrate the social economy's capacity to respond to social needs while taking economic imperatives into consideration. The Quebec experience seems to succeed by: a) expanding markets through new venues for employment that emerge from needs that, at first glance, often seem modest and essential, but not necessarily economically viable; and b) using a blend of commercial (sales of goods and services) and non-commercial (government assistance) activities as well as non-monetary (volunteer) activities, from which the notion of a "plural economy" has been derived (Roustang, et al., (1996). Moving into such an economy entails certain risks, and a recent OECD publication notes three in particular (Sauvage, 1996):

- the risk associated with the "reductionist" trend inherent in industrialized countries, that tolerates experimentation for a limited time, but soon attempts to steer innovative practices into one or other of the two dominant economic models, the most viable towards the conventional private sector, the others to the state, even though partnership would be more beneficial;

- the risk of "ghettoizing" the social economy by seeing it as merely a well of cheap labour, an inexpensive means of privatizing public services or, by limiting enterprises to "collective utility" markets, institutionalizing them as tools for managing poverty and exclusion rather than a means of escape;

- the risk of broadening its mercantile dimension, and the danger of commercializing all facets of human existence with, as a corollary, a diminished concept of the common good and redefinition of state operations and mutual assistance as mere commercial transactions, thereby degrading citizenship to a mercenary consumption of public services.

These dangers exist in every industrialized country: the experience of the Quebec social economy supports this statement. The institutionalization of community-based pilot projects in the health and social services sector (e.g. storefront medical clinics of the 1970s), is an illustration of state takeover of a civil society initiative, and the losses that follow (Lévesque, 1995). Examples of the privatization of local non-profit services (e.g. recycling) also exist. In some cities and towns, services were taken over by private sanitation firms once the community organization showed a profit. Such viability is usually based on a system of home sorting of garbage which, in turn, is inevitably the result of a lot of prior, often quite lengthy, community action to ensure participation by the community. Privatization can erode the community involvement underlying the activity and, in the long run, destroy its profitability.

Moreover, partnerships between the private and education sectors have resulted in the creation of youth job training initiatives designed for potential school dropouts and young welfare recipients (Beauchemin, 1994). The Centre de formation en entreprise et récupération (CFER) in Victoriaville, for example, under the aegis of the local school board, has developed strong ties with many private sector industry partners. It has been able to open new markets, such as one for recycled paint, while training about 150 young people annually, of whom 80% find work thereafter (Bordeleau and Valadou, 1995). This success story is based on the dovetailing of commercial manufacturing activities and non-commercial educational activities, neither of which could have succeeded alone. Institutionalizing or privatizing such practices would substantially alter their innovative character and undermine both democracy and resource mobilization.

For the Quebec Model in Particular

The Quebec social economy experience also faces specific issues regarding state recognition of the social economy, funding, the place occupied by women, local control, and the relationship between old and new social economy enterprises.

State recognition is a major issue entailing both opportunity and risk. As the government of Canada has done implicitly through local development and job creation, the Quebec government is on the right track in recognizing the social economy for its ability to create jobs. A social economy enterprise often accepts lower profits than a private sector enterprise, as it can enlist public funds and count on volunteer human resources to offset various deficiencies, enabling it to hire or retain staff where a capitalist enterprise could not. It has, moreover, a tendency to play an integration role for unemployed individuals with few or no job skills. The social economy can be very useful when it comes to reducing unemployment and poverty, providing the players directly involved have other objectives (e.g., controlling their own development) as well. If it is restricted to collective services, government recognition can hide a desire to cut the costs of these services with home-care cooperatives, early childhood centres and other community-based enterprises. The Quebec social economy experience in other fields is quite good, when it comes to economic development in general and job creation in particular. The task force on the social economy is therefore justified in insisting on exploring a variety of other areas, such as culture, housing, new technologies, natural resource processing and environmental protection (Groupe de travail sur l'économie sociale, 1996).

Moreover, if state recognition of social economy initiatives is simply contractual (delivery of goods and services), the relationship between the state and community and cooperative businesses will decline into a simple commercial subcontract instead of a demonstration of joint solidarity with communities requiring services and the unemployed seeking jobs. In our opinion, the social economy must be developed with the goal of maintaining and strengthening democracy and citizenship. State support is another very important issue for the social economy, with regard to both the start-up of new social economy enterprises and the development of existing ones. Social economy businesses are different from private sector businesses because of their need for a long pre-start-up period to organize the individuals concerned and shape their activities according to target requirements and available resources. Public job creation and public service assistance programs must not ignore this preliminary supply and demand balancing phase in which the process is often as important as the immediate results because of the ties of solidarity and mutual assistance that are developed.

Neither must government jump from the particular to the general. For example the Carrefours jeunesse-emploi project that offered a variety of school dropout prevention activities, job skills development, and business development programs in the Outaouais region was used as the standard for a whole range of programs, with all the risks that entails, in this instance cookie-cutter programs. Replication of models—like restrictive regulation of areas of activity, targeted clienteles, or types of people to hire—may well drain social economy businesses of their versatility and originality. In fact, heads of training businesses and community enterprises receiving public funding have severely criticized the fact that funding is usually based on program structure rather than project support, which usually means inflexibility on the part of public authorities and a lack of local autonomy (Valadou, 1996). The rapid and spontaneous rise in all corners of Quebec of private funding organizations that provide financial support and technical assistance to entrepreneurs suggests an imbalance of supply and demand and the resultant need for public programs to adapt (Lebossé, 1997).

The funding of social economy enterprises is an even more important issue in that the situation is changing rapidly, as witnessed by the creation of many development funds, some of them explicitly targeting social economy enterprises (Lévesque, Mendell and Kemenade, 1997). In the early 90s, the largest and most generalized (funded by the federal government) was undoubtedly related to employment through the Job Development Program, section 25 and the "été Défi" program (Dinel and Bellavance, 1990). The current situation is characterized by a diversity of funding sources (e.g., self-financing by the market, government assistance, development funds, involvement of individuals and the community). If the programs targeting employability development (Human Resources Canada, Ministère de l'Emploi et de la Solidarité du Québec) are widely used by social economy enterprises, the promoters of these enterprises indicate that getting on board is not always easy. In fact, the employability development programs target mainly individual training and return to the job market, whereas the social economy enterprises target community organizations and development that entail continuity and the long term.

The place of women in the social economy is another fundamental concern. At present, few women are active in the conventional social economy, with the exception of the caisses populaires, where the majority of workers are women. However, women are quite active in the new social economy, since its jobs are usually concentrated in the service sector. Indeed, the type of jobs created in these enterprises gives rise to justified fears based on the fact that, in many Quebec initiatives, salaries and benefits are usually quite low, as is the case in child-care centres (D'Amours, 1996). Women are adamant that the jobs created in the social economy be stable, decently paid and provide good working conditions (Comité d'orientation et de concertation sur l'économie sociale, 1996). Ensuring that social economy enterprises do not become underpaid and precarious job ghettos for women is a serious challenge to support organizations. Some polarization does exist in social economy suport structures. The regional social economy committees—technical assistance and support groups made up of women—tend to perceive the social economy as limited to service and mutual assistance initiatives, in other words non-commercial and non-profit activities. On the other hand, the regional development cooperatives often limit their assistance to manufacturing and commercial cooperatives. These two visions, based respectively on need and business development, must be merged.

To a certain extent, the social economy's raison d'être is tied to development of social capital. Social capital is the sum of mutual social debts that individuals and organizations contract in their non-commercial and non-monetary activities (Coleman, 1988). It is a resource, like so many others, that a community can use to satisfy the needs of its members, in that social capital can help reach objectives that could not otherwise be reached. For some, development of social capital is an essential component of a democratic society. Indeed, the success rate in solving social and economic problems is greater in communities where civic commitment is strong (Putnam, 1993). It is necessary to anchor the social economy experiences in local dynamics in order to link all development initiatives and solidify the networks of solidarity that enable a community's optimal use of all its existing resources (Sauvage, 1996). Local control must be directed to ensuring strong ties between the social economy and local development. Recent research (Ninacs, 1993) demonstrates that local, democratically controlled, non-profit intermediary organizations are key to successful local development. In the field, we will have to wait and see how the community development corporations (CDC) announced by the Quebec government in April mesh with the federally supported CFDCs. If the question is unresolved, it must be remembered that local players have shown considerable pragmatism and maturity.

A final concern is the support and networking of old and new social economy enterprises. The former have usually adopted a cooperative framework, the latter a more associative one. The Mouvement Desjardins' provision of financial and human resources to the Task Force on the Social Economy is a kind of sponsorship. However, a lot remains to be done if this support is to balance out the assistance provided by the state for development of the new social economy and favour open-mindedness by the old social economy towards the values put forward by the new social economy, often the basis of their success.

Although opportunities for the social economy in Quebec have never been greater, new challenges abound. The social economy must seize the former and confront the latter in order to contribute, as only it can, to the social and economic development of Quebec. If Rosanvallon (1995) is right, there are only two ways of erasing the line separating the economy and society: either completely integrate society into a market economy or establish an intermediary economy somewhere between market and state. The new social economy is firmly committed to the second option. The challenges are all the greater because they are the hope of all those directly involved, and of society as a whole.

NOTES

This paper, re-published here with permission, was published as part of the conference "Local Strategies for Employment and the Social Economy," hosted in Montréal, June 18 and June 19, 1997, by the Organisation for Economic Co-operation and Development (OECD) in cooperation with Human Resources Development Canada and organized by the Institut de formation en développement économnique communautaire (IFDÉC). The opinions expressed in this article are those of the authors alone.

1. In 1994, 2,374 organizations associated with the social economy were eligible for community organization support service grants from the Ministère de la santé et des services sociaux. These organizations had on their staff 10,107 regular employees and 14,871 casual employees. The payroll for these organizations was 145.18 million dollars (Canadian). See Jean-Pierre Bélanger (1995). Also Y. Vaillancourt (1997).

2. On this point, two comments. Firstly, it must be pointed out that a greater percentage of workers in Quebec are unionized than in Canada as a whole. In 1994, 43.8% of Quebec workers were unionized, compared to 37.5% of Canadian workers and of 17.3% of US workers (Courchernes, 1996:1-2). Secondly, it must be pointed out that the two main

unions, La Fédération des travailleurs du Québec and the CNTU are involved in economic development through investment funds.

3. In 1983, the Fédération des travailleurs du Québec,(FTQ) set up an investment fund to create and maintain jobs, the Fonds de solidarité des travailleurs du Québec whose assets (about \$2 billion) have propelled it to the top of Canadian risk capital venture funds (Lévesque *et al.*, 1996). A few years later, the Confederation of National Trade Unions (CNTU) decided to support the creation of worker co-operatives by setting up a technical assistance group. More recently, in 1995, the CNTU set up a development fund, the Fondaction, for businesses that promote worker participation and sustainable development.

BIBLIOGRAPHY

Michel Albert, *Capitalisme contre capitalisme*. Paris: Seuil, 1991, 318 p.

Jean-Claude Beauchemin, "Recycler et réinsérer:le CFER 'Les Transformateurs,'" in Yvon Leclerc, *Battre le chômage*. Sillery, Québec: Les Éditions du Septentrion, 1994, pp.161-167.

Jean-Pierre Bélanger, *Proposition d'un programme massif de MAD et de création d'emplois permanents pour BAS*. Québec, March 1984 (rev. May 1994).

Jean-Pierre Bélanger, *Les organismes communautaires du réseau: un secteur de l'économie sociale à cosolider et à développer*. Québec, Working Paper (draft), 1995.

Paul R. Bélanger, and Benoît Lévesque, "Le mouvement populaire et communautaire: de la revendication au partenariat (1963-1992)," in Gérard Daigle and Guy Rocher, (eds.), *Le Québec en jeu: comprendre les grands défis*. Montreal: Les Presses de l'Université de Montréal, 1992, pp.713-747.

Jean-Guy Bissonnette, "Le secteur bénévole et communautaire. Faits et tendances," in *Rapport du Comité d'analyse et des tendances sociales. Au tournant des années '90*. Montréal: United Way, 1990, p. 61.

Danièle Bordeleau and Christian Valadou, *Agir pour l'insertion: initiatives d'insertion par l'économique au Quebéc*. Montréal: Institut de formation en développement économique communautaire (IFDÉC), 1995, 91 pages.

Jacques Boucher, "Les syndicats: de la lutte pour la reconnaissance à la concertation conflictuelle," in Gérard Daigle and Guy Rocher (eds.), *Le Québec en jeu: comprendre les grands défis*. Montreal: Les Presses de l'Université de Montréal, 1992, pp. 107-136.

Guy Chevrette, *Politique de soutien au développement local et régional*. Quebec: Secrétariat au développement des régions, 1997, 51 pages.

James S. Coleman, "Social Capital in the Creation of Human Capital," *American Journal of Sociology*, (Supplement), Vol. 94, 1988, S95-S120.

Comité d'orientation et de concertation sur l'économie sociale. *Entre l'espoir et le doute*. Québec: Ministère de la Condition féminine, 1996, 112 pages.

Charles Côté and Yanik G. Harnois, *L'animation au Quebec, sources, apports et limites*. Montréal: Les Éditions Saint-Martin, 1978, 419 pages.

Réjean Courchesne, "La présence syndicale au Québec," *Le marché du travail*, 17, 1996, pp. 1-2.

Martine D'Amours, *Présence de l'économie sociale au Québec*. Report for the social economy task force. Montréal: Institut de formation en développement économique communautaire, 1996, 46 pages.

Jacques Defourny, "L'émergence du secteur d'économie sociale en Wallonie," *Coopératives et développement*, vol. 23, no 1, 1991, pp.151-175.

Henri Desroches, *Pour un traité d'économie sociale*. Paris: CIEM, 1984, 254 pages.

Yvon Dinel et Yves Bellavance, *PDE...quand tu nous tiens! Les impacts du financement PDE sur les groupes populaires et communautaires*. Montréal: Table des OVEP de Montréal, 1990.

Jean-Pierre Dupuis, (ed.), *Le modèle québécois de développement économique. Débats sur son contenu, son efficacité et ses liens avec les modes de gestion des entreprises*. Québec: Presses Inter Universitaires, 1995, 184 p.

Economic Council of Canada, *From the Bottom Up: The Community Economic Development Approach*. Review article. Economic Council of Canada, Ottawa: Supply and Services Canada, 1990.

Louis Favreau and Benoît Lévesque, *Développement économique communautaire: économie sociale et intervention*. Sainte-Foy, Québec: Presses de l'Université du Québec, 1996, 230 pages.

Louis Favreau and William A. Ninacs, *Pratiques de développement économique communautaire au Québec: de l'expérimentation sociale à l'émergence d'une économie solidaire*. Summary fact-finding report for the National Welfare Grants Program, Human Resources Development Canada, 1993, 40 pages (rapport abrégé de recherche produit pour le Programme des Subventions nationales au bien-être social de Développement des ressources humaines Canada, 40 pages).

Fédération québécoise des coopératives de travail, *Les actes du Sommet sur la coopération du travail dans la nouvelle économie*. Sainte-Foy, Québec, 1996, 88 pages.

Jean-Marc Fontan, "Le développement économique communautaire québécois: éléments de synthèse et point de vue critique," *LSP-RIAC [Revue internationale d'action communautaire]*, no 32, 1995, pp.115-130.

M. Fraser, *Québec inc. Les Québécois prennent d'assaut le monde des affaires*. Montréal: Les éditions de l'homme, 1987, 305 p.

Jean-Marc Gareau, *Le Programme Économique de Pointe St-Charles 1983-1989: La percée du développement économique communautaire dans le Sud-Ouest de Montréal*. Montréal: Institut de formation en développement économique communautaire, 1990, 33 pages.

Jean-Pierre Girard, *Connaissance de l'économie coopérative québécoise: quelques repères*. Montréal: Cahiers de la Chaire de coopérative Guy-Bernier, 1995, 94 p.

Groupe de travail sur l'économie sociale. *Osons la solidarité*. Rapport au Sommet sur l'économie et l'emploi. Montréal, 1996, 64 pages.

Jacques Hamel and Éric Forgues, "De la famille à la culture d'entreprise: un modèle québécois de développement," in Jean-Pierre Dupuis, (ed.), *Le modèle québécois de développement économique. Débats sur son contenu, son efficacité et ses liens avec les modes de gestion des entreprises*. Quebec: Presses Inter Universitaire, 1995, pp. 133-150.

Jean-Louis Laville, *Les services de proximité en Europe: pour une économie solidaire*. Paris: Syros/Alternatives, 1992, 247 pages.

Joël Lebossé, *Fonds de développement: les nouveaux outils financiers du développement local?*. Communication à la Semi-annuelle des SADC du Québec. Charny, Québec: ARGOS Consultants inc., 1997, 15 pages.

Frédéric Lesemann and Michel Thiénot, *Animations sociales au Québec*. Fact-finding report. Montréal: École de service social, Université de Montréal, 1972, 501 pages.

Benoît Lévesque, *Animation sociale, entreprises communautaires et coopératives*. Montréal: Éditions coopératives Albert Saint-Martin, 1979, 379 pages.

Benoît Lévesque, "Le mouvement populaire au Québec: de la formule syndicale à la formule coopérative?," *Coopératives et Développement*, vol. 16, no 2, 1984, pp. 83-104.

Benoît Lévesque, "L'institutionnalisation et le financement des services de proximité au Quebec," *Coopératives et développement*, vol. 26, no 2, 1995, 83-104.

Benoît Lévesque and Daniel Côté, "Le changement des principes coopératifs à l'heure de la mondialisation: à la recherche d'une méthodologie," in Alberto Zevi and José Luis Monzon Campos, (eds.), *Coopératives, marchés, principes coopératifs*. Bruxelles: CIRIEC and De Boeck-Wesmael, Inc., 1995, pp. 1-14.

Benoît Lévesque and Marie-Claire Malo, "L'économie sociale au Québec: une notion méconnue mais une réalité économique importante," in Jacques Defourny and José L. Monzon Campos, (eds.), *Économie Sociale: entre économie capitaliste et économie publique/The Third Sector: Cooperative, Mutual and Nonprofit Organizations*. Brussels: CIRIEC and De Boeck-Wesmael, Inc., pp. 385-446.

Benoît Lévesque, Marguerite Mendell and Solange Van Kemenade, *Les fonds régionaux et locaux de développement au Québec: des institutions financières relevant principalement de l'économie sociale*. Montréal, Research paper on social innovations in businesses and unions, Département de sociologie, Université du Québec à Montréal, 1996, 34 pages.

Benoît Lévesque, Margerite Mendell et Solange Van Kemenade, *Profil socio-économique des Fonds de développement local et régional au Québec. Study conducted for FORD-Q*. Ottawa: Supply and Services Canada, 1997, 52 p.

Benoît Lévesque, Jean-Marc Fontan and Juan-Luis Klein, *Les systèmes locaux de production. Condition de mise en place et stratégie d'implantation pour le développement du Projet Angus*. Montréal, Research paper on social innovations in businesses, unions and public services, Université du Québec à Montréal, 2 volumes: 110 pages and 135 pages, 1996.

William A. Ninacs, "L'organisation communautaire en milieu semi-urbain/semi-rural," in Laval Doucet and Louis Favreau, (eds.), *Théorie et pratiques en organisation communautaire*. Sillery, Québec: Presses de l'Université du Québec, 1991, pp. 257-272.

William A. Ninacs, "Synthesizing the Research Results: Where is the Common Ground," *Making Waves*, Vol. 4, no 4, 1993, pp. 18-20

Michel Payette, "Le Forum pour l'emploi: histoire et perspectives," *Interventions économiques pour une alternative sociale*, no 24, 1992, pp. 99-117.

K. Polanyi, *The Great Transformation*. Boston: Beacon Press, 1957, 315 pages.

Jean Proulx, (with Lorraine Guay), *Les épreuves et les défis du partenariat*. Montréal: La Table de concertation des regroupements provinciaux d'organismes communautaires et bénévoles, 1995, 50 pages.

Robert D. Putnam, *Making Democracy Work: Civic Traditions in Modern Italy*. Princeton, New Jersey: Princeton University Press, 1993, 258 pages.

Jack Quarter, "Starting Worker-Owned Enterprises: Problems and Prospects," in Quarter, Jack and George Melnyk, (eds.), *Partners in Enterprise. The Worker Ownership Phenomenon*. Montreal: Black Rose Books, 1989, pp. 33-58.

Pierre Rosanvallon, *La nouvelle question sociale: repenser l'État-providence*. Paris: Éditions du Seuil, 1995, 223 pages.

Guy Roustang, Jean-Louis Laville, Bernard Eme, Daniel Mothé and Bernard Perret, *Vers un nouveau contrat social*. Paris: Desclée de Brouwer, 1996, 187 pages.

Patrice Sauvage, "Summary," in *Reconciling Economy and Society: Towards a Plural Economy*. Paris: OECD, 1996, pp. 9-27.

Yves Vaillancourt, "Sortir de l'alternative entre privatisation et étatisation dans la santé et les services sociaux," in Bernard Eme, Louis Favreau, Jean-Louis Laville, and Yves Vaillancourt, (eds.), *Société civile, État et économie plurielle*. Paris, Montreal and Hull: CRIDA-CNRS, CRISES-UQAM and UQAH, 1996, pp.147-224.

Yves Vaillancourt, *Vers un nouveau partage des responsabilités dans les services sociaux et de santé: Rôle de l'État, du marché, de l'économie sociale et du secteur informel*, Montréal: Cahiers du LAREPPS, no 97-05, 1997, 302 p.

Christian Valadou, *Les entreprises d'insertion au Québec: état des lieux.* étude réalisée pour le Secrétariat à la Concertation, Montréal, Collectif des entreprises d'insertion du Québec, 1995, 83 pages.

Claude Vienney, *L'économie sociale.* Paris: Éditions La Découverte, 1984, 126 pages.

THREE SUCCESSFUL PROJECTS

Housing Co-operatives

Between 1973 and 1994, through three federal funding programs, two provincial programs and one municipal program (Montreal), approximately 21,500 dwellings (1,100 co-operatives) were created (Girard, 1995:67). Most of these co-operatives, which now have over 20,000 members, consist of home renovation projects and projects for recycling institutional buildings for residential purposes. If financial assistance from the various levels of government has produced the desired results, it must be realized that the cornerstone of development is the technical support provided by various programs, especially by the Technical Resource Groups which successfully mobilized the people directly involved in the projects. Although the federal government has not funded any new projects since 1992, its commitments continue to run for periods as long as 35 years. In the social economy as a whole, development of this specific social economy sector has been exemplary for about 20 years. In the opinion of many, it remains a benchmark.

Worker Co-operatives

Beginning in the early 1980s, Quebec promoters of worker co-operatives, inspired by the example of housing co-operatives, promoted relatively rapid development of the sector. Today, of the 250 worker co-operatives in Canada, the great majority (175) are in Quebec, 45 operating in forestry and about 30 as shareholder co-operatives (D'Amours, 1996). The various worker co-operatives can obtain technical assistance, not only from their respective unions but also from regional development co-operatives (RDC). RDCs are financed by the Quebec government on the basis of number of jobs created; in the space of 10 years, they have helped create or save 3,735 jobs in 194 co-operatives (*ibid.*). The criterion of effectiveness (number of jobs created) is important, although clearly insufficient to provide a complete picture of the quality of the advice and assistance to development given by the RDCs. Even though worker co-operatives have some unusual forms of funding available to them—one is an investment plan that provides a reduction in income tax for members who reinvest their share of profits in the co-operatives—under-capitalization is still a major problem. Finally, the financial contribution of the Quebec Industrial Development Corporation (QIDC) has often been a determining factor in the creation of co-operatives.

Child-care Centres

Among collective services, non-profit child-care services or child-care centres clearly illustrate the potential of the new social economy, not only for creating jobs, but also for providing high-quality service with strong commitment by the various players. Quebec non-profit child-care centres, home child-care agencies, and school child-care facilities form a network providing over 90,000 child-care spaces and are considered a part of the social economy. The vast majority of the 659 child-care centres and 134 child-care agencies are under direct parent control, with parents occupying more than two-thirds of the 5,500 seats on the boards of directors. About 15,500 individuals are salaried personnel, with most holding full-time positions (*Ibid.*) As with worker cooperatives, Quebec child-care services can access technical assistance from a government agency, the Office des services de garde du Québec, that oversees development of the network. Funding is mixed, based on user fees and grants—with the exception of start-up and equipment costs—based on spaces occupied. A public support program geared to poorer families and a tax-credit scheme for parents round out the state funding model, at least for the time being. Notwithstanding these regulatory mechanisms, community-based child-care centres have managed to remain independent as to organization of workloads, pedagogy, and internal matters. This has resulted in different models, varying from one centre to another, as well as an involvement of parents and staff rarely found in public or private sector services (Lévesque, 1995).

DEVELOPMENT FUNDS: SOCIAL ECONOMY ENTERPRISES

If Quebec ranks first for risk capital with 40% of funds available in Canada, it is also first in the area of number of regional, local and community development funds. In a study sponsored in part by the FORD-Q, we found at least 254 funds for Quebec with assets approaching one billion (Canadian) dollars. Three-quarters of these funds (73.3%) are associated with the social economy in that they target not only profitable investment but also social objectives such as job creation and regional and local community development. The public sector (and therefore the governments of Canada and Quebec) is the sector most often mentioned (53.4%) as a source of funding. The Government of Canada is involved in 71 out of 224 (31.5%) of funds (we must not forget that a given fund may have a number of funding sources). Next comes the Fonds de solidarité des travailleurs du Québec, which is involved in 69 (30.8%) of the funds, followed by the Government of Quebec, which is involved in 65 (29.0%). The Mouvement Desjardins (Investissement Desjardins, some federations and the Caisses populaires) is in fourth place with 10.6% of investment and the private sector last with 9.6%. Although many of these funds are in competition, they are significantly different from one another in the territory they cover (region, regional county municipality, local community, cultural community), and in the size of the financial participation in the enterprises (e.g. investment below $50,000). Finally, most of these funds are directly or indirectly associated with a regional or local government, so that they try to take strategic planning of economic activities for a given territory into account (see Lévesque, Mendell and Kemenade, 1996 and 1997).

Chapter 9

Social Economy: A Practitioner's Viewpoint

William A. Ninacs

Introduction

Community-based organizations will increasingly act as arbiters and ombudsmen with the larger forces of the marketplace and government, serving as the primary advocates and agents for social and political reform. Third-sector organizations are also likely to take up the task of providing more and more basic services in the wake of cutbacks in government aid and assistance to persons and neighbourhoods in need.[1]

What Rifkin presents as a forecast could well sum up the evolution of community-based organizations (CBOs) in Québec since the mid-1960's. Indeed, their on-going relationship with the State has evolved over time from conflict to collaboration, and, although advocacy is still quite present, it is no longer isolated from an attempt to participate in the search for solutions that will satisfy all of the players involved. The role of CBOs in service-delivery is nevertheless a source of tension and uneasiness, feelings that are also at the heart of the debate on the social economy in Québec.

The success or failure of the social economy here will most likely have a lot to do with the way that CBOs belonging to both the women's movement and the communitarian movement[2] participate in its development, and this, in turn, will inevitably be influenced by their relationship with the State. Over the past two years, a number of events have generated reactions of both optimism and mistrust regarding the social economy in Québec. Stakes are high, since the underlying concerns touch upon a number of fundamental and politically sensitive issues. For example, at stake for the Québec government is its ability to mobilize a significant portion of the women's and communitarian movements—in other words, organizations that are presently dealing with impoverished or otherwise marginalized constituencies—in its efforts to simultaneously reduce its budget deficit, maintain health and social services and provide new ones, and create new jobs for unskilled recipients of welfare and employment insurance benefits. At stake for the women's movement is its search for an alternative to the poverty, job ghettos, and social and economic inequalities that continue to plague the majority of women everywhere. At stake for the labour movement is maintaining public sector jobs for its members while increasing its support for community-based, local development efforts. At stake for the communitarian movement is its autonomy and its resistance to becoming the middle manager of the poor or worse, to exploiting the poor in order to meet its own operational imperatives by being forced to use workfare programmes. At stake for all agents of social change is keeping open the window of opportunity to put forward a true alternative to conventional business development that could help relieve poverty, social exclusion, gender inequalities, and many other social problems.

When it comes to the social economy, all of these players are in fact stakeholders since they have all thus far invested time, money, human resources, goodwill, and sometimes all of these in its development in Québec, and it is not likely that any of them will cease doing so in the near future. There are signs, however, that some support—especially that of the women's and communitarian movements—should not be taken for granted, even though their constituencies probably have the most to gain from the social economy's success. This paper will try to examine the social economy in Québec through the eyes of these stakeholders by exploring their perceived, actual, or potential roles and concerns. In order to do so, it will look at recent events that have shaped the evolution of the social economy, introduce different components of the support system that is being developed for new initiatives, and endeavour to establish the effects that both these events and components have had on the various stakeholders.

The 1996 Socio-Economic Conferences

In 1996, the Québec government organized two major related public events that have had profound consequences on the evolution of the social economy in this province.

The March Conference Zero Deficit

Building on a tradition of regularly bringing together decision-makers to discuss issues of mutual concern and to establish plans of action to deal with them, the Québec government convened the Conference on the Social and Economic Future of Québec in March, 1996, on the general theme of the economy, including public finances, and employment. There were many innovations at this meeting, not the least of which was the inclusion of new partners around the table. These included leaders from the women's movement, from the communitarian sector, from religious groups, and from community-based coalitions. Consensus was reached on the objective to eliminate the government's budget deficit within four years, on the setting up of a commission on taxation, and on the organizing of two major working groups, one governmental, the other private. The mandate of the government working group was to coordinate reforms taking place in the fields on welfare, education, health and social services, and professional training. The private working group was subdivided into four task forces, each headed by an individual from the private sector: 1) business and employment; 2) regional and local development; 3) the revitalization of Montréal; 4) the social economy. Each of the task forces, as well as each of the departments responsible for the various reforms and the commission on taxation, were given six months to find new venues for job creation and economic development within the parameters of reduced public spending.

The setting up of a Task Force on the Social Economy had not been foreseen prior to this conference, although the social economy was already seen as having job creation potential,[3] but was rather the result of convincing arguments put forward by the community-based representatives supported by various labour and business leaders. The creation of this task force as such was considered a significant achievement by many women's groups and community organizations.

However, members of these same organizations also quite vividly recall the icy silence that followed the president of the Québec's Women Federation asking the other partners around the table to indicate what concrete steps they were willing to take to reduce poverty. To a great extent, the Conference ended on an ambivalent note for activists in the women's and communitarian sectors: they now had a chance to demonstrate the potential of non-traditional economic development but they also had the feeling that the more conventional partners were only paying lip service to the issue of poverty and social exclusion and that the objective embodied in the slogan "Déficit zéro" would override all other goals.

The Conference gave the Task Force on the Social Economy a five-point mandate: 1) define the *québécois* model of the social economy while taking into consideration the work already performed by the Québec government's steering and concerted action committee on the social economy;[4] 2) identify promising avenues for development; 3) come up with means to launch job creation projects; 4) specify different players' roles and the responsibilities related to the social economy (government, financial sector, labour unions, communitarian movement, administrative regions, local municipalities, women's groups, etc.); 5) develop an action plan to create jobs in the social economy. The Conference indicated that this mandate was to be accomplished in the following manner: a) establish the Task Force by recruiting participants; b) mobilize practitioners around the idea of creating jobs in the social economy; c) ensure the rapid implementation of the concrete proposals relating to job creation put forward by the various partners during the Conference; d) present an action plan to the fall Summit. To head the Task Force, the Conference named Nancy Neamtan, executive director of RESO (Regroupement pour la relance économique et sociale du sud-ouest de Montréal), a community economic development corporation.

The Task Force wasted no time in getting organized. A steering committee of twelve individuals was rapidly set up with the following sectors being represented: women's groups, cultural organizations, youth, community economic development organizations, labour (the three major trade unions), the Mouvement Desjardins, Hydro-Québec, the private sector, forestry co-operatives, and the Québec Council on Co-operation, as well as a representative from the Québec government's own steering committee on the social economy.

A pragmatic definition was sought by the Task Force, one that would allow the largest number of practitioners to identify with the social economy and that would encompass the largest number of practices. As the background paper for the June, 1997, international conference held under the aegis of Human Resources Development Canada (HRDC) and the Organization for Economic Co-operation and Development (OECD) on local development, job creation, and the social economy highlighted,[5] there is no single definition for the expression "social economy." This lack of clarity was a blessing in disguise since it gave the Task Force some leeway to meet its ends. The definition adopted by the Task Force sees the social economy as being based on principles of solidarity, autonomy, and citizenship, that must be embodied in operational guidelines. The social economy thus promotes the development of initiatives characterized by: a) a primary goal of service to members or the community rather than of accumulating profit; b) autonomous management (independent of public programmes); c) democratic decision-making processes; d) the primacy of persons and work over capital in the redistribution of profits; and e) operations based on principles of participation, empowerment, and individual and collective accountability.[6] In general, the Task Force's perspective argues that the social economy is fundamentally a question of practices tending towards economic democracy and the empowerment of individuals and communities. As such, it overlaps with community economic development (CED).[7] Indeed, many scholars see the two as intrinsically interwoven, with CED being a development strategy within the social economy.[8] Experts generally agree that the main difference between the social economy and CED is that the latter strategy will support the development of conventional businesses that do not possess the characteristics of social economy initiatives. One way or another, this link to CED is of strategic importance since social economy initiatives most often respond to local needs, use local resources as much as possible, and generally rely on the active participation and support of members of the community.

The accomplishments of the Task Force in the six-month interval between the March Conference and the October Summit were remarkable. Supported by a skeleton staff made up of individuals "lent" by various organizations and a few employees paid for out of the Task Force's own budget, it rapidly set up a technical advisory team and a dozen sectorial committees on potential fields of endeavour (forestry, personal services, including, but not limited to, home care and childcare, agriculture, the environment, urban quality of life, tourism and leisure, and culture). Specific networks were mobilized by these committees and this enabled the preparation of a list of projects backed by firm commitments of their sponsors.

The Task Force also formed working groups on financing and technical assistance. It published a newsletter, both on paper and on-line, and organized conferences in almost every region of Québec. These latter events generally brought together activists from the women's, communitarian, and labour movements who spent a day or more discussing the potential benefits of getting involved in the social economy or of supporting it in some other manner, and identified a wide array of markets to be exploited, needs to be rendered financially viable, and examples of possible initiatives. They also often discussed ideological issues, perceived dangers, and real threats stemming from the social economy. As such, the regional conferences were simultaneous mobilization efforts and fact-finding missions. The resulting data was analyzed by the Task Force's staff and collated with ideas generated by its board and committees as well as by other sources, including very public debates in Québec's dailies[9] and journals.[10] Armed with this wealth of information and with a number of firm projects, the Task Force was ready for the October Summit.

The October Summit Zero Impoverishment

Those invited to the Summit Conference on the Economy and Employment were about the same people as the ones who attended the March Conference: seventy players representing almost every facet of Québec society. The general objectives were similar as well, but the Québec government's financial situation had worsened, and this implied that more spending reductions would be required to make up the shortfalls. The priority was nevertheless to set in motion as many projects as possible to stimulate job creation.

The Task Force on the Social Economy put forward twenty-five projects in fields as varied as culture, home care, childcare, forestry, agriculture, the environment, housing, training businesses, and high-tech services. In all, these projects could potentially create up to 20,000 new jobs over three years and most of them were quite advanced in the planning stages, with a few that could be set in motion rather quickly. The Task Force also recommended that the social economy be recognized as a full-fledged economic sector in its own right, but not at the cost of sidestepping key issues such as finding ways to respond to unmet needs without substituting government action, ensuring that the social economy not be a job ghetto for the poor and the excluded, and respecting equity in access to employment, especially for women and youth. The report ended with a series of recommendations to enhance the chances for success.

A consensus was reached during the Summit that adopted the Task Force's proposal and identified the social economy as a way to respond to new and unmet needs, with social economy enterprises producing the required goods and services. Even the private sector made commitments during the Summit to support the social economy. In particular, the Bank of Montreal, the National Bank, the Royal Bank, the Groupe Jean Coutu, the Mouvement Desjardins, and Alcan indicated that they would chip in financially in the setting up of a fund to support the social economy. Other companies also indicated that they were favourable to this idea and that they would evaluate the possibility of contributing as well. This unanimity around the social economy was considered a major breakthrough by all of those involved.

However, for most social activists, the 1996 Summit will also be remembered as the moment when Québec's leaders refused to adopt the Zero Impoverishment proposal. Simply stated, the proposal called for a freeze on all cutbacks to welfare benefits, the reasoning being that balancing the government's books (Zero Deficit) should not be accomplished by sinking the less wealthy twenty percent of the population further into poverty. While the government committed itself to the principle of not impoverishing people who face severe or permanent obstacles in their attempts to re-integrate the labour market, and, among other concrete measures, set up a $250 million dollar fund (spread over three years) to finance job-creating anti-poverty initiatives, it would not agree to a status quo regarding welfare legislation. The women's and communitarian movements' representatives decided that they would not support the government's proposals if the government refused to support theirs, withdrew from the consensus on eliminating the deficit by the year 2000, and left the hall before the Summit ended.

Hence for many social activists, potential social economy practitioners and allies, the October Summit, as was the case with the March Conference, generated both promise and concern. Disappointment, however, was almost palpable for many. While it was not deep enough to preclude further participation, it did have the effect of transforming fledgling cautious enthusiasm into grudging support which, in turn, reduced the momentum generated by the regional conferences, slowed the pace of development, and sparked more ideological debates among many stakeholders.

Supportive Infrastructure

Using the Québec Task Force's definition, the social economy spans a very broad spectrum of formal and informal structures wherein a variable mixture of market forces and public financing—frequently accompanied by volunteer efforts—come into play in order to provide goods and services to targeted individuals as well as to the public at large. Co-operatives and non-profit organizations are usually given as examples of social economy initiatives. The best overview of the social economy in Canada—"Canada's Social Economy" by Jack Quarter[11]—is still quite current, especially regarding organizational structures, even though it was written five years ago. Other recent studies provide specific information on the situation in Québec.[12]

Since the Summit, a variety of structures have been or are on the verge of being set up to support the development of more such initiatives as well as to maintain and strengthen those that are already in place. Taking into consideration that more than a few resources existed in Québec well before the Summit was held, social entrepreneurs here now have a wide array of services available to them, with more still to come, and a number of organizations providing promotion, lobbying, training, and research related to the social economy.

The Task Force on the Social Economy

The Task Force on the Social Economy is still active, incorporated as a not-for-profit corporation and operating as the *Chantier de l'économie sociale* with funding for two years in order to oversee the setting up of some of the projects that it had proposed in its report to the Summit.

No other organization will play as commanding a role in the development of the social economy in Québec as the Task Force will. Its mandate—to serve as an intermediary on all matters relating to the social economy between the Québec government and almost everyone outside of it—will ensure that its way of seeing things will permeate official political and public administration circles. The broad membership of its board of directors should ensure that its vision will seep into the various social and other movements represented on it. Its leadership role on most questions, through its links to the regional committees on the social economy and its seat on the board of the Social Economy Development Fund, will ensure that strategic planners, technical assistance providers, and financial backers share its vision.

The Task Force already wields a considerable amount of clout. For example, even though its view of the social economy is broader in scope than what the Québec government seems to have intended and although other perspectives currently co-exist in Québec, its definition will most likely exert more influence than the others since it has been adopted by the new Social Economy Development Fund as well as by the Québec Minister responsible for regional development. Taking into account that networking and lobbying services will be provided by the Task Force, financial support by the Fund, and technical assistance by the Minister's secretariat (through local development centres), it seems inevitable that this definition will become the social economy's predominant development framework in Québec. In other words, even though other perspectives may continue to be present in debates and even in some policies, the social economy will undoubtedly be recognized by a growing number of practitioners and supporters, as well as by the general public, as a collective, participatory, and somewhat non-profit approach to local economic development.

This definition's advantage is that it identifies the values that can be used to mobilize individuals and organizations in the development of a social economy as well as where opposite points of view can converge in order to engage the greatest number of players in this work. Indeed, the Task Force has thus far been able to obtain surprising compromises from all sectors—including community groups and labour unions—on such thorny issues as home care services for the elderly.

In the year since the Summit, the Task Force reported that 1,000 jobs had been created, about two-thirds of what had been foreseen, in a wide variety of co-operatives including a score of home care agencies (with 55 others in the planning stage), the construction of 1,325 housing units, and a number of forestry-related initiatives. The Task Force noted as well that jobs were maintained in the funeral services sector when seven funeral parlours were bought out by new or existing funeral services co-operatives. The Task Force has also made gains networking with key economic development players. For example, it continues to publish a newsletter but this is now a collective undertaking that includes the *Fondation d'éducation à la coopération* and the

Fondation de l'entrepreneurship. Finally, the Task Force also played a key role in the organizing of the first Québec Cultural Days, a province-wide project to stimulate cultural activities on a yearly basis.

The Social Economy Development Fund and Other Sources of Financing

The Social Economy Development Fund emerged from the Québec Task Force on the Social Economy's work prior to the October Summit and from the commitments made by the private sector to concretely support the social economy. Officially incorporated in June, 1997, as a not-for-profit corporation, the Fund will be under the joint control of the conventional private sector and the social economy, since each have an equal number of seats on the board of directors. When its initial capitalization is completed, it will attain $23 million, $19 million of which will have been provided by the private sector with the government of Québec picking up the balance.

The Fund has two main objectives: 1) contribute to the capitalization of social economy enterprises; 2) provide these initiatives with administrative support. To achieve its first goal, the Fund will invest up to 20% of a social economy enterprise's initial capital needs up to a $50,000 maximum. It is expected that the enterprise will in turn leverage this investment to obtain "love money" (loan or investments from friends and families) or other more conventional financing. The Fund will not require mortgages or other guarantees in order to make it easier for the venture to obtain loans and investments from other partners. To reach its second objective, the Fund will provide the initiative with technical assistance or training, depending on specific needs, on a fee basis. In both cases, the Fund will expect the social economy enterprise to reimburse the investment or to pay for services rendered, but it is expected that terms will be relatively flexible and non-detrimental to the enterprise's financial well-being. The Fund will operate with a minimal staff and will sub-contract its technical assistance and training services to local organizations. Moreover, analysis of business plans will be provided by the *Société de développement industriel* (SDI), Québec's industrial development agency, which will also manage the Fund's own investment and working capital.

It should be noted that Québec already abounds with venture capital funds, including many that support local development initiatives and co-operatives.[13] Furthermore, the SDI can make non-collateral loans to all small and medium-sized companies, including co-operatives and not-for-profit corporations that have a business component. There are also income tax incentives available to worker co-operative members who reinvest their dividends. Such public and private financial support has often been a key factor in the creation of co-operatives in Québec. Undercapitalization is nevertheless still a major problem for co-operatives and not-for-profit organizations.

Indeed, that it has been necessary to set up a specific development fund for social economy initiatives is indicative that their financial needs are unique in many ways. This is especially true during the pre-start-up phase that enables the initiatives to detect new needs and to identify how to respond to them by mobilizing resources that neither capitalist business nor public service are able to enlist. It is not a step to be ignored, but all practitioners recognize that it is a very lengthy phase and that the promoters of these initiatives hardly ever have the capital required to finance it outright. The Fund will, unfortunately, not really offer much to solve this problem.

Local Development Centres and Other Technical Assistance Resources

There is a deep concern among all practitioners and stakeholders that new social entrepreneurs will not possess the knowledge and skills required to run economic initiatives. This fear is echoed by activists from the social movements themselves, especially since, based on CED research in Québec, most of these entrepreneurs will likely stem from their ranks and a "qualitative leap" is required to move from purely social goals to economic ones.[14] While community activists are quite often very successful at managing organizations on shoe-string budgets, this does not mean that they possess the know-how to market and produce goods and services in a competitive arena where quality control and cost-effectiveness are the rule.

Technical assistance will therefore be crucial to the success of most social economy enterprises. In its report to the October Summit, the Task Force listed an impressive number of organizations developed, ostensibly, to support social economy enterprises and organizations. The list includes regional development co-operatives (8), community development corporations (17), community economic development corporations (CDÉC) (8), Community Futures Committees (55), and community organizers working in Local Community Service Centres (CLSC), about 325 practitioners in approximately 100 CLSCs. To a certain extent, this information is misleading, since many of these organizations, especially community development corporations, do not have staff that is qualified to provide technical assistance to social economy enterprises. Indeed, most community organizers do not possess knowledge related to business planning, developing marketing strategies, and calculating break-even analyses, all of which are essential to the success of the business of social economy enterprises. Similarly, most of the analysts working with Community Futures Committees lack expertise in the social side of a social economy enterprise's operations. For example, social economy initiatives usually depend on donations of time. At the very least, members of their boards of directors contribute the time that they spend attending meetings, since they cannot be paid for this work, while other members quite often play key, unpaid roles chairing committees or otherwise participating in them, and frequently help out during special activities. Quarter goes so far as to consider volunteerism as a "salient characteristic" of the social economy.[15] The issue here is that volunteers become a part of a social economy initiative's human resources, one that it cannot function without. But volunteering cannot be decreed, since volunteers freely choose to donate their time and usually leave organizations that take them for granted. Volunteers simply cannot be managed in the same way that paid staff can. They cannot be ordered to accomplish a task and monitoring functions that they do accept requires both diplomatic skills and a lot of time. Most management training programmes rarely take such factors into account and conventional business development tools do not deal with such issues.

Some of these support structures, such as some regional development co-operatives, refuse to offer assistance to ventures outside of conventional manufacturing or commercial activities, while others, such as community development corporations, tend to perceive the social economy as limited to service and mutual assistance initiatives, and therefore restrict their services to non-commercial and non-profit activities. There seems to be a kind of polarization of technical assistance taking place with services being offered in either a business or a service organization mode depending on the perspective adopted by the different providers of support services.

There is clearly a need for specialized technical assistance for social economy enterprises and a few organizations offering such support have been developed in recent years. A few CDÉCs, at least one community development corporation, the *Regroupement québécois des coopérateurs et coopératrices du travail* (an association of co-operative workers), and the *Groupe de consultation pour le maintien et développement de l'emploi de la CSN* (a consulting arm of the Confederation of National Trade-Unions) all provide knowledgeable assistance on both the economic and social components of social economy enterprises. However, such resources are scarce. The Québec government has recognized the need for additional support, and legislation tabled just before Christmas, 1997, calls for the setting up of a local development centre (LDC) in each county (*municipalité régionale de comté*) or its equivalent in urban neighbourhoods by April 1st, 1998. Each LDC will be a multi-service outlet managed by the community to provide technical assistance and other development services to potential or existing businesses. Each one will also provide technical assistance to existing or potential social economy initiatives, and a portion of its budget will be earmarked specifically for business development in the social economy. While some LDCs may sub-contract this work where resources already exist, it is believed that most will hire new staff to do the job. The overall policy related to the implementing of local development centres has been severely criticized, since many LDCs will overlap with existing development organizations, especially Community Futures Committees and community economic development corporations. However, from a narrow social economy perspective, the advent of local, qualified technical resources for the social economy is seen as a giant step in the right direction.

Networking Organizations and Other Training Resources

An overview of the co-operative movement indicates that the worker co-operative has historically been the most difficult of all forms of co-operatives to sustain just about everywhere in the world.[16] This was recently confirmed by the outgoing director of the Québec worker co-operative federation, in a workshop presentation at an international conference, who stated that of the 25 or so worker co-operatives created every year in Québec, about 15 die "in absolute silence."[17] Since the worker co-operative (or some version of it) is the framework of choice for new social economy enterprises, this rate of failure is of great concern, especially in the case of personal care services requiring medium and long term intervention. The new Social Economy Development Fund is planning for a default rate of 18% on its investments.[18] Although this isn't the rate of actual foreseen failures (since not all ventures require the same amount of money), the figure still scares people who have doubts about adopting the social economy as a strategy for personal services and who don't want to have to pick up the pieces for every one in five initiatives that will stop providing essential services. Horror stories, such as that of the daily Le Fleuve, where lack of business sense by its journalist-managers and lack of understanding of how a co-operative operates by its lenders contributed to the demise of Rimouski's only daily newspaper and to the loss of over 40 jobs in an area hard-hit by lack of employment opportunities,[19] certainly don't help.

Knowledge and skills will likely be acquired primarily through experience for some time to come, with practitioners calling upon providers of professional services for advice and information, and this will probably often turn into informal, on-the-job training of sorts. There is nevertheless a clear need for technically competent and value knowledgeable professional training. Unfortunately, the dearth of educational programmes that integrate both economic and social development training has been decried for many years to little avail. Schools of social work still do not include business planning and market analysis in their curricula, and business schools still do not include social intervention and popular education in theirs. This means that new training programmes adapted to the specific needs of social economy practitioners have to rapidly be developed if this approach is to prosper. At least one private, non-profit CED training intermediary is presently working on a short training package along these lines, and Montréal's Concordia University is in the process of setting up a formal graduate diploma programme in CED with a concentration being considered on social enterprise development and social entrepreneurship. While these projects are encouraging, they will unfortunately only make a small dent in learning needs.

Networking can often bridge learning and technical assistance gaps by providing peer support on specific problems or at crucial moments. Two types of networks seem to be the most helpful. Local ones tend to be mixed in terms of fields of practice but bring together individuals and organizations who share common problems tied to the specific community that they belong to. Social capital[20] can also be produced at this level. Moreover, grounding the social economy experiences in local dynamics is necessary in order to link all development initiatives and, by doing so, to strengthen the bonds of solidarity that enable a community to make optimal use of all its existing resources. Recent research suggests that local, democratically controlled, non-profit intermediary organizations are key to successful local development.[21] In Québec, a variety of local networking structures exist, but their ability to recruit social economy enterprises remains to be seen.

A second type of networking is through sectorial intermediary organizations, such as the *Fédération québécoise des coopératives de travail* (FQCT), the Québec federation of worker co-operatives, that brings together organizations with common interests. Such intermediaries can assess knowledge and skill gaps. The FQCT has, for example, been able to develop a number of short training sessions on various narrowly-focused subjects based on needs expressed by its members. Moreover, some practitioners believe that setting up social economy enterprises independently from one another can have a negative effect on their eventual solidarity and that sectorial networks should play a greater role in the first stages of development. It isn't clear, however, what ties organizations such as the FQCT will have with technical assistance providers, such as local development centres, who will be doing this work.

The Social Economy Regional Committees[22]

In the wake of the Women's March Against Poverty and the Québec government's commitment to invest $250 million over five years for "social infrastructure," an initial outlay of $15 million was made available in 1995. The money was under the tutelage of the Québec government's regional development secretariat (*Secrétariat au développement des régions*), the SDR, that promptly set up Social Economy Regional Committees (CRES) in every administrative region. Their objectives were to: 1) promote the social economy; 2) encourage the creation of new ventures or consolidate existing initiatives; 3) participate in local and regional development strategies; 4) evaluate the different projects and make recommendations to regional job development funds. Each CRES was made up of four representatives from women's groups, representatives of four provincial departments and agencies (the SDR, the regional welfare board, the regional health and social services board, the regional manpower development agency), a representative from the Québec Council on the Status of Women, a representative from the regional development council, and, in a few regions, a representative of the labour movement. Their accomplishments have varied from region to region, but all have experienced similar problems related to financing. There simply wasn't very much money with each region receiving between $40,000 and $350,000 per year. As for the other moneys committed by the Québec government, women's groups soon found out that these were the recycling of existing programmes. The participation of women's groups, however, has ensured that issues related to poverty and social exclusion have maintained a high profile in regional discussions and development plans thus far.

There have been major changes since June, 1997, when each CRES became affiliated to its regional development council. In line with the Québec government's new policy supporting local and regional development, their membership changed: all government delegates were forced to leave and new representatives from community-based organizations and the co-operative movement were added. Their role is now to: 1) develop the portion of the region's strategic planning devoted to the social economy; 2) ensure that representatives of the local social economy are represented on each local development centre's board of directors; 3) coordinate actions between local and regional players in the social economy. Since local development centres have not yet been established, the CRESs have been working on strategic planning. It is anticipated that each CRES will also serve as a relay of sorts to the Task Force on the Social Economy, but nothing formal has yet been clearly defined.

The Québec Government [23]

Documents used by the government of Québec for information purposes and for the training of various public sector workers foresee that job growth in the public sector will be very weak and that jobs created in the private sector will continue to be extremely demanding when it comes to qualifications and extremely limited when it comes to numbers. The challenge of enabling the least qualified segment of the population to integrate the labour force is therefore quite daunting, since it would seem to require expanding the job supply outside of the private and public sectors. This is where the Québec government sees the social economy as fitting in. Its document explains that potential markets exist for the social economy because the Welfare State has reached its limits, because there are growing unsatisfied needs, and because the private sector has shown little interest to engage in low-profit activities. By satisfying these needs, the social economy can generate new economic activity and thereby enlarge the job supply by opening less qualified positions. While not wanting to confine the social economy to cheap labour markets or tiny business ventures, it is a fact that many unmet needs often require less specialized people.

The government considers the word "enterprise" as being the key to the success of the social economy. It believes that an enterprise produces goods and services, provides real jobs, and is financially viable. To the Québec government, an enterprise can be financially viable even when it receives government funds. The example of childcare centres is given to show how public support to parents does not make these centres any less viable. The government document also stresses that the commitment made at the Summit is for social economy enterprises and not for non-entrepreneurial programmes. Its support can take various forms: 1) start-up funds; 2) direct transfers to low-income families in order to enable them to access services provided by these enterprises; 3) direct purchases of goods and services by public departments and organizations; 4) entrepreneurial support; 5) opening up existing business development programmes to social economy initiatives; 6) creating new tools such as loan guarantees by its development agencies. It believes that such support is required to encourage a portion of the communitarian sector to adopt an entrepreneurial mindset—indeed, a paradigm shift that should not be underestimated.

The government document notes that it will support social economy enterprises in markets that are financially viable. Although it recognizes that the social economy can and does operate in other types of markets, it is clear that its priority is to support development where job creation will be highest and least costly. This is cause for concern, especially among women's groups, since it means that there seems to be a distinction between social economy initiatives given a priority since the Summit and its "social infrastructure" projects that include the core financing of community-based organizations. In fact, the document makes it clear that social utility is not the main criterion for government support. There is also concern that highly standardized government programmes will not take into account the fact that the social component of the social economy initiatives cannot be financed by market forces alone, that programmes will be more focused on their business side since the financial bottom line is easier to evaluate than the results on the social side. Indeed, the belief is that quantitatively-based evaluations perceived as being the standard focus of public programmes will be the norm here as well, and that this in turn will have a negative effect on the quality of services provided if qualitative criteria are not included.

Key Stakeholders

With the advent of this network of resources and especially with the announcement that free technical assistance and affordable financing will soon be available province-wide for ventures in the social economy, more and more organizations and institutions have become or will soon be involved in this domain. Key players warrant specific scrutiny since many, often because of different constituencies, interests and resources, do not necessarily share a common perspective on the social economy. A number of practice and policy issues emerge from this diversity.

Womens Groups

The women's movement has been at the forefront of the development of the social economy. Most observers agree that the renewed interest in the social economy was triggered by the Women's March Against Poverty in late spring of 1995. The March called for a programme of "social infrastructures" which would encompass the support for all types of community groups, including those of the communitarian movement, and the development of a new economy that would speak to the issue of women's exclusion from the labour market and that would recognize the often unpaid and otherwise usually underpaid work that women accomplish for society's benefit. Indeed, since the beginning of the 1990's, various segments of the women's movement had already begun investigating how women's centres were being used to help alleviate poverty among women.[24] In preparation for the March, 1996, Conference, women's groups held seminars in order to explore different issues related to the involvement of women's organizations in local and regional development.[25]

However, it was the marchers' demand for a programme of "social infrastructures" that sparked a second look at the social economy to see if it could play a role in the struggle against unemployment and social exclusion that were victimizing women.[26]

The women's movement has been generally disappointed with the way that "their" field of the inquiry has been usurped by both the Québec government and the Task Force on the social economy who, in turn, have relegated its more fundamental issues to the sidelines.[27] For example, the women's movement argues that the social economy should include all initiatives that build social solidarity while the Task Force argues that some form of commercial activity is an essential component. Mutual non-profits serving specific interest groups and voluntary organizations that may have economic activities (usually fundraising) but that are not really business transactions as such, are therefore not part of the social economy[28] according to the Task Force and, by default, the Québec government. Even the communitarian movement, by its efforts to disassociate itself from the social economy, has adopted what the women's movement sees as a restrictive view of the social economy. The women's movement is, in fact, genuinely dismayed at what it perceives as its allies not defending a vision of the economy that would address all social concerns. This has become a source of tension, especially between the women's and the communitarian movements, but it is not a rift, since both agree on a great number of other fundamental issues.

There are other complaints as well, but the overall effect has been a great deal of confusion among women's groups. As it stands now, some women's groups unequivocally support involvement in the social economy while others believe that it is, at best, an illusion or, at worst, a hoax. As is the case among many progressive elements in Québec, some think that the social economy should not substitute what is available from the private sector nor what is produced by the public sector. Others take this vision one step further, arguing that organizations belonging to the social economy should not have any commercial transactions at all—these are seen as the exclusive domain of the private sector—while simultaneously remaining independent from government programmes. Still others hold that the place of the social economy is between the private and public sectors, that it should not overlap either one, that its role is to complement them or to temporarily increase the supply of their production where necessary, until such time as it becomes economically feasible for either the private or public sector to take over.

Different versions of this last view are quite prevalent among women's groups—and, for that matter, among many anti-poverty action committees and community organizations in general. The reasoning behind it stems from the idea that the development of a completely new economy—one based on solidarity and whose role is to strengthen civil society, not the other way around—must be achieved if oppression and exploitation are to be countered.[29] While the social economy seems to be a step in this direction and, as such, part of a broader social change movement, practitioners in these groups believe that if it is nothing more than a more collective way of doing business, then its social goals will eventually be subordinated to what become, with time, economic imperatives.[30] In the same vein, if the social economy is just another form of State service delivery, then its only advantage would seem to be cheap labour or less expensive management and infrastructures or both, practices that these organizations will not condone because of the resulting losses of public sector jobs and because they insist on equitable wages and benefits for workers of all types.

The women's movement realistically sees personal services as the main avenue for short term development of the social economy. Women, more than men, will most likely be on the front lines of such activities and hence, do most of the routine tasks and bear the brunt of the problems, since personal care of some kind has always been relegated to women in the home and has been their traditional source of employment for as long as anyone can remember. Moreover, the type of jobs created in social economy enterprises gives rise to justified fears about cheap labour, since salaries and benefits are usually quite low in the field of personal services. All women's groups are adamant that the jobs created in the social economy have to be stable, decently paid, and provide good working conditions. In the eyes of the women's movement, ensuring that social economy enterprises do not become underpaid and precarious job ghettos for women is therefore a serious challenge to promoters and social entrepreneurs as well as to providers of technical assistance and financing.

The Communitarian Movement

The advent of the social economy was looked at with trepidation by the communitarian movement. Generally speaking, it feared being forced into an entrepreneurial mode which, it believed, would have the effect of fundamentally changing its prime vocation which is to provide services and not to engage in commercial activities. In order to protect itself, the communitarian movement successfully lobbied its major funder, the secretariat for non-governmental community action (*Secrétariat à l'action communautaire autonome*), to ensure that not-for-profit advocacy and community service agencies would not be considered as being part of the social economy and that funding already attributed to them—$195 million in 1995-1996, excluding childcare centres[31]—would not be reallocated to the social economy.

There seems to be an anomaly here, since the communitarian movement in Québec is made up of two main types of organizations: community service organizations and advocacy groups. Many of the community service organizations have been used as examples of non-profit organizations in the social economy! Childcare centres, home care service providers, and thrift shops have all been used to illustrate how market forces and public financing can be combined to ensure community controlled service delivery in poor communities. On the other hand, most advocacy and many popular education groups receive grants for core funding or for programmes that are not tied to specific service provision or outcomes. These organizations will not be directly involved in the development of a social economy, and indeed, lead the movement not to be assimilated into it. However, many have become stakeholders where social economy initiatives overlap into their realm. For example, future training businesses in the field of residential building maintenance will probably not be able to succeed without working relationships with tenants' rights groups. Moreover, some of the communitarian movement's federations and umbrella groups will likely participate in coordinating bodies and some may even provide some technical assistance to social entrepreneurs, especially on the social aspects of their ventures.

The idea that social economy initiatives must have a business component is generally shared by those who believe that the social economy must contribute to economic development as does any other economic sector. While networking and mutual support (that characterize most communitarian organizations and women's groups) are fundamental to local development, their specific contribution to the economy is quite difficult to establish. Local development practitioners, supporters from the private sector, and policy-makers see the business side of social economy enterprises as fostering entrepreneurial capacity, their profits as producing taxable income, and their associative structure as encouraging local control and member participation. Many communitarian activists believe that this perspective is inherently dangerous, since market forces play on inequalities, favouring the most resourceful at the expense of those who are less so, in other words, those who are their constituencies. It follows that they believe that there should be some kind of collective control over the business side of the social economy just as there should be over any economic entity providing personal care services. There is some merit to this view since the social economy is not an informal nor an unregulated economy. Even though it challenges the assumption that the market is the most efficient means of regulating economic activity, it does not in any way disavow the laws of supply and demand. Viable businesses require profitable markets. In practice, needs that spur the social economy are most often those that have been ignored or abandoned by the private sector. Indeed, with the decline of both Keynesian and Welfare State models, the social economy will be called upon to play an increasingly important role in labour-intensive service provision because of its capacity to enlist both users and professionals in such activities. Influential European studies[32] tend to confirm this trend.

This leads practitioners stemming from the communitarian movement to believe that most new social economy initiatives will be concentrated in fields that are not profitable for the private sector or too costly for the public one. In turn, because the enrollment of local volunteer efforts will never be adequate enough to compensate for the differential between revenues and labour costs or stable enough to ensure on-going quality and quantity of services, it seems inevitable that new social enterprises will have to rely on low salaries and few fringe benefits to make ends meet since labour costs will be their major expense. Many thus fear that only exploiting people receiving welfare or employment insurance benefits or substituting public sector jobs with cheap labour can ensure the continued existence of social economy enterprises. They also suspect that training and organizational start-up costs will be financed through job skills development programmes, or worse, workfare schemes,[33] since this is the way that most personal care co-operatives and non-profits have gotten off the ground until now in Québec. Activists of every kind, including members of the Task Force, are opposed to this, since the social economy is supposed to alleviate poverty, not contribute to building a bastion of working poor. In other words, to many, social economy enterprises are doomed or dangerous unless public programmes are available to offset losses and unless worker participation is voluntary (which is generally not the case with workfare programmes), even when workers are drawn from the ranks of the unemployed.[34]

The Co-operative Movement

Many, although not all, co-operative development professionals see the social economy in terms of legal structure and consider it to be made up of organizations that have legal status as co-operatives or that formally embody principles[35] that regulate co-operatives in their governance and operational rules and structures. People using this definition see all types of co-operatives and mutuals as being inherently part of the social economy, as long as they are legally structured. They believe that social goals are attained through the structural components themselves, since democratic decision-making levels the relationship between rich and poor members, because local participation in economic development is ensured through boards of directors made up of members of the community served by the organization, because dividends are based on services received by members and not on personal wealth, and because the non-transferability of accumulated reserves guarantees local control over assets. Indeed, they have a point, especially in Québec, where progress on the economic front has gone hand in hand, since the turn of the century, with the growth of the co-operative movement. Today, the Desjardins network of credit unions (Québec's largest bank), insurance mutuals and investment firms is among the top ten suppliers of financial services in Canada, the *Coopérative fédérée* provides employment to close to 6,000 people,[36] over 20,000 Québec families live in housing co-operatives, and Québec has the largest concentration of worker co-operatives in North America.

These success stories help justify the idea that the co-operative model is advantageous in itself. Even so, the legal model is rarely proposed to budding entrepreneurs, often because a co-operative requires twelve founding members in Québec, except for worker co-operatives that need only three. This membership constraint impedes all potential one and two person start-ups from adopting the model. Moreover, the co-operative capital structure is not conducive to obtaining private venture funds and fiscal policies are much less generous to new co-operatives than to other types of businesses. Economic development practitioners—including credit managers in *caisses populaires*—therefore often balk at recommending the model except in cases where an immediate, direct advantage, such as access to a specific financing programme, can be identified. As the Task Force noted in its report, this is why specific programmes to support social economy enterprises are essential.

The advent of renewed interest for the social economy has been quite beneficial to the co-operative movement in general, providing it with much more visibility, highlighting its numerous achievements, and sparking increased fervour among its leaders.

To illustrate this last point, it could be argued that, had the women's movement not succeeded in getting the social economy on the public agenda, the Québec Council on Co-operation, *Conseil de la coopération du Québec* (CCQ), would have continued to play the rather discreet lobbying and representative role that was its hallmark before 1995. The CCQ is an umbrella group that brings together Québec's co-operative confederations and federations. As such, it is identified with the "old guard" of the co-operative movement. However, because of its strategic position, it was invited to participate in the Task Force on the Social Economy, and has sat on its steering committee and its subsequent board of directors ever since. Heeding the call for some new mechanism that could bridge co-operative and local development principles and actions, the CCQ developed a new structure, *coopérative de solidarité*, based on an Italian model. The uniqueness of the solidarity co-operative is not so much the type of services rendered, but rather its governance structure. In this type of co-operative, two groups of members must be present: users of the services provided and the co-operative's workers. A third membership group is also possible, one that brings together other individuals or organizations who have a vested social or economic interest in the co-operative's success. This last group can be made up of community members who are neither workers nor users, as well as suppliers, representatives of key players, etc. Each group has the right to elect at least one member of the board of directors, but the third group cannot occupy more than a third of the total number of seats on the board. This is a very significant undertaking by the CCQ, since this type of co-operative is well suited for all kinds of personal services. The CCQ was also recently instrumental in setting up a task force on co-operation. Modeling itself on the Task Force on the Social Economy, the *Chantier coopératif* brings together co-operatives from different sectors and other partners, including the Department of Industry and Commerce, to explore how the co-operative model can contribute even more to Québec's social and economic revitalization.

The Labour Movement

The labour movement's attitude towards the social economy is one of simultaneous resistance and support. Most existing social economy best practices in Québec are in the personal services field.[37] Since this focus on personal services comes at a time of cutbacks in a great number of public programmes, it bolsters the idea that the social economy could be an easy vehicle for the privatization[38] of some public services. Aside from concerns about the elimination of public sector jobs, there are also fears that services could wind up being provided only to people whose problems require less time, energy, and other resources, or, alternatively, who have greater financial means available, or both, since these types of clients are likely to cost less to service and can therefore more easily ensure economic viability. Since job displacement can also occur when paid jobs are replaced by volunteer ones, this shift *en douceur* towards the social economy is seen as an additional threat by trade unions and some professional associations. Their apprehension is that the resulting public sector job losses will actually increase unemployment and, further down the road, poverty and exclusion, since not all of them will be picked up by social economy enterprises and since many of the ones that will be, will be paid less and will have poor working conditions. There are therefore calls, within the ranks of the labour movement, to clearly define where and how the social economy fits in as a complement to the existing public service infrastructure.[39]

Moreover, many of the larger co-operatives have engaged in practices, such as lock-outs, union-bashing, and massive layoffs, that have likely increased problems that the social economy is supposed to redress. In spite of this, some trade unions in Québec, the Confederation of National Trade Unions (CNTU) in particular, have a long history of working closely with social economy enterprises.[40] Well before the 1996 Conference, the CNTU even issued what amounted to a plea to its members to support new initiatives in this field.[41] Moreover, building on the success of the Québec Federation of Labour's Solidarity Fund, the CNTU set up a new one, FondAction. The Solidarity Fund has been active in saving jobs in the private sector and in supporting local development and its outlook is to continue to do so.[42] FondAction will concentrate primarily on smaller initiatives, especially those in the social economy in tandem with the CNTU's co-operative development consulting arm.

Conclusion

The social economy is not a new phenomenon, with the expression dating back to the 1830's, and the organizations making it up having been around for at least as long a period of time.[43] Its history in Québec is a little more recent, since the phrase was in use here in the late 19th century, and the province's first co-operatives go back over one hundred years as well.[44] Other expressions are also frequently used to identify the same idea and, in English language publications, the social economy is referred to as the "third sector," the "non-profit" sector, the "voluntary sector," and, to lesser extent, as the "community sector."[45] In general, however, no matter what words are used to describe it, the social economy is seen as occupying the space between the private (first) sector and the public (second) one, at times overlapping one or both of these as well.

The situation in Québec is similar to that found in many industrialized countries facing financial problems and social unrest stemming from ever-increasing unemployment and poverty. The complexity of these social problems, the variety of perspectives on the social economy, and the large number of stakeholders and constituencies all contribute to making this a very difficult situation to understand. It is no wonder, therefore, that practitioners are desperate for ways to solve their confusion and not surprising, therefore, that over 500 people attended a one-day conference last spring on the social economy and health and social services,[46] and that at least 20% of this year's sessions at the Institute in Management and Community Development's Summer Programme dealt with issues directly related to using economic tools and business development to meet social goals.[47] There is a very strong demand for help in understanding the role of the social economy in addressing contemporary social and economic problems, a fact that should be of interest to both educators and policy-makers alike. It follows that there is therefore a need for much more research into the social economy and, indeed, into all fields that attempt to erase the boundaries between economic and social issues including community economic development and sustainable development.

Until recently, the social economy was often seen as a marginal notion, one that did not belong in the "major leagues" of economic development.[48] In truth, this is still the case although its credibility is progressing and recognition of its merits is growing. However, for practitioners, recognition, especially State recognition, is worrisome. Practitioners know that a social economy enterprise will often accept lower profits than a private sector one, since it can usually obtain public funds of some kind and count on a minimum of volunteer resources, enabling it to hire or retain staff where a capitalist business cannot. Its initiatives can also be very useful when it comes to reducing unemployment and poverty, providing job opportunities for unemployed individuals with few or no job skills. However, if social economy enterprises are limited to the field of personal services (as practitioners believe that many would like it to be), State recognition is no more than an opportunistic attempt to cut the costs of such services with home care co-operatives, early childcare centres and similar community-based enterprises.

Since the social economy's track record is quite positive in Québec when it comes to economic development in general and job creation in particular, the Task Force on the Social Economy's insistence on exploring a variety of other fields, such as culture, housing, new technologies, natural resources, and environmental protection,[49] seems quite warranted. On the other hand, practitioners believe that if the government's recognition of social economy initiatives is simply contractual, based only on the delivery of goods and services as is often the case with private entrepreneurs, then they fear that the relationship between the State and the social movements will likely degenerate into a simple commercial subcontract instead of being a demonstration of joint solidarity towards communities requiring services and the unemployed seeking jobs. All activists agree that the social economy must be developed in such a way as to support and strengthen democracy and citizenship.

Practitioners also worry about the tendency that government departments have to want to rapidly replicate best practice models. They are opposed to a cookie-cutter approach since, in their eyes, duplication of models—just like restricting fields of activity, targeting specific clienteles, or requiring that only certain types of people be hired—may drain social economy businesses of their versatility and originality. Until quite recently, the experience of Québec's training businesses was rife with the lack of flexibility on the part of State authorities and the resulting lack of local autonomy.[50] Practitioners are keeping a close watch on the most recent funding programme to see if more leeway will be allowed. This is especially important for supporters of the social economy, since the Québec Task Force played a key role during negotiations. There are indeed reasons to be wary, since examples of State interference on sensitive issues are common. For example, bureaucrats have recently had an enormous role in setting the agenda for co-operative development—shareholder co-operatives holding 49% or less of an employer's voting shares now *the* priority—and reform—non-members can now hold up to 25% of a co-operative's voting rights.[51] These were clearly not the ideas of the Québec worker co-operative federation. Similar past experiences—from the institutionalization of community-based initiatives to the privatization of local not-for-profit services—give good cause for all kinds of concerns. Practitioners are thus justified in being apprehensive about the future of the social economy if the government seems too keen on it.

As for private sector recognition, it isn't clear what it really means. Some see pledges by chartered banks to the Social Economy Development Fund as a relatively inexpensive face-saving device in an era of billion-dollar profits and million-dollar salaries while poverty is on the rise. Others see private sector interest as a way to co-opt social movements into the capitalist system even more than before. What is known is that partnerships are growing in Québec between the private sector, labour unions, community-based organizations, and the women's movement, and that private sector recognition of the social economy appeared, for the first time, at the Summit. Optimists, on all sides, believe that such collective efforts between previous antagonists are part of a positive trend that could lead to social change. Only time will tell if any of these opinions is valid.

The fundamental issue is that the social economy must not become a strategy for managing poverty and social exclusion. Instead, it has to be a tool to eliminate them. It seems to have a great deal of potential on this front, but it is not a panacea. Indeed, if it is to work it must be part of a broad, multi-faceted attack on unemployment and poverty[52] that should include a variety of measures such as reduction in and reallocation of paid working hours, equitable sharing of productivity gains between workers and owners, commitment to the idea and the practice of good corporate citizenship, local development strategies that mobilize community resources and encourage community participation and empowerment, and support for community economic development.[53] In other words, the social economy must be much more than the adopting up of formal legal structures and social change must be its fundamental goal.

This can only work if the social economy is on an equal footing with the private and public "economies" and becomes an active part of what some refer to as a "plural economy"[54] that gives new value to reciprocal non-commercial and non-monetary transactions by recognizing them as economic activities in their own right. Some observers see the social economy as having two generations, an older one which operated in strongly competitive sectors, such as financial services, agriculture and forestry, and where markets imposed their will on profitability, and a newer one, wherein groups of people tend to play a more deciding role in enterprise viability. The "new social economy" perspective sees itself as calling upon both market forces and public redistribution mechanisms, notably when it operates in the local service sector. The resulting enterprise, and thus the new social economy, is characterized by a hybrid economic mix of commercial activities (self-financing through sales), non-commercial but monetary activities (public funding, donations from churches, foundations, and other institutions), and non-monetary activities (voluntary work and donations by members and other supporters). Even though this view was developed primarily in France where it is referred to as an economy based on solidarity,[55] it has a great number of fans in Québec who can be divided into two groups: a) academics striving to build a theory of the social economy and who are enthused by the economic model that builds on Polanyian theory;[56] b) practitioners and organizations who hope to use this definition to help advance the cause of providing personal services using nonprofit or co-operative organizations supported, in whole or in part, by public funds. These people recognize that market forces cannot alone transform latent demand stemming from unmet personal needs and other local services into profitable niches. But they also see government funding of, as is often stated, the social side of these initiatives as only another, albeit essential, part of the solution. The major innovation in thinking is the idea that other local resources, such as volunteer efforts and donations in kind, must be mobilized by social economy enterprises if they are to succeed. In this sense, it is easy to understand why social economy organizations are sometimes referred to as "public-private projects" in Japan or as "community partnerships" in Europe.[57]

The "new social economy" perspective is based upon the premise that the more recent social economy ventures emerge from a reciprocal impulse that brings together potential users (eventual clients) and professionals (eventual staff) who jointly shape the supply and demand of services. This process, wherein ongoing trust and mutual support is essential, transforms individual needs into collective ones through discussion and exchange. Meetings around a kitchen table and study groups become "incubators" for the ensuing enterprises. This somewhat idyllic picture, in fact, describes the way that many consumer co-operatives and early community-based service agencies were developed in Québec and elsewhere in the world. While some new social economy initiatives will certainly follow this same path, the trend seems to be more market-focused since the advent of the Task Force, with the impetus stemming from individuals who will be neither likely users nor potential staff. This will, inevitably, result in less participation of those needing jobs and of those needing services, and it will unfortunately produce little direct empowerment of these constituencies. It is therefore difficult to see such new initiatives as being a strong segment of a movement for social change, although the practitioners who support and initiate them probably are, unless a clear focus on individual and community empowerment supersedes the goals of job creation and service provision, however laudable these last goals may be.

Indeed, in order for the Third Sector to become Rifkin's agent for social and political reform, it must speak to the issue of community control. In an era of global markets, it is possible to justify the social economy from a purely economic perspective: local markets for services already exist, these markets are relatively impervious to the fluctuations of the global economy, exploiting them requires little start-up capital and can make use of local labour. But there are more than economic issues at stake, since local communities must possess the capacity to develop such markets and to identify and take advantage of whatever comparative advantages that they may have. Such capacity is directly related to both local control over resources and community well-being, issues that are basic to community economic development. This is why developing the social economy should not be disassociated from CED efforts and why much more public and private support of experimentation, innovation, and research into both the social economy and community economic development is needed.

To a great extent, the social economy is much more about citizenship than about economics. The main issue has a lot to do with the way that control is exercised, since it must encourage the participation of all of the community's members, especially those who are usually left out, in order to harness all possible resources, to see that the resulting development will benefit all people in society, and to ensure that all social concerns are part of the agenda for change. This, I believe, is the type of economic development that the women's movement in Québec is striving for, one that would be more in line with feminist values such as power sharing, consensus decision-making, and integrated individual and collective concerns. This means that concepts such as productivity and compensation have to be looked at through new lenses and that social and economic organizations have to make room for people simply because they are people, not because they are the best and the brightest, not because they are the most technically competent. The development of the social economy has the potential to embrace some of these values and to experiment their practice in an economic context. But this new economic development goes beyond what a social economy can offer and thus requires the emergence of—or the return to—a reciprocal economy. The social economy can, however, contribute to the advent of such an economy, even if only in a limited fashion, since neither the women's movement nor other social change movements have the upper hand in its development. Indeed, the women's and communitarian movements in fact possess exactly what is needed to ensure that the social economy takes on this challenge: a vision of the type of an economy that is required, and a skills and knowledge base to build on. Their support of the social economy is therefore vital to make it part of the process of building a new society based on mutuality and solidarity.

NOTES

The Employability and Social Partnerships Division of Human Resources Development Canada is pleased to have provided financial support for this project. The views expressed in this publication do not necessarily reflect those of HRDC.

1. Jeremy Rifkin, *The End of Work*. New York: G. P. Putnam's Sons, 1995, p. 249.

2. The term "mouvement populaire et communautaire" refers to an amalgamation of somewhat diverse democratically-controlled organizations in Québec, many of which have been called community groups, alternative service organizations, community-based organizations, communitarian and popular organizations, and popular groups. Of all of these, the word "communitarian," defined as "of or relating to social organization in small cooperative partially collectivist communities" (Webster's Ninth New Collegiate Dictionary, 1985, p. 267) seems most appropriate to designate them. More specifically, they include consumer, housing, and worker co-operatives, not-for-profit service organizations and private community-based social service agencies, advocacy groups, other community-based organizations including environmental groups and Third World solidarity groups, and their related federations, umbrella groups, and coalitions.

3. Gouvernement du Québec, *Un Québec de responsabilité et de solidarité: oser choisir ensemble*, document de réflexion préparatoire à la Conférence sur le devenir social et économique du Québec, March, 1996, p. 43.

4. Its report was handed down two months after the Conference. See: Comité d'orientation et de concertation sur l'économie sociale, *Entre l'espoir et le doute*. Québec: Ministère de la Condition féminine, 1996, 112 pages.

5. Benoît Lévesque and William A. Ninacs, "The Social Economy in Canada: The Quebec Model," in *Local Strategies for Employment and the Social Economy*. Proceedings of the Conference. Montréal: Les publications de l'IFDÉC, 1997, pp. 123-136.

6. Groupe de travail sur l'économie sociale, *Osons la solidarité, rapport au Sommet sur l'économie et l'emploi*. Montréal: Gouvernement du Québec, 1996, 64 pages. For all intents and purposes, the Task Force adopted the definition used by the Walloon Council for the Social Economy. The fifth rule, however, is not found in the Walloon framework and was added by the Task Force intent on developing a *québécois* model. See: Jacques Defourny, "L'émergence du secteur d'économie sociale en Wallonie," *Coopératives et développement*, Vol. 23, No 1, 1991, pp.151-175.

7. Mike Campbell, "The Social Economy and Local Strategies for Employment," in *Local Strategies for Employment and the Social Economy*. 1997, op. cit., pp. 115-116: "We shall proceed as if the most generic approach is taken to the term social economy wherein what is envisaged is an approach to local development which is community based, or at least community oriented—what we may call community economic development."

8. Louis Favreau and Benoît Lévesque, *Développement économique communautaire: économie sociale et intervention*. Sainte-Foy, Québec: Presses de l'Université du Québec, 1996, pp. xxii-xxiii. This idea is also prevalent elsewhere in Canada—see: Jack Quarter, *Canada's Social Economy: Co-operatives, Non-profits, and Other Community Enterprises*. Toronto: James Lorimer & Company, Publishers, 1992, pp. 89-111.

9. For example: André Joyal, "Peut-on se priver de l'économie sociale?," *Le Devoir*, April 15, 1996; Jean-Marc Fontan and Eric Shragge, "L'économie sociale: une économie pour les pauvres?," *La Presse*, April 30, 1996; Henri Lamoureux, "De l'économie sociale à

l'économisme social," *Le Devoir*, May 23, 1996; Benoît Lévesque and Yves Vaillancourt, "Une économie plurielle," *Le Devoir*, May 16, 1996; Jean Panet-Raymond, Nicole Galarneau, Eric Shragge and Lucie Bernier, "L'économie sociale a ses limites," *La Presse*, May 17, 1996.

10. For example: Louis Favreau and Carol Saucier, "Économie sociale et développement économique communautaire: de nouvelles réponses à la crise de l'emploi?," *Économie et Solidarités*, Vol. 28, No 1, 1996, pp. 5-17; Christiane Gagnon, "Développement local viable: approches, stratégies et défis pour les communautés," *Coopératives et développement*, Vol. 26, No 2, 1996, pp. 61-82; Gabriel Gagnon, "Faire payer les pauvres," *Possibles*, Vol. 20, No 3, 1996, pp. 124-128; Pierre Jean, "L'économie sociale: autre chose qu'un gadget pour occuper les victimes de la restructuration," *Nouvelles pratiques sociales*, Vol. 9, No 1, 1996, pp. 15-32.

11. See: Quarter, 1992, *op. cit.* Other works on the same theme include: Brett Fairbairn, June Bold, Murray Fulton, Lou Hammond Ketilson, and Daniel Ish, *Co-operatives and Community Development: Economics in Social Perspective*. Saskatoon: Centre for the Study of Co-operatives, University of Saskatoon, 1991; George Melnyk, *The Search For Community: From Utopia to a Co-operative Society*. Montréal: Black Rose Books, 1989; David P. Ross and Peter J. Usher, *From the Roots Up: Economic Development as if Community Mattered*. Toronto: James Lorimer & Company, 1986.

12. Unfortunately, few, if any, are available in English, with the exception of the summary of a seminal overview of the Québec situation five years ago. See: Benoît Lévesque and Marie-Claire Malo, "The 'Social Economy' in Québec: A Misunderstood Concept, a Significant Economic Fact," in Jacques Defourny and José Luis Monzón Campos, (Editors), *Économie Sociale: entre économie capitaliste et économie publique/The Third Sector: Cooperative, Mutual and Nonprofit Organizations*. Brussels: CIRIEC and De Boeck-Wesmael, Inc., 1992, pp. 386-389. On occasion, *Économie et Solidarités*, like its predecessor, *Coopératives et développement*, the official publication of CIRIEC Canada (Centre interuniversitaire de recherche, d'information et d'enseignement sur les coopératives), an international research network on co-operatives and the social economy, will contain an article in English.

Among studies written in French, the following are noteworthy: Comité international de la Marche des femmes contre la pauvreté, *Les actes du séminaire international sur l'économie sociale tenu les 6 et 7 juin 1995*, Montréal: Relais-femmes, 1995, 73 pages; Conseil québécois de développement social, *L'économie sociale: dérision ou panacée*. Montréal: Conseil québécois de développement social, 1997, 33 pages; Chantal Martel, *L'économie sociale et les femmes: garder l'oeil ouvert*. Québec: Conseil du statut de la femme, 1996, 37 pages.

13. Benoît Lévesque, Marguerite Mendell and Solange Van Kemenade, *Les fonds régionaux et locaux de développement au Québec: des institutions financières relevant principalement de l'économie sociale*. Montréal: Collectif de recherche sur les innovations sociales dans les entreprises et les syndicats, Université du Québec à Montréal, 1996, 34 pages.

14. Research suggests that new "social entrepreneurs" who innovate in the field of economic development or who redirect existing projects are often former community leaders. See: William A. Ninacs and Louis Favreau, "CED in Québec: New Features in the Early 1990s," *Making Waves*, Vol. 4, No 4, 1993, pp. 8-11; Louis Favreau and William A. Ninacs, "The Innovative Profile of Community Economic Development in Quebec," in Burt Galaway and Joe Hudson, (Editors), *Community Economic Development: Perspectives on Research and Policy*. Toronto: Thompson Educational Publishing, 1994, pp. 153-165.

14. Quarter, 1992, *op. cit.*, p. 11.

15. *Ibid.*, p. 28.

16. Marcel Arteau, *Co-operative Movements in Quebec*. Workshop presentation, Global Awareness Society International Annual Conference, Montréal, May 23rd, 1997.

17. Unpublished internal working paper of the Fonds de développement de l'économie sociale, p.2.

18. Jacques Bérubé, "Autopsie d'un consternant gâchis," *Le Mouton Noir*, Vol. III, No 1, June, 1997, p. 2.

19. The sum of mutual social debts that individuals and organizations contract in their non-commercial and non-monetary activities. See: James S. Coleman, "Social Capital," in *The Foundations of Social Theory*. Cambridge: Harvard University Press, 1990, pp. 301-321; Robert D. Putnam, *Making Democracy Work: Civic Traditions in Modern Italy*. Princeton (New Jersey): Princeton University Press, 1993, 258 pages.

20. William A. Ninacs, "Synthesizing the Research Results: Where is the Common Ground?," *Making Waves*, Vol. 4, No 4, 1993, pp. 18-20.

21. See: Thérèse Belley, "L'économie sociale, « saveur » régionale," *Relations*, No 635, November, 1997, pp. 272-274; Claire Gagnon, Johanne Lauzon and Isabelle Rivet, "Économie sociale: une tour de Babel?," *La Gazette des femmes*, No.19, N$ 4, November-December, 1997, pp. 13-14.

22. Currently, the following have commitments towards the social economy: Department of State for Employment and Solidarity, the Secretariat for Regional Development, Department of Health and Social Services, Department of Education, Department of Agriculture, Department of the Environment, Department of Justice.

23. Josée Belleau and Martine D'Amours, *Tous les moyens du bord. Les centres de femmes: des chantiers économiques*. Montréal: L'R des centres de femmes du Québec, 1993, 47 pages.

24. Josée Belleau and Martine D'Amours, *Tous les moyens du bord. Les centres de femmes: des chantiers économiques*. Montréal: L'R des centres de femmes du Québec, 1993, 47 pages.

25. Francine Pelletier, *Les centres de femmes: des sentiers et des chantiers économiques*. Montréal: L'R des centres de femmes du Québec, 1995, 87 pages.

26. Lorraine Guay, "La Marche des femmes *Du pain et des roses* contre la pauvreté" in *Du néolibéralisme à l'économie sociale: le combat des femmes*. Actes du deuxième séminaire international sur l'économie solidaire. Montréal: Relais-femmes, 1997, pp. 41-50.

27. Françoise David, *Le mouvement des femmes et l'économie sociale: où en sommes-nous?*. Montréal: Fédération des femmes du Québec, October 14, 1997, 6 pages.

28. An idea espoused by Lévesque and Malo (1992, *op. cit.*, 409-410) not shared by Quarter (1992, *op. cit.*, 63-86).

29. This perspective is also found among a number of women authors engaged in redefining economic development. See: Barbara Brandt, *Whole Life Economics: Revaluing Daily Life*. Philadelphia, PA, and Gabriola Island, BC: New Society Publishers, 1995, 243 pages; Hazel Henderson, *Paradigms in Progress: Life Beyond Economics*. San Francisco: Berrett-Koehler Publishers, 1995, 293 pages; Marcia Nozick, *No Place Like Home: Building Sustainable Communities*. Ottawa: Canadian Council on Social Development, 1992, 237 pages.

30. An opinion that research seems to confirm. See: André Joyal, "Les entreprises alternatives au Québec," in Benoît Lévesque, André Joyal, and Omer Chouinard, (Editors), *L'autre économie: une économie alternative?*. Sillery, Québec: Presses de l'Université du Québec, 1989, pp. 165-184, and "Les entreprises alternatives québécoises: à l'image de leurs homologues européennes," *Coopératives et développement*, Vol.20, No 2, 1988-1989, pp. 69-88; Jean-Louis Laville, "Les coopératives de travail en Europe. Éléments pour un bilan 1970-1990," *Coopératives et développement*, Vol. 25, No 1, 1993, 5-29.

31. Jean-Pierre Bélanger, *L'économie sociale: quelques dimensions (texte préliminaire)*. Internal report. Québec: Ministère de la Santé et des services sociaux du Québec, 1996, 99 pages, pp. 36-37.

32. The European Commission identifies 17 "job areas" and estimates that these could provide an additional 140,000 jobs in its member countries. These are: home services, childcare, assisting youth with social integration problems, housing improvements, security, local public transport, local shops, tourism, cultural heritage, local cultural development, waste management, protection and maintenance of green areas, and pollution control. See: Commission européenne, *Les initiatives locales de développement et d'emploi: enquête dans l'Union européenne*. Luxembourg: Office des publications officielles des Communautés européennes, 1995, 122 pages (in English: *A European Strategy for Encouraging Local Development and Employment Initiatives*. COM 273/95).

33. See: Nicole Dallaire, *Le Workfare: pour quoi faire?*. Montréal: Conseil québécois de développement social, 32 pages; Eric Shragge and Marc-André Deniger, "Workfare in Quebec," in Eric Shragge, (Editor), *Workfare: Ideology for a New Under-Class*. Toronto: Garamond Press, pp. 59-83.

34. See: "Regeneration through Work: creating jobs in the social economy," *Local Work*, No 72, December 1996/January 1997, Manchester, England: Centre for Local Economic Strategies, pp. 1-7.

35. The principles regulating co-operatives are based on the axiom of "people before capital": 1) democratic control based upon the principle of one member/one vote; 2) mandatory retaining, by the organization, of a portion or all surplus earnings; 3) distribution of non-retained surplus earnings based on either patronage or membership and never on personal capital; 4) no distribution among members of accumulated reserves upon dissolution.

36. Ranked in *Canadian Business*, Vol. 70, No 7, June 1997, pp. 150-151 and pp. 154-155.

37. Martine D'Amours, *Présence de l'économie sociale au Québec: une illustration dans six secteurs et sept régions*. Montréal: Chantier de l'économie sociale, 1996, 46 pages.

38. The distinction between privatization and communitarization has not yet filtered out of the halls of academia and the concept of community care, that is quite common in English literature on social issues, is relatively unknown in Québec. For a notable exception see: Yves Vaillancourt, "Sortir de l'alternative entre privatisation et étatisation dans la santé et les services sociaux," in Bernard Eme, Louis Favreau, Jean-Louis Laville and Yves Vaillancourt, (Editors), *Société civile, État et économie plurielle*. Paris, Montréal, and Hull: CRIDA-CNRS, CRISES-UQAM, and UQAH, 1996, pp. 147-224.

39. René Lachapelle, "Arrimer syndicats et entreprises communautaires," and Louis Roy, "Organismes communautaires, syndicats et réseau de la santé et des services sociaux: jusqu'où vont les alliances?," in Denis Plamondon, Sylvie Dubord, Danielle Maltais, Sylvie Brassard, Huguette Boivin and Mario Couture, (Editors), *Au-delà de la tourmente: de nouvelles alliances à bâtir*. Chicoutimi, Québec: Groupe de recherche et d'intervention régionales (GRIR), Université du Québec à Chicoutimi, pp. 205-218 and 81-90.

40. Benoît Lévesque, "De promoteur à entrepreneur," *Le Devoir*, Saturday/Sunday, March 22/23, 1997, p. A-11.

41. François Aubry and Jean Charest, *Développer l'économie solidaire—Éléments d'orientation*. Montréal: Confédération des syndicats nationaux, 1995, 40 pages.

42. Clément Godbout, "The example of local investment societies for employment development as a mobilising tool for local capital by the trade union movement," in *Local Strategies for Employment and the Social Economy*, 1997, op. cit., pp. 73-76.

43. Jacques Defourny, "The Origins, Forms and Roles of a Third Major Sector," in Defourny and Monzón Campos, 1992, *op. cit.*, pp. 29-32.

44. Jean-Paul Gravel, *Les coopératives au Canada: le cas du Québec*. Sherbrooke, Québec: Institut de recherche et d'enseignement pour les coopératives de l'Université de Sherbrooke (IRECUS), 1992, 21 pages, pp. 5-6; Lévesque and Malo, 1992, *op. cit.*

45. Campbell, *op. cit.*, p. 1; Quarter, 1992, *op.cit.*, p. x.

46. *Nouvelles pratiques sociales*, an academic journal devoted to social work, heath and welfare services delivery, and related fields, holds an annual conference on controversial issues. The 1997 event was held in March in Montréal, and the topic was "L'économie sociale et les services sociaux et de santé: enjeux et perspectives." Information can be obtained from Yves Vaillancourt, the journal's director, at the Département de travail social, Université du Québec à Montréal, C.P. 8888, succ. Centre-ville, Montréal, Québec, H3C 3P8; phone (514) 987-3000, extension 4721; fax (514) 987-4494.

47. Every June, Concordia University's Institute in Management and Community Development (Continuing Education) provides a few days of training, in both English and French, aimed at community development and community economic development practitioners. Over 650 participants attended in 1997, with about a quarter coming from other provinces. Information can be obtained from Lance Evoy, Coordinator, Institute in Management and Community Development, Concordia University, Loyola Campus, 7141, rue Sherbrooke Ouest, CC 326, Montréal, Québec, H4B 1R5; phone (514) 848-3956; fax (514) 848-4598.

48. Nancy Neamtan, who today chairs the Québec Task Force on the Social Economy, was quoted in precisely these terms a few years ago: "la notion d'économie sociale, c'est une notion marginale, par rapport à ce qu'on appelle les ligues majeures," in Benoît Lévesque and Daniel Côté, "L'état du mouvement coopératif au Québec," *Coopératives et développement*, Vol. 22, No 2, 1990-1991, p. 154.

49. Groupe de travail sur l'économie sociale, 1996, *op. cit.*

50. Christian Valadou, *Les entreprises d'insertion au Québec: état des lieux*. Montréal: Collectif des entreprises d'insertion du Québec, 1995, 83 pages.

51. Arteau, 1997, *op. cit.*

52. A position taken by some worker co-operative activists: Perusse, Madeleine, *Prendre notre place: la position du RQCCT*. Montréal: Regroupement québécois des coopérateurs et coopératrices du travail, 1997, 7 pages.

53. Danielle Lapointe and Bernard Vachon, "Création de services d'aide à domicile," *Économie locale et territoires*, Vol. 1, No 3, April 1997, p. 3.

54. Guy Roustang, Jean-Louis Laville, Bernard Eme, Daniel Mothé and Bernard Perret, *Vers un nouveau contrat social*. Paris: Desclée de Brouwer, 1996, 187 pages.

55. Jean-Louis Laville, *An Approach of Non Profit Organizations and Welfare Mix: the "Proximity Services."* Paris: Centre de recherche et d'information sur la démocratie et l'autonomie, Laboratoire de sociologie du changement des institutions, 1996, 47 pages.

56. Karl Polanyi, *The Great Transformation*. Boston: Beacon Press, 1957, 315 pages.

57. Keitaro Ishigami, *New Approaches to Public-Private Projects in Japan*. Nomura Research Institute, Ltd., 1995; Richard Macfarlane and Jean-Louis Laville, *Developing Community Partnerships in Europe: New Ways of Meeting Social Needs in Europe*. London, England: Directory of Social Change and Calouste Gulbenkian Foundation, 1992, 121 pages.

Chapter 10

The Development of Mutual Benefit Societies in the Loire-Atlantique Region: A Tradition of Solidarity for Ten Generations

Jean-Luc Souchet

The quest for efficiency has combined with the breakdown since the 1970s of a number of beliefs and practices, such that many enterprise leaders have begun to question the process of socio-historical reflection. Can we take the time to look back at the past? Are there not more essential areas in which to invest time and energy? The mutual benefit societies of the Loire-Atlantique answer thus: "Any institution with years of experience behind it is inclined to reexamine its past in order to be able to face the challenges of the future with greater confidence."[1] And there are many challenges facing the mutual benefit system in France, including competition from private for-profit insurance and changes in the rules of trade resulting from the opening up of European borders. Inside the movement, there is often heated debate between those who subscribe to traditional values and those who, in the name of realism, support an evolution of the social economy in a more liberal direction, albeit with a social conscience. It is in this context that the Union of Loire-Atlantique mutual insurance companies asked the Nantes Centre for the History of Work[2] to undertake a study of its history. The democratic spirit and the maturity of those associated with the project have enabled the research to be driven by their desire for truth and authenticity, while eschewing hagiography. This is a history of two centuries of cooperative efforts to provide complete social protection for the greatest number of people possible, two centuries of building towards today's achievements and tomorrow's plans: "it is the tangible traces of a thousand and one events which we set out to capture, not for our own satisfaction, but so that this history might be carried on."[3]

The Plight of the Isolated Individual

Before turning to the history of the mutual benefit societies, we should note that the need for solidarity dates from the very origins of humanity; ancient methods of organization sowed the seeds for its modern foundations. These practices encouraged mutual aid over debates around beliefs or convictions, and they sought to substitute mutually supportive methods of organization and management for charity and dependence. Right from the start, they inscribed democratic rules in the statutes, enabling participants to decide for themselves the nature, limits and conditions of their activities. Very early on, the powers that be, whether religious or political, expressed their uneasiness faced with the potential for coalition generated by such groups. From their midst, in urban areas, in villages, within trades, there "emerged the key actors who liberated the communes from the authoritarianism of feudal power."[4] However, these groups fulfilled "functions which had neither been foreseen nor regulated sufficiently by those associations deemed necessary"[5]; "the established authorities" were therefore compelled to tolerate them and to strike a balance between repression and control. Granting official authorization was one of the means employed to keep an eye on them. The statement[6] it required relieved the authorities of the ongoing and systematic work of investigation. It had the advantage of coupling the "carrot and stick" as "the privileges usually granted attracted both new members and benefactors."[7] Any perceived suspicious developments in ideas or acts of an "approved" association would lead the organization to be banned and deprived of resources—an outcome that might prove fatal.[8]

The Nantes Region and the Lower Loire: A Fertile Breeding Ground?

The Loire-Atlantique region has a singular history in many respects marked by a tradition of solidarity which gave rise to the mutual insurance system.

Lying between Brittany and Aquitaine on France's North-South axis and extending through the prosperous towns on the banks of the Loire towards the Atlantic shores on the East-West axis, the bishopric of Nantes is a very old inhabited area, which archeological exploration dates back to prehistoric times. The estuary which leads this fertilizing and nourishing river to the ocean is a place of transit: there is heard the call of the sea and far away places; the hope of fortune beckons and the spectre of shipwrecks looms. "Neptunus faveat euntes ..." proclaims the coat of arms of the city of Nantes. Marked by the Loire which runs through it and by its Atlantic facade, "it is a zone of transition, a crossroads of influences, of landscapes linked by the charm of the Loire."[9]

Up until the 17th century, local activity was primarily rural: livestock, forests and grain North of the Loire, salt in the Guerande region, fishing on the coast and the river, vineyards in the southern Loire (the first mention of the famous "muscadet"[10] appears in the local archives in 1655). In this rural world, many forms of solidarity took shape in the traditional customs of the community, such as the exchange of services or products, mutual aid at work, assistance to strangers and the poor, visits to the sick, funeral rites and so on.

In the Nantes region, in addition to neighborhood activities undertaken in the parishes, crafts and trades provided the basis of practices designed to protect corporate interests, as well as aid and prevention: "Here professional mutual aid found an ideal foundation. The marked tendency towards trade guilds has probably lent the mutual insurance system a certain sense of discipline."[11]

Following upon the 17th century, which saw the development of trade, owing in part to Dutch savoir-faire, the 18th century was a period of prosperity for Nantes and witnessed the dawn of its industry (textiles and shipbuilding).

The origins of this development lay in the pernicious triangular trade[12] of which the West African peoples were the victim. The "good works" practiced by many local notables made wealthy by this traffic do not erase the shame: such facts of local history remain, to this day, a sensitive issue for the people of Nantes.

After the French Revolution of 1789, the bishopric of Nantes became the Départment de Loire-Inferieure. Modern industrialization took place in the 19th century, with the development of metallurgy, shipbuilding, canning and the foodstuffs industry. This period also saw an unprecedented influx of people to urban areas: rural folk arrived from the neighbouring countryside, but also from Brittany and the Vendée, to do service on the production lines of the new factories.

Thus unfolds a portrait of a three-faceted region:

- In the cities, we find an urban working class population, close to the rural culture of its origins. Mutualism was often part and parcel of the traditional forms of worker solidarity.

- In the area North of the Loire, with its conservative Christian rural population, agricultural modernization was spurred on by the notables and industrialists of Nantes. The latter began to see rural areas as interesting target of capital investment and an important outlet for their various businesses such as: land clearing, livestock selection, introducing the use of fertilizers in agriculture.[13] The entire region became particularly hospitable first to the spread of social Catholicism, and then, at the beginning of the 20th century, to the Christian mutualism of the Rue de Bel-Air.

- The region South of the Loire, where the protests of winegrowers over vine plantations[14] came close to the trade unionism of the late 19th century, was an important area for the development of Désiré Colombe's[15] lay mutual association.

These three elements constituted the breeding ground of the modern mutual societies, as well as of trade union activity, in a type of association that combined resistance, charity and contingency funds.

The Birth of the French Mutualist Movement

Several years prior to the revolution of 1789, the national and local mutualist movement entered the modern world marked by a deep contradiction. At the very moment when it was designated a social movement, the Le Chapelier law[16] banned it, along with all other popular movements. "It is up to the Nation and its representatives to provide assistance to those who need it."[17]

However, the movement continued to develop in spite of the repressive inclinations of first the revolutionary rulers and then the imperial powers.

Up until the 1848 Revolution, and in the Lower Loire perhaps more than anywhere else, it was the bearer of a great social ideal.

The Aborted Dream of a Society Governed by the Mutualist Principle

After 1830,[18] mutual societies represented the only option to bring together the most humble social elements, issuing from the trades or the nascent industrial world. However, the great social ideal that took shape for a time was nipped in the bud: the failure in Nantes during 1848 of a cooperative bakery set up by the universal Fraternal Benefit society was a symbolic turning point. At the behest of the mayor of Nantes, Guepin and his friends wished to make the Society an official benevolent society. The bakery workers, on the other hand, chose to make it a socialist and revolutionary undertaking. City Hall withdrew its support from the workers and the police and judiciary moved in: the Society was shut down.

The Mutualism of the Notables

From then on, however, the reality of popular forces eager for change registered loudly in the socio-political debates of the time.[19] "The politicians who resolved the crisis triggered in February 1848 by the coup d'état of December 2, 1851, fought workers' separatism with the essential weapon of social reform, namely: contingency planning through association."[20] Thus was born with Napoleon III the idea of an obligatory mutual insurance system geared towards providing protection against illness, old age and the vagaries of life. Notables would have to contribute through taxes, while workers paid dues deducted from their salaries. The architect of this reform, Viscount Armand de Melun, was involved in Social Catholicism. His avowed goal was: "to extend the spirit and practice of mutualism throughout the smallest villages."[21] However, he took issue with the President-Prince on the matter of obligation. "Between the dangers of an association at the mercy of the inexperience, caprices and whims of worker members, and having the State assume complete responsibility, there is a path safer than the former and more liberal than the latter."[22] Armand de Melun carried the day on this point and membership in mutual associations remained voluntary. However, his wish to confer upon the Church a key role in the organization of mutual aid was rejected: "If there is something the Church can do to combat socialist ideas, it is through its appeals and by setting an example, rather than by becoming involved in the management of the secular public assistance system."[23]

Out of these debates came the laws of 1850 and 1852 which constituted the first pieces of legislation governing mutualism in France. They distinguish among three types of mutual society:

- The first is described as an "establishment of public utility": it enjoys significant rights and benefits, but is subject to "the authority of a restrictive public administration ruling."[24]
- The societies which did not seek official recognition found themselves in a precarious position. Sometimes incorrectly designated "free" because of the statement required to constitute themselves, they were explicitly subject to the

laws governing associations (article 291 of the penal code and the 1834 law conveniently brought back into effect on the eve of the proclamation of the 1852 law on mutual societies). "This is the status usually adopted by the pre-union worker mutual societies, which aimed both at resistance and contingency planning."[25]

- The authorized society was added in 1852. With more extensive rights and a lighter framework of supervision, "the authorized society operated in the communal context under the authority of the mayor and the priest, with the express purpose of dissociating the practice of mutualism from professional activity."[26]

The Social Catholics of the Lower Loire

In the Lower-Loire region during the 1830s, an influential social Catholic movement directed by the Abbé Fournier, a priest at Saint Nicholas,[27] brought together progressive notables. It laid the foundations of mixed trade unionism uniting workers and notables in activities which combined wage demands and the provision of various social services, such as mutual insurance, loans and training.

In several ways it served as a source of inspiration for the national movement: when Albert de Mun set up the Catholic workers' circles, he was inspired by the work of Abbé Peigne, Abbé Fournier's vicar and creator of the Notre-Dames-de-Toutes-Joies foundation for apprentices.[28] Under the Empire, the influence of these local social Catholics, closely aligned with the reformist ideas of de Melun, facilitated the deployment of a network of societies throughout the region, as did the decision by many older societies to seek authorization. If we also take into account company-based societies,[29] as well as the creation of the new professional mutual societies,[30] it can be said that this period, widely known for the rise of the mutualism of the notables, was also important spur to the growth of mutualism throughout the region. This development took a particular direction, however. "It established the politically 'clean' role of the mutualism by conferring on it the unofficial mission of providing health insurance on a voluntary basis."[31] It also marked a new relationship between the working class and the mutualist movement.

Napoleonic paternalism and the patronage of the notables cut the movement off from the workers who henceforth chose to carry on their struggles inside the trade union movement. In the Lower-Loire region, many workers maintained their membership in mutual societies, which began in the 1850s to extend coverage to the whole family. However, these societies no longer constituted a significant site of self-expression and representation:

A subtle balance in the relation between the mutual societies and the trade unions was established, a unique development in the history of mutualism in this region. It bespeaks a conscious will to respect two independent sovereignties, at once creating the conditions for mutual enrichment.[32]

Republican Mutualism

At the time when Léon Bourgeois and his radical friends were formulating the political doctrine of mutual aid, the mutualist movement became a partner of the Republican State. This partnership opened a new phase in laying the foundations of modern social protection.

In the Lower Loire, various forms of solidarity continued to take shape, building on the momentum of the previous period. And original initiatives also developed, based on new types of affinities and the new needs. Some of these were "pilot projects," such as the Union Générale founded in 1881 by Eugene Pedu as "a reinsurance fund for member associations, the first of its kind to be created in France,"[33] or the Syndicat mutualiste de Loire-Inferieure. The latter was established in keeping with the legal framework for professional trade unions, which was set out on March 21, 1884, due to the persistent dearth of guidelines pertaining to the mutual benefit movement. It enabled the mutualists of the Lower Loire to play an important role in formulating the 1898 Mutualist Charter and, subsequently, in setting up the National Federation.

This epoch also witnessed a major struggle by the mutualists to keep medical costs under control. They negotiated agreements with pharmacists, as well as the first bitterly disputed medical conventions, in particular in Nantes, and undertook certain projects such as the cooperative pharmacy in Trignac. The Republican decree of April 25, 1877, officially opened the way to the social economy: thenceforth, the mutualists were classified not as clients but as partners with the authority to run clinics, pharmacies and medical centers for their own use, without risking prosecution for unfair competition. The debate, however, was far from over.

The 1898 Charter

The major document desired by the mutualists was slow in coming, and the question arises as to why the Third Republic hesitated so long before freeing the mutualist movement from "the laws of imperial servitude." The answer is that the large-scale insurance industry increasingly won over political decision makers of every stripe. At the same time, there were persistent doubts as to the efficacy of the democratic management practiced by the mutualist movement. At a time when the economic stakes of contingency planning were becoming increasingly important, "the political powers remained relatively wary of the mutualist movement's managerial capabilities." On April 1, 1898, the mutual movement was finally given (more than fourteen years after the trade unions) a major emancipatory republican legislative framework, "on a par with those concerning schools, public assembly, the press, trade unions and associations."[34] From then on, the ability to form unions gave the mutual benefit societies an organizational capacity which enabled them to handle coverage of major risks. Article 24 of the charter gave birth to independent funds.[35] It allowed for continuity in the services provided. The financial benefits reflected the social role of the mutual benefit movement, which some members of parliament saw as "a genuine public service." While the three categories of association were maintained, the partial access to civil authorities granted to authorized or "free societies" situates them within the emancipatory trends that were revitalizing the movement.

The 1904 Congress of Nantes

The 1904 national congress was an opportunity for Nantes to assume a particular role in these seminal debates. In 1902, in the wake of the creation of the FNMF[36] presided over by Léopold Mabilleau, a friend of Léon Bourgois, the Nantes mutualists, Gabriel Guist'hau, Adolphe Pion and Aristide Lecomte participated in the delegation sent to the State Council to discuss the conditions of authorization for mutual societies. In the Lower Loire, active members created a Mutualist Federation on March 29, 1903. The successor of the mutualist trade union, the Federation was also established following upon the creation of a legal arbitration committee centred around the lawyer Alexis Ricordeau and assigned the task of settling mutualist disputes. The members immediately nominated Gabriel Guist'hau as a candidate for the High Council of the Mutual Society, to which he was elected.

Nantes was then ready to host the 1904 national congress, attended by more than 1200 delegates from all over France. For a week, the town of Namnète was lit up by the mutualists' debates and festivities. In addition to the extraordinary effect the event had on local residents, it took on great significance for the entire mutualist movement. Apart from the federalization of the movement, the focus was on the question of mandatory coverage,[37] in anticipation of the more extensive social protection measures planned by the state.

The traditionalists in the movement were in favor of "full mutualist freedom" in the form of voluntary membership. Faced with a majority, Léopold Mabilleau subjected to critical scrutiny this notion of freedom, "so equivocal beneath its unassailable image." Was this "freedom," he asked, or a "status quo" of inequality?[38] And he was persuasive: the motion to extend access to risk coverage carried with only two votes opposed. A certain form of mandatory coverage was accepted as the mutualist movement abandoned the principle of voluntary adherence to its guarantees and accepted a partnership with the state for a universal and compulsory insurance system.

Another key argument was advanced which drew a distinction between mutualism and insurance companies. Unlike the companies, the mutual benefit associations were not to be under the auspices of the ministry of trade. Rather, management of the newly instituted mutual benefit system was to be governed by the ministry of labour, which was being set up and which officially came into being two years later.

The modern character of French mutualism was thus mapped out, as was its status within a social economy distinct from both the market economy and state management. As a direct result of the congress, the Lower Loire Departmental Union succeeded the Lower Loire Federation on February 12,

1905. Gabriel Guist'hau was its first president. Two hundred associations joined from the outset. The new president's first major project was to extend the General Union's activities, then limited to the Nantes area, to the entire region. Thus began the slow process of linking all 200 fiercely independent member associations in a network within the departmental union.

The Singular History of the Lower Loire

At the beginning of the 20th century, the working class, organized by the C.G.T.,[39] was subject to strong secular and radical influences. Over time, however, social Catholicism came to compete for hegemony. Its activities extended far beyond the professional realm, into areas such as housing, health, credit, recreation, culture and training, among others. While very much a minor trend up until 1939-45, represented by clerks and notables, social Catholic action became the "second leg" of the local workers' movement in the Lower Loire from the mid-1950s. Largely organized within a revitalized CFTC, it helped to bring about a balanced situation and encouraged a desire—rather unique in French history[40]—for unity of action between lay and Catholic militants, both in the trade unions and the mutual societies. "What is noteworthy here, in addition to the exceptional effort to sustain close ties between the mutual benefit and the labour movements, is the creation of internal unity based on turning difference to advantage—a rather daring gamble in a country like ours which is so enamoured of division."[41]

The Mutualist Movement and General Social Security

The dream of the radical Republic continued to be pursued at the dawn of the 20th century, and it was celebrated in particular in the Lower Loire. In addition to finding expression in events, the cooperation between the state and the mutual benefit movement was the main focus of concern. The departmental mutualist movement redoubled its efforts. On October 4, 1904, a mutualist pharmacy was established at 10 rue Scribe in Nantes, and the pharmaceutical third party payer[42] scheme was born. The Saint-Nazaire canton union was set up in 1909 and succeeded from 1910 on in putting an agreement into practice with local doctors. In Nantes, similar negotiations were not bearing fruit.

1910 was also the year when the law on worker and peasant pensions came into effect. The response of the mutualists was not overwhelmingly enthusiastic. Their agreement to become responsible for managing this compulsory insurance had made the mutualists hopeful of obtaining a monopoly, which the state did not accord them. It relied, pragmatically, on two criteria. The first was the defense of mutualist interests, and the second was knowing how to intervene in a high-stakes social question. In 1911, the Departmental Union created its mutualist worker pension fund. Although the application of the law was a failure, the law did spell out the right to a pension: "a truly fundamental debate on social security opened up. It would come to fruition in 1945."[43]

The First World War put a halt to all these undertakings. The disasters it wrought for the people, and the delicate situation created by the return to French hands of Alsace Lorraine and its system of employee protection inherited from Bismarck, drove home, as of 1918, the inescapable need to set up a social security system for the whole country. It would have been unthinkable to reduce the level of protection for the people of Alsace-Lorraine and dangerous to create a regional exception; it was thus necessary to raise the level of social security for the rest of the country at least up to that of Alsace-Lorraine. For more than ten years, elected representatives, senators, the medical establishment, employers' associations and workers' union confederations debated a plan for social legislation aiming to institute: "compulsory insurance against the risk of disability, old age and especially illness, which constituted the key areas of intervention for mutual aid societies."[44] On the mutualists' side, opposition to obligatory programs revived, especially as they were denied a monopoly of social insurance management: in fact, organizations dependent on employers, the church, unions, found themselves in competition with the mutualists over management. On April 5, 1928, an unenforceable law was passed, immediately corrected by a law of April 30, 1930, introducing social insurance. "It was to be continuously modified and supplemented by a series of texts up until the war."[45]

Mutualist Competition and Conflict

The development and implementation of social insurance renewed various differences of opinion pertaining to social questions in the Lower Loire.

Christian trade unionism could not but get involved in the debate given the eagerness of the leadership to cover all services liable to improve members' quality of life. Thus, on May 1, 1922, the Mutual Aid Society of the unionized Christian workers of the Lower Loire came into being at 6, rue de Bel Air in Nantes, the CFTC trade union headquarters.[46] Initially reserved for members of the Christian trade union movement, as well as their spouses and children, it became, the Lower Loire Christian Workers mutual society in 1927, through the efforts of Léon Buerne, Alphonse Beillevaire, André Duhamel and Gaston Pressensé. At the outset, relations with the Departmental Mutualist Union were consensual: Léon Buerne, Gaston Pressensé and many others were members of the powerful Trade and Industry employees' mutual society. On April 19, 1925, the general assembly of the Bel-Air Mutual society ratified its decision to join the departmental Union. Forming unions to manage social insurance seemed to be the typical practice, when an article by Edouard Leriche de Tourcoing published in December 1927 in *La Vie Catholique* and reprinted in *Le Messager Syndical*, the CFTC's journal in the Lower Loire, ignited controversy. The article called for the creation of funds specifically for the Christian trade union movement. The dream of unity harboured by Emile Bastit, the president of the Departmental Mutualist Union, crumbled. The Saint-Nazaire union of Christian trade unions took up Leriche's idea and, in the end, the Bel-Air mutual society opted for the Catholic fund, La Famille.

For their part, the CGT[47] labour unions announced the affiliation of the unions in the Lower Loire with the labor union fund, le Travail, in a September 1928 letter from their secretary Auguste Peneau. They rejected the practice of joint management with employers which was typical of the administration of mutualist funds or departmental funds reserved for non-members of a mutual society. As for the managers of the CRIFO,[48] an organization founded in 1919 to manage employers' aid for large families, they decided to set up their own fund, the SMIC.[49] However, in a gesture of conciliation towards the mutualist movement, they restricted their activities to those individuals who did not belong to mutualist societies, and they accepted the complete redistribution to their respective societies of employers' contributions to the SMIC for mutual society members. There were three conditions attached to this compromise: first, that the benefits associated with these societies be at least equal to those of the SMIC; second, that employers' contributions be limited to society members whose companies contributed; and third, that the latter's directors be admitted as honorary members for the purposes of administering these societies. Abel Durand, Departmental Union administrator and legal advisor to the CRIFO, doubtless had a hand in maintaining these good relations.

The Mutualist Enterprise

These events gave rise to two distinct mutualist enterprises in the Lower Loire. Both the Departmental Union, Désiré Colombe, and the Bel-Air mutual society required new premises, organizations and employees. For Désiré Colombe, these changes caused severe tensions which led to the departure of Emile Bastit and the election of Marcel Chabirand as head of the Departmental Union. This was also a period in which intense competition between Bel-Air and Désiré Colombe spurred a number of projects, namely, Bel-Air's mutualist surgical fund (1935) and Désiré Colombe's major clinic (1936) which failed in the short-term. For its part, the Departmental Union opened a mutualist medical center in 1935 and a small surgical clinic in 1936.

In keeping with its traditions, the mutualist movement remained relatively silent on the events surrounding the French Popular Front of 1936. A number of militants who made their mark at the time by occupying businesses and taking their protests and demands to the streets were doubtless the same people who were responsible for a large part of the social security funds within their mutual benefit societies. The mutualist movement was clearly no longer the locus of such struggles.

The Dark Years of 1939-1945

The Popular Front's strong momentum was thwarted and the unity of the anti-fascist forces was broken by the combined effect of weakness on the part of the political class and mass indecisiveness in the face of the rising "Brown Plague." The mutualist movement, one of the only professional organizations not targeted by the law of August 16, 1940,[50] began an ignoble chapter in its history.

The positions taken by its leadership committed the movement, without ado, to the support of Pétain's policies and the Work Charter.

For its part, the mutual movement of the Lower-Loire recommended that its members keep quiet and exercise caution. By virtue of its status as a neutral manager, the movement was granted a degree of tolerance which it was reluctant to give up. Each organization was allowed to conduct its activities as usual, despite the restrictions imposed by the Germans on the right of assembly. However, under the circumstances, the scope of these activities was extended to include giving aid to prisoners of war and their families. In addition to the action they took as members of the mutualist movement, many active members engaged in more general acts of solidarity, such as aid to displaced persons, food aid for the general population, mobilization for non-violent civil disobedience. Sometimes the hardships of the period led the movement to rediscover its roots in struggle through more radical resistance activities, which claimed the lives of some members.

Throughout this period, the mutualist institutions carried on their activities to the extent possible, under what were often arduous conditions. In 1942, a mutualist surgical fund was created at Désiré Colombe. André Duhamel (one of the founders of the Bel-Air mutual benefit society) was appointed director. At Bel-Air, a mutual benefit society for families was set up in 1942, in order to accommodate the many workers who would periodically replace prisoners of war in the various organizations.

Beginning in 1943, the national mutualists' enthusiasm for the Work Charter seemed to wane; the tide was turning. The mutual society of trade and commerce employees' in Nantes even mounted official opposition to the share allotted by the Work Charter to employers' mutual societies. Employers were able to encourage their employees to join such societies because of the special benefits allowed. Further, the widespread destruction caused by the bombing (to which the Désiré Colombe building also fell victim) added to the usual work of solidarity. New problems and challenges arose, such as dealing with the dispersion of the membership. The organization also sought to reconstruct the documented history that had partly disappeared with the destruction of the archives in the bombing which obliterated management records, administrative records, and the records of each mutual society's particular history.

After victory in 1945, a major social security plan was worked out. Although the workforce at both the Désiré Colombe departmental union and the Bel-Air mutual society were much larger than before the war, anxiety reigned due to a number of concerns: the threat of a single social security fund, the attack on a fundamental right through the suppression of free choice, the injustice of ousting the mutualists from the management of social contingency funds, and the dangers faced by the mutualist movement. The resolution of mutualist delegates at the general assembly of the departmental union on June 10, 1945, did not reflect a spirit of optimism.[51]

The Mutualist Movement and Social Security, 1945-1947

After the war, three edicts were issued in response to the growing demand for social protection.

That of February 22, 1945, entrusted shop committees with the social responsibilities, for which the mutualist societies provided a "model of social institutions."[52]

On October 4, 1945, the edict instituting social security was promulgated.

On October 19, 1945, an edict was issued defining the mutualist movement's new fields of activity, which were to complement that of social security. All areas in which mutual aid and contingency funds were applicable were to be opened up; work was to be undertaken in the traditional health-related fields, but also in the medical-social and social sectors. Thus modern social security was born.

In the Lower Loire, the future was embraced without ado and no time was wasted on regrets. This attitude was due both to the persuasiveness of Pierre Laroque, one of the most determined founders of the French Social Security system, and the rapprochement with the mutualists made possible by the Morice law.[53] Large-scale civil servants' mutual societies were set up which immediately took advantage of the opportunity to manage their own social security system rendered possible by the extension of the Morice law.

On April 19, 1946, the first meeting of the Nantes Primary Fund board of directors took place, presided over by Auguste Peneau, general secretary of the CGT Departmental Union. In 1947, Alexandre Bazin, president of the accountants' mutual benefits fund became the first elected president.

The Mutualist Movement and the Social Security System, 1947-1967

After participating actively on the Nantes Primary Social Security Fund's board of directors and passing down their traditions and expertise in the field of social security, the Désiré Colombe mutualists gradually withdrew. The Bel-Air unionists and mutualists, on the other hand, felt at home there. They gradually consolidated their activities and, from the mid-fifties until 1967, occupied the most important positions, such as the presidency of the Regional Social Security Fund and the presidency of the Nantes Primary Fund. They were the leaders of a new bold and committed generation which set its goal as complete social security coverage for everyone. During the same period, Bel-Air built up its mutualist, departmental and family activities by coordinating and fine-tuning the actions of its members.

By contrast, the Désiré Colombe mutualists concentrated more on internal matters. They cultivated their specialties (mutualist endeavours, company mutual benefit societies, prevention), drawing on the legitimacy they gained through their official representation within the FNMF.

Then dawned a period of joint struggles to defend social security, driven by the new idea that tampering with social security was tantamount to attacking a form of mutualism which went far beyond compensating for the accounting deficits of health insurance. In 1964, while the first early retirement programs were being negotiated in Saint-Nazaire to mitigate the effects of unemployment following the closing of the foundries, mutualists of all tendencies, unionists and politicians took to the streets of Nantes in huge numbers. The measures taken by Gilbert Grandval against the mutualist third party payer system, as well as against the mutualist pharmacies and optical centers, "affected the entire social fabric,"[54] as was noted at the time. That same year, most of the mutualist or Christian trade unionist in the department became involved in the move to transform the CFTC union into the secular CFDT.[55] This constituted an important step towards unity of action.

The 1967 edicts gave rise to new struggles: Nantes was the last French fund to persistently reject joint management. In those places where democratic elections brought a "comfortable" union majority to the boards of the primary health insurance funds, joint management arbitrarily placed union and employers representatives on an equal footing. It often enabled employers to use alliances to exercise a deciding role. From then on, for many participants, the mutualist movement became a favoured channel of democratic activism in defense of social security.

The Road to Unification, 1967-1976

As the national mutualist movement broached the possibility of joint action with the professional trade unions, the watchword of "active social independence" replaced the now suspect slogan of "mutualist neutrality."

After 1967, a new activism energized the departmental mutualist movement. The challenge was to mitigate the effects of the recent edicts and to resist the drive of private insurance companies towards contingency funds and more specifically collective contingency funds for businesses. Thenceforth, the two arms of the departmental movement found themselves, for better or worse, on the road to unification.

Unification came about in two stages. The first stage took shape in 1971 with the Loire-Atlantique mutualist Federation under the terms of which each side retained its independence and saw to its own management. In 1976, a Union of the Loire-Atlantique Mutual Benefit societies was forged. It demanded the complete commitment of the department's two mutualist tendencies and solidarity between them.

Building the Future: 1976-1996

The traditional principle of the mutualist movement survived. With the implementation of a progressive contribution system, solidarity in face of the vagaries of life was to be equally shared. Did this constitute a realistic response to competition from the private insurance industry? Since the retreat of the welfare state in the 1980s, the field of complementary health insurance has been wide open and insurers have been effective in cornering the youth market with contributions indexed to personal risk.

Did the change reflect a social revolution taking place? Today, elderly people are in a relatively favourable position with respect to resource allocation in comparison to youths who are often deprived. How then can young people be asked to bear the cost of social security for the more privileged age groups?

A new mutualist endeavour, Atlantique Santé, was launched in 1989 in the Loire Atlantique, offering preferential conditions for young members. In 1996, this mutual society could claim 26,000 members, but more importantly, it compelled all the mutual benefit societies in the union to raise the question of adjusted contributions[56] instead of traditional linear system of contributions, as a means to renew their own membership.

Contingency fund guarantees have also been one of the major growth sectors in the departmental mutualist movement since 1990. "As a complement to the compulsory programs, it only makes sense for us to manage the problems of income loss in cases of illness by proposing contingency fund guarantees to mutual fund members."[57]

With respect to mutualist endeavours, the movement's objectives are now being evaluated in terms of controlling costs, and in terms of the value of experimentation and innovation. It is not a matter of competing with what already exists but rather of looking at unsatisfied needs and effecting change where necessary. Hence the widespread introduction of agreements on third party pharmaceutical reimbursements will put an end to the proliferation of mutualist dispensaries, and instead of expanding drug distribution attention will turn to the analysis of how medications are distributed.[58] The clinics are increasingly focused on offering "highly specialized" services.[59] Dentists continue to wage their fight against unregulated prices, particularly in the area of prostheses.[60] The network of optical centers accounts for one-third of the departmental market. Community-run seniors' residences and home care services for the elderly have become one of the mutualist movement's recognized areas of expertise, and it is often asked to partner with local communities or retirement organizations. Other fields of activity in which the Loire Atlantique mutualists are involved include recreation, social housing and measures to combat social exclusion.

In 1985, a new code governing the mutualist movement made it possible to broaden the sphere of action and responsibility. The traditional skills and know-how of the Désiré Colombe branch were put to work once again, together with the dynamic activism of the Bel-Air branch, to undertake a complete reorganization of the departmental mutualist movement.

Driven by a spirit of innovation, competence and complementary expertise, the mutualists of Loire-Atlantique launched a new type of enterprise in October 1995. Sphéria brought together, the Union of Loire-Atlantique mutual fund guarantees, the Loiret Mutual Association and the Bordeaux Myriade Mutual association, linking them not only at an institutional level, but also tying them together economically in a permanent way.

If one element were to be singled out to characterize the endeavours of the Loire-Atlantique mutualists, it would have to be the stimulating effect of the ongoing albeit sometimes difficult dialogue between two forces. On the one hand, was the powerful, dynamic and innovative Christian trade union and mutualist movement concerned with ensuring unity and efficiency. On the other hand, there was the lay movement in which worker activists, mindful of the mutualist principle of independence, working side by side with republican notables, paradoxically maintained the ties with the Christian trade unionists and a sense of rootedness in local workers' traditions. This continued to open up possibilities for common action, while maintaining respect for the basic values held by each group. It demonstrated the wisdom of remaining open to change and of being able to distinguish between what is essential to preserve the identity of the movement and the need to make certain concessions in the interest of compromise. Some questions remain open, as expressed by journalist Denis Roux in the last chapter of the study referred to at the outset of this chapter. They revolve around the future of the mutualist enterprise now faced with the prospect of new European legislation. At issue are the new roles to be played by the members who are the lifeblood of the mutualist movement. The future remains in the hands of these men and women who are often torn between the temptation to cling to the past and the illusion of an all powerful technocracy and neo-liberal efficiency.

NOTES

1. André Delêtre, President of the Union of Loire-Atlantique mutual benefit societies, in the preface to *La Mutualité en Loire-Atlantique*, Jean-Luc Souchet and Denis Roux, Éditions Mutuelles de Loire-Atlantique, 1996, p. 8.

2. The Centre d'archives et de mémoire du mouvement syndical ouvrier et paysan, 6, bd Léon Bureau, 44200 Nantes

3. André Delêtre, ibid., p. 9.

4. G. Fourquin, les Soulèvements populaires au Moyen âge, PUF, 1972

5. Gabriel Le Bras, Études de Sociologie religieuse, PUF, 1955, v2, p. 419.

6. These questions were a constant concern of French Statism, as borne out by the French parliamentary debates surrounding the vote on the July 1901 law concerning associations. Cf Waldeck Rousseau, Associations et Congregations. Eugène Fasquelle Éditeur, 1901.

7. G. Le Bras, Ch. Lefèvre et J. Rambaud, Histoire du Droit et des Institutions de l'Église en Occident, v.7, p. 208. Sirey, 1965.

8. Notwithstanding its avowed aims, the traditional discretion of the French mutualist movement with respect to its internal debates is thus deeply rooted.

9. Robert Cheize, in La Loire-Atlantique des origines à nos jours, Édition Bordessoules, 1984, p. 24.

10. A fruity white wine served with oysters and seafood responsible for current renown of the vineyards in the southern Loire.

11. Bernard Gibaud, "Histoire mutualiste, la singularité du cas nantais", review of La Mutualité de Loire-Atlantique, Revue d'Études Coopératives, Mutualistes et Associatives-Revue Internationale d'Économie sociale, no. 264, second quarter 1997. Cf the work of Émile Cornaert, Les corporations en France avant 1789, Gallimard, 1941; William H. Sewell,

Gens de Métier et révolution, Aubier Montaigne, 1983, and "Du compagnonnage aux sociétés de secours mutuels," Revue de l'Économie sociale, October/December, 1984; E. Martin Saint-Léon, Le Compagnonnage, Armand Colin, 1901.

12. The ships left from Nantes for West Africa loaded with calico and objects for barter. They took Africans on board on the Senegalese coast and transported them to the West Indies or to Martinique to be sold as slaves. The ships returned to Nantes loaded with spices and exotic products.

13. We can note especially a significant use of animal black produced by local factories. Cf Rene Bourrigaud, Le développement agricole au 19e siècle en Loire-Atlantique, Centre d'Histoire du Travail, 1993.

14. More than 11,000 growers revolted, threatened with expulsion by the wealthy owners of the vines they tended. A phylloxera epidemic forced them to dig up the vines, which led the owners to consider themselves released from the ancestral rights that reserved their lands for these winegrowers who cultivated the vines in return for a share of the harvest. The law of March 8, 1898, came down on the side of the growers, putting an end to the revolt.

15. Bel-Air for the Christian mutualist movement, Désiré-Colombe (associated with the Bourse du Travail) for the secular mutualist movement. Apart from simply referring to the locations of their respective headquarters, this is a symbolic nomenclature identifying each of the movements.

16. Article 2 of this law passed unanimously on June 14, 1791, by the French Constituent Assembly, forbade professinal associations for almost a century.

17. Bernard Gibaud, "La Loi Le Chapelier et ses prolongements", in La Mutualité en Loire-Atlantique, p. 24.

18. Abdication of King Charles X, extremely hostile to all forms of mass organization.

19. Cf Jacques Le Goff, Du silence à la parole. Droit du Travail, société, État (1830-1989), éditions Calligrammes, 1989.

20. Pierre Legendre, Trésor Historique de l'État en France, Fayard, 1992, pp. 250-260.

21. "Mémoires d'Armand de Melun," cited by J.B. Duroselle, Les débuts du catholicisme social en France, PUF, 1951, p. 507.

22. Letter from Armand de Melun cited by J.B. Duroselle, op. cit., p. 499.

23. Note to Armand de Melun from the Minister of the Interior, cited by J.B. Duroselle, op. cit., p. 507.

24. Bernard Gibaud, La Mutualité..., p. 43.

25. Bernard Gibaud, La Mutualité, op. cit, p. 44.

26. Bernard Gibaud, La Mutualité, op cit, p. 44.

27. Fournier became an elected representative after 1848, and the Bishop of Nantes during the 1870s. He symbolizes the modernist current amd was concerned with social reform of a part of the clergy in this department, sometime in open conflict with an influential conservative wing.

28. Marius Faugeras, Le diocèse de Nantes sous la Monarchie censitaire, Thesis, volume 2, Fontenay le Comte, 1964.

29. Forgerons et Chaudronniers d'Indret, Société Saint-Charles à la manufacture des tabacs de Nantes...

30. Société des instituteurs et institutrices, Employés du commerce et de l'industrie de la ville de Nantes...

31. Bernard Gibaud, La Mutualité... op cit, p. 44.

32. Bernard Gibaud, Revue Internationale de l'Économie sociale, op. cit.

33. G Goullin, Institutions de prévoyance et de mutualité en Loire-Inférieure, 1898, Médiathèque de Nantes, 217017.

34. Bernard Gibaud, *La Mutualité... op cit.*, p. 67.

35. Reinsurance funds which allow major long-term health risk coverage by bringing together the greatest possible numebr of members.

36. Fédération Nationale de la Mutualité Française.

37. Namely, that of knowing whether, contrary to its principles recommending voluntary membership, the mutual society could participate in managing a universal and manadatory insurance program.

38. Bernard Gibaud citing Léopold Mabilleau, *La Mutualité...op cit*, p. 78.

39. Confédération Générale du Travail.

40. Except perhaps in Alsace-Lorraine.

41. Bernard Gibaud, "Histoire mutualiste, la singularité du cas nantais." Review of *La Mutualité en Loire-Atlantique, Revue d'Études Coopératives, Mutualistes et Associatives-Revue Internationale d'Économie Sociale*, no 264, second quarter 1997.

42. The mutual society pays directly for medications supplied to member pharmacies and associated pharmacies, thus relieving them of the burden of paying in advance.

43. Richard Vercauteren, la Mutualité en Loire-Atlantique p. 87.

44. Philippe-Jean Hesse, "Les lois d'assurances sociales," *la Mutualité en Loire-Atlantique, op.cit.*, pp. 100-101.

45. In addition to the article by Philippe-Jean Hesse, a good source on the historical development of social protection in France is Henri Hatzfeld's classic thesis, *Du paupérisme à la sécurité sociale*, Armand Colin, reissued by PUF de Nancy, 1989, as well as volume 2 (1870-1945) of the series *La sécurité sociale par les textes*, published by the Comité d'Histoire de la sécurité sociale, Paris, 1996.

46. Confédération Française des Travailleurs Chrétiens.

47. Confédération Générale du Travail.

48. Caisse Régionale des Institutions Familiales de l'Ouest. This employer's fund is the precursor of the Caisse d'allocations familiales.

49. Société de Secours Mutuels de l'Industrie et du Commerce.

50. This law heralded the dissolution of trade union confederations syndicales in November 1940.

51. La Mutualité en Loire-Atlantique pp 148-149.

52. Ambroise Croizat, Compte rendu du XIXème congrès de la FNMF, Mai 1948, p. 44.

53. André Morice, Minister and parlementarian in the Nantes region, won the vote in parliament on January 22, 1947, of the law which carries his name. It enables mutual societies to take part in the administration of social security.

54. Louis Guénégues, President of the CPAM de Nantes, l'Éclair, February 3, 1964.

55. Confédération Française Du Travail.

56. This adjustment is set out contractually by each mutual society. It is therefore easy to plan for. By contrast, the practice of many insurance companies is to index increases in premiums to increases in personal risk. They can thus prove significantly higher than young people expect.

57. David Mazurelle, General Manager of the Union des Mutuelles de Loire-Atlantique. *La Mutualité en... op. cit.* p. 2.

58. The recent book by FNMF President, Jean-Pierre Davant, on generic drugs illustrates this development.

59. In Loire-Atlantique, hand surgery for example.

60. In France there is a 1 to 10 gap in this field.

Chapter 11

Globalization and Social Economy: A North-South Perspective[1]

Louis Favreau

Three main ideas are outlined in this presentation: the current revival of social economy, its close connection with social movements and non-governmental organizations in the North and South, and its linkage with a new societal and developmental model. The content represents a synthesis of the research conducted in those areas, divided into four main topics: 1) an overview of the dominant contemporary trends which are emerging in societies of both the North and South; 2) a review of the reconfiguration process taking place in societies North and South, in regards to their social classes, social movements and economies; 3) a proposed assessment of social economy and of its contributions; 4) a number of directions for the renewal of international solidarity and cooperation, taking the notions of conflict management through cooperation, social economy and solidarity, and local development as a starting point, these notions being rooted in the wider framework of the new social contracts that are emerging at the national and international level. The common thread running through these ideas is that NGOs are at the centre of the relationship between local communities, social economy and development.

The dynamics of social economy in the North and community movements in the South are becoming increasingly similar. The community movement[2] represents an unprecedented opportunity for social innovation in the midst of the present crisis. We will first outline the dominant trends within the current transformation in societies of both the North and the South; then we will examine a number of these new trends within various social movements and NGOs. Lastly, we will highlight several new directions for international cooperation, in the context of social economy and solidarity economics.

North and South Societies: An Overview of Common Challenges
Both in the North and in the South, society is undergoing radical transformation. Several analytical studies concur in stating that we are at a major historical turning point, that we have reached a crisis in our search for a new societal and developmental model and that the time for action has almost run out. We can no longer talk about a continuous development process for the countries of the South nor about a favourable juncture for an international "Pro-third-world" solidarity movement. As for the North, gone are the days where we could talk

about societies where the Welfare State would guarantee a better future for everyone and full employment for all. In other words, the future has become, once again, uncertain. In the North, democracies are being tested by higher unemployment and precarious living conditions (Perret, 1995). In most countries in the South, economic and social destabilization seems to have gained the upper hand over development (Laidi, 1997). One main question remains: what model do we have for society and development as we enter the 21st century? What role can the social economy play in the North as well as in the South?

Globalization as we know it today is fraught with ambiguities; at most, it could eventually bring about a broadening of cooperative endeavours between nations, but for now it seems more bent on reinforcing inequalities and threatening democracies. The social question is re-emerging (Castel, 1995) and is increasingly becoming a core issue in the North. Meanwhile, in the South, marginalization is the main factor in the isolation of several countries. Thus we are witnessing a profound realignment, I would even say the emergence of a new North and a new South, made up of vast slum areas, running from New York or Paris to Mexico, Sao Paulo, Bombay or Jakarta.

Our current situation is influenced by three main trends: Globalization and its corollary: the monetarization of the economy; the spread of precarious living conditions and marginalization on a global scale; the changing role of the state including its weaker position in the global balance of power equation.

Globalization and Its Corollary: The Monetarization of the Economy

The internationalization of markets is not a new phenomenon. What is new is its scale and portent. Today, internationalization goes hand in hand with the rearranging of large regions into tight economic blocs (Europe, the Americas, South-East Asia). It is driven by financial globalization, stemming from the abolition of the systems which used to regulate the cross-border currency flow. The deregulation and liberalization of trade, the communication opportunities made possible by rapidly evolving technology are all factors that reinforce the internationalization of markets. The results are ambiguous: on the one hand, businesses are focussing their efforts much more on external markets, at the expense of domestic ones. Their outward focus is growing constantly. They are continually readjusting themselves (Boyer and Saillard, 1995) by entrusting the work to sub-contractors, by intensifying their rate of technological changes, by trimming their workforce and retaining better-qualified personnel, etc.

In this new social and economic landscape, the employment crisis, and loss of social cohesion has moved to the top of the list of national and international social concerns, reflecting the widening of the gap between unqualified and qualified workforce in the North, and increased competition between the nations of the South. This has resulted in the proliferation of these groups, which have gone underground into an informal economy, the only cushion left to absorb this social tremor.[3]

The Spread of Precarious Living Conditions and
Marginalization On a Global Scale: Marginalization In the North

Until the 1980s, in the societies of the North, it was assumed that development was a permanent fixture of social progress.[4] Today, those same societies are revisited by social conditions that afflict the developing world (extremes of poverty, for example). This explains why the social and economic sciences prefer to use the terms disqualification (Paugam, 1995), exclusion and disaffiliation (Castel, 1995), and of social breakdown instead of the term poverty (Lipietz, 1996). In short, after "the post-war boom years" we are now witnessing, in the countries of the North, a steady rise in the marginalization of people with a corresponding collapse of social stability. The disappearance of full-time work, and the disintegration of northern societies industrial base, have contributed to the suppression of their working classes, the loss of their social status and a weakening of union power. At the same time the collective handling of public services is being phased out to sub-contractors (to community organizations, for example).

In conclusion: Work is still the core activity for the major part of the population, but for the rest, a non-working life (unemployment, infrequent bouts of employment) is becoming their main life-experience. Social economy and local development are emerging at the intersection of those two trends and give us some reason for hope. Why? 1) Because they can play a key-role in creating employment and in starting or reviving businesses; 2) because they can encourage the local control of land development; 3) because they can foster empowerment of local communities and encourage them to mobilise their members. At least, these are the conclusions that are proposed by several studies on Québec (Favreau and Lévesque, 1996), on countries in the North (Defourny and Favreau, 1998) and on countries in the South (Ortiz, 1994 and Razeto, 1990 for Latin America; Jacob and Delville, 1994 for Africa).

Social Economy: A Question of Definition

According to those studies that have gained international recognition (Defourny and Monzon Campos, 1992; Laville, 1994; Vienney, 1994) the term "social economy" refers to a relatively well defined system, composed of businesses and organizations having for the most part adopted the same legal structures as cooperatives, credit unions, or other non profit organizations. The main characteristics of these businesses and organizations are the associative structure they have adopted, which give priority to people over assets (and thus to democratic processes), and the adaptivity of the services they give to their members. Therefore, they usually function through a process of supply and demand developed jointly by users and professional service providers (Laville, 1994). These businesses and organizations, therefore, are created in general by individuals that are dominated in some way (popular classes, women, youth, etc.), in partnership with middle-class advocacy groups (community organisers). These experiments, which contribute to the empowerment of those groups involved, presupposes a voluntary mobilization, combining initiative and solidarity. From this perspective, "social enterprises" (Defourny, 1994) are clearly different from capitalist and governmental enterprises.

However, as far as social economy is concerned, it is possible to consider both enterprises and organizations (micro level), and problems associated with social and economic regulation (macro level). The debate around "Social Economy" has more to do with the place and the role it plays in the reshaping of the Welfare State and in the modernization of the economy than with the experiences it merely provides. It is true to say that, because of the adaptability of their services, because of their structures and because of the people they involve, social enterprises offer, at local level, new opportunities in job creation and services development, particularly in communities where the accessibility of these services and the participation of users are being insisted upon.

On the other hand, in a more general sense, it must be stated that social economy does not represent a global remedy to social ills and is not by itself a project that runs counter to society. It can, however, contribute to the implementation of a new social contract, which implies both the renewal of the Welfare State and the modernization of the system of production (Lévesque, 1997; Favreau and Lévesque, 1996). Given this context, it would be wise not to eschew the analysis of contemporary society which, in the last twenty years has been so transformed that the mere attempt at preserving hard-won social advantages means isolation, and, more often than not, powerlessness.

Marginalization In the South

In the North, as in the South, marginalization is the consequence of a common economic and social rationale. It stems from a state of acute instability which itself is closely related to the increased splitting of society into two separate camps and to the globalization of certain social problems (ecological crises, mass migration, working children, the threat of social implosion in those countries that are "losing" the battle for survival, etc.).

In the 80s and 90s, these gaps between North an South have widened considerably, as the South transferred more money to the North (in total repayment of capital and interests) than they received in new capital (Comeliau, 1991). Even worse, for those countries that are at the bottom-end of international trading (about fifty in all, two-thirds being African countries), the influence of undeveloped countries is constantly being eroded. To such an extent that soon, for many of them, neo-colonial domination will no longer be an issue since marginalization has fully replaced it.

The economic crisis has also had another consequence: Developing countries (in all about fifty), under pressure from the IMF—who imposed such drastic economic measures on them as to mortgage for years ahead the future of their working peoples—have cancelled their already meagre social programs.[5] The composition of the working population has been profoundly transformed by this process. The informal economy and the independent worker have thus become the new economic and social protagonists.

The Diminishing Role of the State and
Its Disempowerment by the Forces of Globalization

With the onset of globalization, the states of the North have seen their role challenged, as economic and financial networks have become more autonomous and considerably more powerful. Used to being the leading force in the management of human affairs on the international scene, the authority of the state is now being eroded not only from the top by its elite in the economic and cultural fields, but from the base, albeit in a lesser measure, notably by local governments (and a few small and medium-size enterprises) who make cooperative agreements independently.

In the South, developing country governments who in the 60s and 70s were invested with every power and who carried every hope, have been disempowered by the structural adjustment policies imposed upon them by IMF and the World Bank. Development is further hindered or nullified by the "landlord states." Within such system, whole populations will have to "invest" their future in the informal sector.

Is There No Alternative To the Present Globalization System?

Is there no alternative to the present globalization system, a system promoted by the IMF and the World Bank, who see market-forces as the only viable solution to development? There are, in our view, many trends and movements that run counter to this view point: 1) the rise of a global socially-responsible society and the proliferation of NGOs (De Ravignan, 1996); 2) the emergence of grassroots enterprises; 3) new political trends (which value work-sharing, the development of a solidarity economics, new forms of international cooperation, etc.) (Lipietz, 1996); 4) democratic reforms advanced by some social movements (control by local populations of their own territories, mobilization of individuals and groups for the protection of the environment, etc.,) (Durning,1989); 5) the exploring of new socio-economic alternatives and the pioneering of new strategies within the dynamics of social economy and of local development (Annis, 1988; Ortiz, 1994). Albeit timidly, a new world-embracing social contract is being developed. It gives local government an important role to play, while resurrecting the concept of collective welfare and the need to control economic and financial activity (Groupe de Lisbonne, 1995).

Social Classes, Social Movements and
Social Economy in the Countries of the North and of the South

Social Classes, Social Movements and Social Economy In the North

Every social movement has felt the brunt of the present crisis. From a short-term perspective, the situation seems more worrisome than encouraging. A look at history can, however, offer us another angle. In the North, after the period of capitalist exploitation that was the hallmark of society from the 19th century to the end of the 30s, we moved into a period characterised by the conflict-ridden integration of workers and the marginalized poor; a society which earned for, its thirty years duration (1945-1975), the title of "Post War Boom." During these "three glorious decades," the 30s crisis was replaced by the rise of the Mighty Welfare State, and social laws and agreements negotiated under the auspices of a "New Deal." From the 80s onwards, social integration has been halted by the emergence of a new kind of social exclusion, which brought in its wake a dualist society. This new crisis has led to the birth or rebirth of social economy.

Since the 80s, social mobilization has become more diffuse and has been brought about by a wide variety of movements (unions, women's groups, environmental groups, popular and community organizations, youth groups). Given this new reality, we will present, as our central hypothesis, that social movements, with the community movement leading the way, are generating innovative solutions, because they occupy a unique midway position in the space created by the relationship between the state and civil society, between local communities and development and between the 'economic' and 'social' arenas. We might add that this new dynamic is part of a new social contract within which the community movement is given a new role, and occupies a place midway between the 'local' and the 'global'. Step by step, notions such as partnership, and conflict management through cooperation (Dommergues, 1988), economic and social revitalization (Vidal, 1992), local development and community economic development (Favreau and Lévesque, 1996; Tremblay and Fontan, 1994)), solidarity economics (Laville, 1994) and emerging non-profit sector (Salamon and Anheier, 1996), are coming in by the side door.

Social Movements And Social Economy In the South
In the South also, because of the pervasiveness of the ongoing exclusion process, social movements are going through a period of extreme change. The 70s had witnessed the emergence of a strong urban movement, which grouped community, urban and rural workers around a common socialist initiative. The recession of the 80s provoked a fragmentation of these movements, while the 90s introduced new players on the social scene, notably women and youth, who worked within local communities and developed concrete strategies for survival and development (Castadena, 1993; Rodrigo, 1990).

It is from this matrix of the 80s and 90s that a new type social economy was able to emerge, in the wake of social struggles for democracy. It is those struggles, which have accelerated the retreat and exhaustion of several authoritarian regimes and military dictatorships. Indeed it is true to say that although the 70s served to highlight North-South inequality, it is the 80s and 90s which are playing a part in renewing democracy and in throwing off the economic straightjacket of present-day globalization. This is being made possible through the emergence of non-competitive regions and of new multi-nations contracts (the Lisbon group, 1995). In this context, social movements, and in particular the shantytown popular movement, seem to gain in strength and to be ready to take the lead, supported by NGOs and church groups, who have been cast, somewhat unwillingly, with the role of opposition forces.

In many countries of the South, shantytown movements seem to have taken the lead, on both the political and social front. It is from them that concepts such as popular economy, solidarity economics (Larrachea and Nyssens, 1994) have emerged, following those of informal sector or subsistence economy. To illustrate the point, let's take the example of Villa El Salvador, a shantytown with some 300,000 inhabitants, situated on the outskirts of Lima, Peru. Today, Villa El Salvador is autonomous and manages its own territory. It has divided its residential blocks into organised neighbourhoods, and established public services around its 120 public squares and co-ordinated a network of small businesses, all in the spirit of solidarity economics (Favreau, 1993).

Social Economy and the New Societal and Development Model: A Proposed Evaluation

The Renewal Of Social Economy In the North

For the last two decades, in most of the countries of the North, new social economy initiatives, very different from those of the past, are being implemented involving new players, new answers to new social needs, new organizations systems. Let's see how they are different. Since social economy is built on productive activities governed by three modes of action, and since it is at once a grouping of diverse organizations rooted in an institutional framework and carrying a particular culture (a development project), it is necessary to evaluate its present nature and what it is becoming within these three modes.

a) Development Projects

The promoters of these new social economy projects foster the revival of communities by creating a localised series of structuring impacts which help communities to take control of the development of their territories (Community Development Corporations in the U.S. and in Canada, Régies de quartier in France, or Agences de développement local in Belgium, for example). In other cases, and for obvious reasons, these projects are created and implemented either under contract from the public or private sector or are managed jointly with them.

In other words, both the "new social economy" (NSE) and "community economic development" (CED) possess a potential which enable them to discard the ancillary role they play in their interactions with the private and government sector, while maintaining close ties of collaboration with them, in particular at the regional and local level. Even if the NSE and the CED cannot be really considered as "alternative" global models, they can contribute to the democratization of economy and of society.

b) Institutions

Support from the community and from governments can encourage the emergence of local mechanisms for social integration and development, in the context of negotiated partnerships. These initiatives, however, are confronted by two seemingly contradictory systems, on one hand the management of public programs aimed at specific targets (through subcontracting, etc.), and on the other, the motivation of the community (empowerment and local responsibility and control approach).

c) Organizations

Through their management methods, social enterprises seek to reconcile both the need to make a profit and to meet the social needs of their stakeholders, in other words economic viability and social mandate. They do not always succeed, because of commercial pressures and the weak support they receive from the state. They are able to succeed, however, when the pressures of social movement add weight to their endeavours.

In brief, from a global perspective, these initiatives can become levers for social transformation, providing that they act simultaneously on several levels: 1) defending threatened groups by suggesting "alternatives" (creation of workers cooperatives, community enterprises, etc.); 2) imposing new local methods of social regulation to counter the impacts of crises; 3) experimenting with other methods for business and policy development.

At the macro-social level, the NSE and the CED. can contribute to the democratization of work relationships in enterprises and of relationships between users and public utilities. This influence may be felt most keenly when these initiatives, by means of growing number of partnerships, spread their network and take hold of a sizeable part of the market.

It is clear, however, that these initiatives are in keeping with national alternative development scenarios, which means that their influence is limited: 1) in the context of a strong neo-liberal economy, this NSE, rooted in the informal sector, runs the risk of being used as a mere palliative; 2) in the context of a state-run economy, the NSE is used to complement traditional social policies, without transforming these policy in a significant manner; 3) in the context of an economy and of a society undergoing profound changes, the NSE creates a solidarity-oriented society, potentially able to generate a strong drive towards the reconfiguration of "economic" and "social" relationships, and towards democracy. In short, the scope of these initiatives can be defined and measured differently, depending on the path followed by each national developmental model.

The Emergence of Social Economy In the South

When social economy in the South is mentioned, the first thing that comes to mind is the physical improvement of shantytowns (Boucher, 1986), the development of solidarity economics, primarily through the informal sector (micro-credit, micro-enterprises, etc.) and through sustainable development (urban wastes recycling etc.). It is important to point something out, however: Although the informal sector can be used as a starting point for developing solidarity economics, it would be unwise to confuse social economy with the informal sector. The informal sector is not a real development mechanism. It is mainly a survival mechanism. On the other hand, social economy represent a definite development strategy rooted within a long-term development project, and in which stakeholders become fully conscious participants.

In the South, the emergence of social economy is due, to a great extent, to the development' NGOs. They are its lifeline. These NGOs are grouped around what is commonly termed as community development (Sanchez, 1994). This community development work has three aspects (Doucet and Favreau, 1991):

- micro-project support work in local communities motivated by the changes they experience in their living conditions in the areas of work, health, housing and education;

- defence of social rights through the organization of neighbourhood committees, around vital issues such as access to water, electricity etc., and to collective facilities, for example health and education;

- implementation of measures for local and integrated socio-economic development, which allow local communities to organize themselves.

The North as well as the South, however, are still debating the functions of relays and levers in the context of the contribution made by social economy to the development of a society. Just like their cousins in the North, the new social economy and solidarity economics initiatives in the South are running the same risk of farming out responsibilities. In order to counter the social impacts of structural adjustment programs, they could very well find themselves replacing the state in the same the areas that the latter has abandoned.

Social Economy In the North and In the South:
An Analysis of Common Trends

There is no easy answer to those questions. Some see social enterprises as perfect partners to replace public services. The qualities generally attributed to social economy initiatives (flexibility, speed, creativity, responsibility, and closeness to the people, etc.) are seen as means to offer better services at a lesser cost. Others declare that on the contrary, social economy is the means by which public policies pursue privatization, and through which social gains are progressively eroded. The first of these answers seems to trivialise the tensions created as the result of the position occupied by social enterprises within an international framework heavily controlled by neo-liberal forces. The second answer is the opposite. It underestimates the capacity of the different players to develop their own strategies, that is to say their ability to explore fully the possibilities offered by that type of enterprises, for example, by responding to new social needs, by supporting the construction of new types of communities, and by creating public opportunities for the revival of democratic practices.

A third hypothesis, offering both positive and critical arguments, can be considered. It points out the fact that our societies are moving towards a redefinition of the relationships that exist between different communities, between the intermediary structures of civil society, between market forces and the state. This redefinition could be leaning towards a greater degree of democratization. In brief, in the option we favour, nothing is cast in stone. In the North as in the South, the kind of society unfolding from this crisis could be oriented towards a redistribution of responsibilities between the different levels of government, private producers and social economy organizations (Lévesque, 1995).

This hypothesis has the advantage of opening a theoretical and political window, which will give us the opportunity to understand those social economy initiatives that are solidly anchored in the on-going process of social transformation. Are we talking about specks in the ocean or the dawn of a new system? It is difficult, at this stage, to advance a definite answer, simply because the parameters of this future society are not yet fully determined. That is why, at this juncture, a historical look at social economy in the societies of the North, would be useful.

One of the first lessons to be learnt, a century and a half after its birth, is that the social economy has grown, mainly through cooperation, amidst exploited working classes who were struggling to improve their living conditions. Cooperation was at first, an answer to a number of social needs.

This is the very first socio-economic dimension of our reading chart. As a direct result, one of the roles played by social economy is brought to the fore: that of a relay mechanism in the event of market, or state, failure. For example, consumers' cooperatives were at first an expression, on the part of certain segments of the population, of collective endeavours meant to meet basic needs at the lowest cost possible. For their part, workers co-operatives have been their own response to a capitalist industrialization system that was robbing them of their work. Social economy took the relay of a market/public economy rendered unable or powerless to resist the tide of new social challenges. But necessity or interest are not enough to explain the success of social economy in mobilising people. The creation of social enterprises can also be explained by the strong need in people to be part of groups or communities (whether in their working environment, their neighbourhood or their village), the need to have an identity, the need to live together.

In the last analysis, we could even suggest a third dimension, insofar as the mobilization undertaken to build social economy has a greater importance than each of these initiatives, since it needs not only an identity, but also a project which will give a sense to this identity—this desire to live together (Touraine, 1973). This is the dimension of movement or lever in the social transformation process. An example of this is the story of the cooperative housing complex in Mondragon, where the Basque identity has been the prime 'mover'. The same thing is happening in many countries of the South where practices are being developed, according to methods rooted in social economy principles such as Villa El Salvador, in Peru, an initiative which can be considered as a southern replica of Mondragon.

Some will wonder if social economy is not also the story of initiatives that became institutionalised when they lost this levering dimension? It is true that there is a tendency for a part of these institutions to operate as subsidiary components of the public economy (credit unions) or the market economy (financial cooperatives), in areas where the development model of post-war boom years still has a strong influence. It is precisely during this period that the large institutions of civil society, have, to varying degrees, found that their interest was best served within the framework of a strong social state (working class parties, unions, credit unions and cooperatives). It is also during this period that all the social movements of the day became strongly institutionalised, and consequently saw their proactive mandate considerably weakened. One must also add, however, that during this same period, social economy made, simultaneously, significant contributions to the construction of a social state.

Today, under what conditions can social economy play the role of lever in the transformation of society? In the light of several studies that have been conducted in this field, we conclude that the experimental nature of the NSE and the CED initiatives in the North, and of Solidarity Economics in the South can be replicated and used elsewhere provided certain conditions exist:

- a stronger entrepreneurial capacity in the launching stages of projects, in the search for opportunities, in the networking of projects and enterprises, in the search for self-financing, in the negotiation of a share of the markets, in the implementation of follow-up and support measures. In brief, stronger economic foundations, underpinned by an entrepreneurial culture, would be valuable assets (Defourny, 1994);

- an integrated system of local development, enabling enterprises to firmly root themselves in the reconstruction of their local territories through the forging of relevant partnerships. This reconstruction goal can be served more particularly through agreements and contracts between community organizations, NGOs, municipalities and cooperative financial institutions (Reilly, 1995);

- a commitment to develop a pluralistic economy (Roustang, 1996), which implies a more explicit loyalty to another rationale than simply adapting to the market place;

- the establishment of linkages with powerful and traditional labour institutions such as large cooperatives, mutual trusts and union organizations (Favreau and Lévesque, 1996).

Ways of Renewing North-South Cooperation Through Solidarity Economics

We cannot speak of North-South cooperation in the context of social economy without mentioning the burgeoning projects and movements around the world which directly reflect a renunciation of social duality. As we have stated earlier, various counter-trends to free-market globalization are combining to create "alternative" structures as a reaction against exclusively market-determined ones. Although weak, these new structures are none the less very real.

In terms of international cooperation, social economy will only be fully effective if the following three requirements are met: first, international cooperation will have to position itself more explicitly within the emerging global civil society and new social contract (Chesneaux, 1992 and 1993); second, governments and leading international NGOs will have to be more willing to support social economy and find other ways of taming market forces (Petrella, 1996); and, finally, project agencies, both in the North and the South, will have to develop a more conscious mutual recognition that they share, a) a common enemy in the form of neo-liberal globalization, b) a common goal in the form of responses to economic and social problems, both in the North and the South, which are increasingly interrelated, c) a possibly common outlook in the form of participation in creating of a new societal and developmental model.[6]

However, it is also going to be necessary that social movement leaders work more in areas such as federating local initiatives, making linkages at the national level, creating national NGO networks and developing closer collaboration with the North's international cooperation organizations (ICO). This type of cooperation increasingly has a ripple effect, as far as the UN.[7] In sum, it would be a mistake to underestimate the political or economic importance of contemporary forces and movements.

First of all, so far as the political arena is concerned, several recent studies on Latin America and Africa have clearly shown the emergence of two powerful new social forces: the NGOs, which, by adapting their approaches, have become, at least partly, "social outcome" enterprises; and certain local governments, which have been getting more and more involved in genuine partnerships or "joint ventures" with both popular movements and the NGOs (Reilly, 1995; Jacob and Lavigne Delville, 1994). Secondly, in the economic area, several studies have clearly shown the growing importance of social economy in both North and South (Salamon and Anheir, 1996): representing many millions of jobs, nearly 5% of GDP, 5-7% of jobs, 75% of the business in four key sectors (education, health and social services, culture and recreation) and 13% of all new jobs during the decade 1980-90.[8]

Overall, from now on, it is going to be necessary to take into account the existence of almost 500,000 non-governmental organizations (NGOs) in the world, more than 50,000 of whom are already networked and linked together by the Internet (the Association for Progressive Communications Network or APC Network[9]). In this context, the challenge is to increase the number of intervention levels (local, regional or federated, national and international) and come to have a major world-wide influence by judiciously adjusting the action level, from the 'micro', i.e., local government, to the 'macro', i.e., global policy.

North-South Cooperation: The Community Movement and
Social Economy as Levers of International Solidarity and Development

Providing they broaden the circle of their partners, NGOs, together with social economy and local development initiatives, can fill a large portion of the gap between "local" and "global" activity? But how can we make them more effective socially? As a first response, current experience indicates that NGOs should set up an authentic international system of funding local development and social economy.[10]

Secondly, experience also suggests we should not only support local development by setting up community organizations, lending systems, and different forms of cooperative and community enterprises, we should also increase the number of "North-South" and "Association-NGO-local government" partnerships (and small business if possible) in a general community revival. Recent developments also point to the value of thinking along the lines of multi-partner projects focusing on specific challenges: for example, joint ventures between unions and cooperatives, Northern and Southern associations, municipalities, Northern small business and their budding Southern counterparts and so on.[11]

Lastly, recent developments also highlight the need to give greater emphasis to research and thought on certain themes which are more closely linked to the main social protagonists: namely the factors which encourage the development and durability of social economy enterprises and the role of NGOs and churches in the emergence of a new model of society.

Although these ideas may not appear earth shattering, they are based on certain core elements, i.e., concrete challenges and specific local and international groups. They are not especially revolutionary because they avoid both important classic approaches: major confrontation or humanitarian intervention. Their positive value lies in their contribution to the implementation of the four global contracts presented by the Group of Lisbon: the basic needs contract (removal of inequality); the cultural contract (aimed at improving inter-cultural communication); the democratic contract (the world-wide application of new political regulations) and the Earth contract (sustainable development).

NOTES

1. The content of this document has been drawn and developed from the initial research which was undertaken to produce two presentations for the opening of two international conferences: The International Conference on Social Economy in the North and in the South, held in Ostende in March 1997. This conference was organized by the Secretariat of State for Cooperation and Development, in collaboration with third sector organizations and academic professionals from Liège and Louvain universities (the Conference attracted 400 participants, representing over 30 countries North and South); The International Symposium on Solidarity Economics, held in Lima in July 1997. This conference was attended by 225 people (NGO and Community organizations) representing 32 countries, mainly from the South.

2. The expression "community movement" embraces three realities: 1) an emergence (or renaissance) of this movement in the 60s; 2) organizations which are working to transform living and working conditions within local communities; 3) the empowerment of neighbourhoods or local communities, and their autonomy from government.

3. In the urban centres of developing countries, about 50% of the population draw their living from the informal sector (Lautier, 1994).

4. We are referring here to the passage from the proletarian system of the last century (social marginalization, paucity of jobs and absence of rights) to the labour system. This evolution was made possible by the struggles of the worker's movement (who gained certain rights and carved for themselves a place in society). This labour system has been transformed into a salary-based system, with full rights as equal citizens.

5. The neo-liberal remedy, advocated by the IMF and the World Bank under the form of structural adjustment policies can be summarized as follows; 1) maximizing insertion in the world market; 2) privatizing government enterprises; 3) reducing social expenses (education, health, housing, etc.).

6. For example, it is necessary to simultaneously 1) organize local financing, obtain the development of a pertinent budgetary policy at national level, request a greater control of financial fluctuation as well as long term government financing to support development at international level; 2) manage employment opportunities (on a local level), request the development of a national policy on employment in the areas where reduction of working hours is important and at international level, request the development of a social clause (regarding the fundamental rights of the salaried work force); 3) stimulate partnerships to encourage local development and define priority investment policies regarding personnel and work force training, research activities, etc., at the national and international level. The actions proposed here are both feasible and desirable, but their implementation depends on the capacity of the various players to mobilize themselves (see "Que faire et à quel niveau?," *Alternatives économiques*, #138, June 1996, p.37).

7. This international influence is demonstrated by the regular participation of NGOs in the major United Nation's conferences organized during the last five years (Environment and Development—Rio, 1992; Population and Development—Cairo, 1994; Condition of Women—Beijing, 1995; Social Issues—Copenhagen, also in 1995, Urbanization Istanbul, 1996).

8. The authors still insist in underlining several key-problems: little visibility, little legal protection, unstable situation between agent (in the shape of government) and partner (with a recognized status and collaborating in an autonomous manner), precariousness of the sources of financial support, excessive focusing on local issues.

9. For further information, visit their internet site at: http://www.apc.org

10. Proposed by Holzer and Lenoir (1989), drawn from the french experiment: Société d'investissement et de développement international (SIDI), developed in greater depth by Vigier (1995).

11. Criterias proposed more and more often when support is being given to solidarity projects at international level: 1) capacity to mobilize stakeholders around economic activities; 2) long-term development; 3) innovation and experimentation in the areas of sustainable and concrete economic alternatives; 4) networking; 5) capacity to place pressure on the global policies in a given region or country; 6) capacity to combine community organization and enterprises.

BIBLIOGRAPHY

M. Aglietta, *Macro-économie financière*. Paris: La Découverte, "Repères," 1995.

Sheldon Annis, "Can small-scale development be a large-scale policy? The case of Latin America," in S. Annis and P. Hakim, *Direct to the Poor: Grassroots Development in Latin America*. Boulder and London: Lynne Rienner Publishers, 1988.

J.-D. Boucher, *Volontaires pour le Tiers monde*. Paris: Karthala, 1986.

R. Boyer, and Y. Saillard, (eds.), *Théorie de la régulation. L'état des savoirs*. Paris: La Découverte, 1995.

R. Castel, *Les métamorphoses de la question sociale*. Paris: Fayard, 1995.

J.G. Castadena, *L'utopie désarmée, l'Amérique latine après la guerre froide*. Paris: Grasset, 1993.

J. Chesneaux, "La société civile internationale face au Sommet de la Terre," *L'événement européen*, March 1992, pp.195-200.

J. Chesneaux, "Les ONG, ferment d'une société civile mondiale," *Transversales*, #24, Paris, nov.-déc 1993.

C. Comeliau, *Les relations Nord-Sud*. Paris: La Découverte, "Repères," 1991.

J. Defourny, and L. Favreau, *Insertion et nouvelle économie sociale: un bilan international*. Paris: Desclée de Brouwer, 1998 (Forthcoming).

J. Defourny, *Développer l'entreprise sociale*. Belgique: Fondation du roi Baudoin, 1994.

J. Defourny, and J.L. Monzon Campos, *Économie sociale, entre économie capitaliste et économie publique*. CIRIEC, Belgique: De Boeck Université, 1992.

A. De Ravignan, "Les nouveaux rôles des ONG dans le concert mondial," in *État du Monde 1997*, Paris, 1996, pp.50-53.

P. Dommergues, (ed.), *La société de partenariat (économie-territoire et revitalization régionale aux États-Unis et en France)*. Paris: Afnor-Anthropos, 1988.

L. Doucet and L. Favreau, "L'organization communautaire dans les pays du tiers monde: L'Afrique et l'Amérique latine," in L. Doucet and L. Favreau, *Théorie et pratiques d'organization communautaire*. Sainte-Foy: Presses de l'Université du Québec, 1991, pp.379-388.

Alan B. Durning, "Mobiliser les communautés de base," in Lester R. Brown, *L'état de la planète*. Paris: Economica, 1989, pp.253-284.

B. Fairbain, *Co-operatives & Community Development*. Saskatoon: Centre for the Study of Co-operatives, University of Saskatchewan, 1991.

L. Favreau, "Du bidonville à la municipalité autogérée: acquis et tensions à Villa el Salvador," *Economie et Humanisme*, #326, October 1993, pp.14- 20.

L. Favreau, and B. Lévesque, *Développement économique communautaire, économie sociale et intervention*. Sainte-Foy, Canada: Presses de l'Université du Québec, 1996.

Groupe de Lisbonne, *Limites à la compétitivité*. Canada: Boréal, Belgique: Labor and Paris: La Découverte, 1995.

B. Holzer, and F. Renoir, *Les risques de la solidarité*. Paris: Fayard, 1989.

J.-P. Jacob, and Ph. Lavigne Delville, (eds.), *Les associations paysannes en Afrique: organization et dynamiques*. Paris: APAD/Karthala/IUED, 1994.

Z. Laïdi, *Malaise dans la mondialization*. Paris: Textuel, 1997.

I. Larraechea, and M. Nyssens, "Les défis de l'économie populaire au Chili," RECMA, vol.49, no 252, 1994, pp.43-53.

B. Lautier, *L'économie informelle dans le tiers monde*. Paris: La Découverte, "repères," 1994.

J.L. Laville, (ed.), *L'économie solidaire, une perspective internationale.* Paris: Desclée de Brouwer, 1994.

B. Lévesque, "Repenser l'économie pour contrer l'exclusion: de l'utopie à la nécessité," in J.L. Klein and B. Lévesque (eds.), *Contre l'exclusion, repenser l'économie.* Sainte-Foy: Presses de l'Université du Québec, 1995, p. 17-44.

B. Lévesque, *Démocratie et économie sociale: un scénario pour contrer le chômage et l'exclusion.* Cahier du CRISES, Département de sociologie, UQAM, Montréal, 1997.

A. Lipietz, *La société en sablier (le partage du travail contre la déchirure sociale).* Paris: La Découverte, 1996.

Muller, *Les politiques publiques.* Paris: Presses universitaires de France, 1994.

H. Ortiz, *Las organizaciones economicas populares (semillas pequenas para grandes cambios).* Lima: Servicios Educativos El Agustino, 1994.

S. Paugam, (ed.), *L'exclusion. L'état des savoirs.* Paris: La Découverte, 1996.

B. Perret, *L'avenir du travail: les démocraties face au chômage.* Paris: Seuil, 1995.

R. Petrella, *Économie sociale et mondialization de l'économie.* Montreal: SUCO, 1997.

L. Razeto, et. al., *Las organizaciones economicas populares.* Santiago: PET, 1990.

C.A. Reilly, (ed.), *New Paths to Democratic Development in Latin America: the Rise of NGO-Municipal Collaboration.* Boulder (USA) and London (UK): Lynne Rienner Publishers, 1995.

J.-M. Rodrigo, *Le sentier de l'audace. Les organizations populaires à la conquête du Pérou.* Paris: L'Harmattan, 1990.

G. Roustang, J.-L. Laville, B. Eme, D. Mothé, and B. Perret, *Vers un nouveau contrat social.* Paris: Desclée de Brouwer, 1996.

L.M. Salamon and H. K. Anheier, *The Emerging Nonprofit Sector, an overview.* Manchester and New York: Manchester University Press, Johns Hopkins Nonprofit Sector Series 1, 1996.

G. Salamé, *Appels d'empire.* Paris: Fayard, 1996.

N. Sanchez, "Community Development and the Role of NGOs: a New Perspective for Latin America in the 1990s," *Community Development Journal,* Vol.29, No.4, London, 1994, pp.307-319.

A. Touraine, *La production de la société.* Paris: Seuil, 1973.

D.G. Tremblay and J.-M. Fontan, *Le développement économique local.* Sillery: PUQ,

A.C. Vidal, *Rebuilding Communities. A National Study of Urban Community Development Corporations.* New York: New School for Social Research, Community Development Research Center, 1992.

J.P. Vigier, *Finances et solidarité, votre épargne pour le développement.* Paris: Syros, 1995.

C. Vienney, *L'économie sociale.* Paris: La Découverte, "repères," 1994.

Chapter 12

Selected Resources on the Social Economy

Michael Toye

Print Documents:

Y. Comeau and J. L. Boucher, "L'économie sociale est-elle un projet de développement crédible?," in *Économies et Solidarités,* Vol. 28, No.2, 1997, pp. 1-10.

Comité d'orientation et de concertation sur l'économie sociale, *Entre l'espoir et le doute.* Québec, May, 1996.

Conseil québécois de développement social, *L'économie sociale, dérision ou panacée?* Proceedings of the Round Table, 1997.

Martine D'Amours, *Présence de l'économie sociale au Québec, une illustration dans six secteurs et sept régions.* Montreal: Institut de formation en développement économique communautaire, 1997. This 46 page document, available in French only, looks at the problem of defining the social economy, the cooperative movement, the community movement by sector of activity and by geographic territory, and finally the organizations and networks that exist in Québec to support the social economy.

Martine D'Amours, editor and coordinator, *L'économie sociale au Québec: cadre théorique, histoire, réalities et défis.* Montreal: L'Institut de formation en développement économique communautaire, 1997. This 80 page book succinctly summarizes the major components of the social economy—its definitions, history, similarities and differences with related concepts and the particular challenges that the Quebec context brings to its growth. It is available only in French.

Jacques Defourny and José L. Monzón Campos (Eds.), *Économie sociale, entre économie capitaliste et économie publique / The Third Sector, Cooperative, Mutual and Nonprofit Organizations.* Bruxelles: CIRIEC, De Boeck Université, 1992. 459 pages of articles in both English and French, with each article summarized in a 4 to 7 page translation. The 11 essays provide a brief introduction and survey the status of the social economy in 7 European countries, the US and Québec.

H. Desroches, *Pour un traité d'économie sociale.* France: Coopérative d'information et d'édition mutualiste, 1983.

Economic & Industrial Democracy. Thousand Oaks, CA: SAGE Publications. Sponsored by the Swedish National Institute for Working Life, this international journal "covers all aspects of industrial democracy, from the practical problems of democratic management to wide-ranging social, political and economic analysis. Economic and Industrial Democracy focuses on the study of policies and other initiatives designed to enhance the quality of working life and the democratic control of workers in the workplace and in the economy. A central theme is participation in management, and how initiatives in that direction are affected by wider political, economic and technological factors. Special emphasis is placed on international coverage of empirical findings including discussion of the changing social and economic conditions in various countries and of the market economy." Information is available at http://www.sagepub.co.uk/journals/usdetails/j0017.html

L. Favreau and B. Lévesque, *Développement économique communautaire, Économie sociale et intervention.* Quebec: Presses de l'Université du Québec, 1996.

Groupe de travail sur l'économie sociale, *Osons la solidarité! Rapport du groupe du travail sur l'économie sociale.* Chantier sur l'économie sociale. Octobre 1996.

J.L. Laville, "L'économie solidaire: une nouvelle forme d'économie sociale?" *Revue des études coopératives, mutualistes et associatives,* No. 255, 1995, pp.70-80.

B. Lévesque, *Démocratixation de l'économie et économie sociale: un scénario radical pour de nouveaux partages.* Montreal: Cahiers du CRISES No.970549, 1997.

Local Strategies for Employment and the Social Economy: Proceedings of the Conference. Montréal: Les Publications de l'IFDÉC, 1997. The 136 page (almost 300 pages altogether with the entire French translation) Proceedings of the Conference hosted by the Organization for Economic Co-operation and Development (OECD) in co-operation with Human Resources Development Canada (HRDC) and organized by the Institut de formation en développement économique communautaire (IFDÉC). 23 articles of 2 to 10 pages each from prominent practitioners, academics politicians and bureaucrats discuss policy and practice issues in Québec and abroad.

M.C. Malo, "Les associations au sein de l'économie sociale," in *Inter-Action spécial,* October, 1991, pp.39-47.

J. Moreau, "Où en est l'économie sociale?," in *Humanisme & Entreprise,* 100 27, 1997, pp.97-221.

Nonprofit and Voluntary Sector Quarterly. Thousand Oaks, CA: SAGE Publications. This journal of the Association for Research on Nonprofit Organization and Voluntary Action is "an international forum for a vital and expanding area of study in which overlapping fields meet to examine nonprofit organizations, philanthropy and voluntary action around the world." It focuses on four areas: organization and leadership, philanthropy,

volunteerism and public policy. More information is available at
http://www.sagepub.co.uk/journals/usdetails/j0052.html

Jack Quarter, *Canada's Social Economy*. Toronto: James Lorimer & Company,
1992.

Review of Social Economy. New York: Routledge. The quarterly Journal for the
Association for Social Economics has over 50 years of papers on the
relationships between social values and economics. Subjects addressed include:
income distribution, justice and equity, poverty, cooperation, human dignity,
labour, workplace organization, gender, need, the environment, economic
institutions, economics methodology, and class. Each issue also contains short
papers and comments, book reviews and review essays, and announcements of
future meetings. More information on the Journal is available at
http://www.heinle.com/routledge/journal/rse.html, and further information can
be obtained from Routledge at: journals@routledge.com

Jeremy Rifkin, *The End of Work*. New York: G. P. Putnam's Sons, 1995. The 350
page book deals more broadly with the current economic context, but the last
4 chapters (Part V of the book) specifically address Rifkin's suggestions for the
development of the social economy or the third sector as an alternative.

Y. Robitaille, "Vous avez dit 'économie sociale'?," *Revue Possibles*. Montreal,
1997, pp. 82-93.

C. Vienney, *Les activités, les acteurs et les règles des organisations de l'économie
sociale*. Paris I: Centre d'Éducation permanente, D.E. Sup. Économie sociale,
1986.

C. Vienney, *L'économie sociale*. Paris: La Découverte, 1994.

Internet Sites:

http://www.aries.eu.int
  The European Social Economy Electronic Information Network. Largely
  funded by the European Commission's Social Economy Unit, this site
  contains online information, a documentation centre, databases and bulletin
  board/information exchange. Access to the information requires a
  membership, however, which cost 50 ECU for an annual basic membership
  in January 1998. This site is entirely in English.

http://www.ulg.ac.be/ciriec/ciriec.htm
  Originally called the "International Centre of Research and Information on
  Collective Economy" and set up in Geneva in 1947, CIRIEC has been
  operating in Liège, Belgium since 1957. Their website describes their
  quarterly journal, "The Annals of Public and Cooperative Economics," some
  of their recent publications, and information about the biennial
  International Congresses (for which the site indicates the 23rd International
  Congress in the year 2000 should be held in Canada). This site is available in
  English, French and German.

http://www.unites.uqam.ca/crises

The Collectif de recherche sur les innovations sociales dans les entreprises et les syndicats is a collective of a dozen researchers and about 40 graduate students from 6 universities in Quebec. The website includes a description of CRISES and associated individuals, a listing of all publications (45 workbooks), of which 21 are available on the website. It also has an excellent listing of other related sites. The site is completely in French.

http://www.francomedia.qc.ca/~col-ei

The website of the Collectif des entreprises d'insertion du Québec [Quebec Training Businesses Collective] gives a description of the Collective, lists and describes members and associated organizations and presents their newsletter. This site is entirely in French.

http://www.clsc.org/solidaire/index.html

Hosted by the Quebec network of CLSCs [Local Community Service Centres], this site is dedicated to discussions surrounding the idea of a solidarity-based economy [économie solidaire] and other related questions, such as the social economy, community services, social utility and territorial services. It is entirely in French.

http://www.ilo.org/public/english/65entrep/coop/index.htm

Wide-ranging information on the extensive activities of the Cooperative Branch of the International Labour Organization's Enterprise & Cooperative Development Department. The page on Social Services particularly empasizes the broader concepts of the social economy. It contains links to the International Cooperative Alliance, the International Committee for the Promotion & Advancement of Cooperatives and the World Council of Credit Unions. All of this information is available in English.

http://www.coop.org/

The International Cooperative Alliance's Cooperative website contains information on the ICA itself, it's aims and activities, and details on the cooperative movement by sector and by region around the world. Links to related sites and an interesting Research Register round out the site.

http://www.legacoop.it/index.html

This site, put together by the Institute for Cooperative Studies "Luigi Luzzatti" offers an interesting Italian perspective, with contacts for the cooperative movement in Italy. The site is not yet complete but still offers substantial information. English is available from the second page.

http://www.globenet.org/horizon-local/horizong.html

Local Horizon is a site dedicated to local development, North-South cooperation, the solidarity-based economy and their micro-projects. It contains 15 interesting papers related to the social economy, all in French, many useful links and suggestions for discussion groups. The majority of the site is in French, but a few pages are available in English, starting with the one indicated above.

http://www.sfu.ca/cedc

The people at Simon Fraser's Community Economic Development (CED) Centre in Vancouver have good reason to feel that they have put together one of the most comprehensive sites on the web pertaining to CED. There is lots to find your way around, including the full on-line version of their latest publication *Sharing Stories,* dozens of other articles and papers and a wide array of links. The clearest overview of the contents of the site is given on the "Gateway Contents" page. The entire site is in English.

http://www.personal.u-net.com/~varos/links2.htm

This site on Cooperatives and the Social Economy contains over 80 links to sites related to cooperation, listing coops by sector, networks, documents and archives, mostly from Britian and North America. Almost all links are English language sites.

http://solar.rtd.utk.edu/~ccsi/ccsihome.html

Centre for Civil Society International is a private, non-partisan educational organization based in Seattle, Washington, which supports the "development of civil society by fostering relationships between the nonprofit sector in the West and the grassroots & nonprofit organizations that have emerged in the states of the former Soviet Union and Central & Eastern Europe." Their site describes the CCSI, lists organizations in the former Soviet Union by country and activity, has a list of organizations in the US by sector of activity, contains a listing of on-line and print resources, and a page for research and opinion on civil society.

http://www.jhu.edu/~istr

The International Society for Third Sector Research was founded in 1992 at Johns Hopkins University to promote "research and education in the fields of philanthropy, civil society and the nonprofit sector." It seeks to provide a permanent forum for international research and build a global scholarly community in the field. Their site contains: an archive of the tables of contents of past issues of *Voluntas,* their International Journal of Voluntary and Non-Profit Organizations; information on their biennial conferences; a ListServ on third sector news and views (which is based out of York University, Toronto, for some reason); information on their quarterly newsletter; and contacts for regional networks.

http://fdncenter.org/lnps/index.html

This is the site of the on-line database of the Foundation Center, an independent nonprofit information clearinghouse established in 1956 and now operating in 5 US cities, with headquarters in New York. Their searchable library, entitled "The Literature of the Nonprofit Sector," contains the contents of their 5 libraries, totalling 15,196 full bibliographic citations, 9,129 of which have descriptive abstracts.

THE PUBLIC PLACE
Citizen Participation in the Neighbourhood and the City
Dimitrios I. Roussopoulos

Drawing on his experience in community journalism, Roussopoulos writes on a broad range of issues that affect the daily life of neighbourhoods and cities, using the 'public place' as a source of citizen participation.

Dimitrios I. Roussopoulos is an editor, writer, and ecologist. He has written widely on international politics, democracy, and social change. His most recent books are *Dissidence: Essays Against the Mainstream* (1992), and *Political Ecology* (1993) Black Rose Books.

200 pages, bibliography, index
Paperback ISBN: 1-55164-156-9 $19.99
Hardcover ISBN: 1-55164-157-7 $48.99
1999

BRINGING THE ECONOMY HOME FROM THE MARKET
Ross V.G. Dobson

An examination of the contemporary and historical processes by which local communities and individuals have been made dependent on the global market.

The most intelligent appraisal of LETS that I have ever seen.
Liz Shepard, UK LETS coordinator

...[This book] has a gripping eloquence when philosophizing about human nature, economics, and the demonstrated possibilities of LETS.
Chaos Review

...a simple and practical way to initiate community economic development.
Journal of Economic Literature

235 pages, index
Paperback ISBN: 1-895431-50-6 $19.99
Hardcover ISBN: 1-895431-51-4 $48.99
1990

FIRST PERSON PLURAL
A Community Development Approach to Social Change
David Smith

Smith's approach to adult education and community development methods help people build locally-controlled, democratic institutions and effective, broad-based social movements.

176 pages
Paperback ISBN: 1-55164-024-4 $19.99
Hardcover ISBN: 1-55164-025-2 $48.99
1994

MYTH OF THE MARKET
Promises and Illusions
Jeremy Seabrook

Dicusses how the spreading of market values is leading to social disintegration and the destruction of indigenous cultures.

A strong indictment of the market system. The argument is timely.
Peace and Environment News

189 pages
Paperback ISBN: 1-895431-08-5 $18.99
Hardcover ISBN: 1-895431-09-3 $47.99
1993

SHELTER, HOUSING, AND HOMES
A Social Right
Arnold Bennett

This useful book, the result of hands on experience, provides tools for understanding how any city can be made to work for its tenants.

Comes at a critical time to examine the deteriorating state of social housing.
Hour Magazine

236 pages, index
Paperback ISBN: 1-55164-042-2 $19.99
Hardcover ISBN: 1-55164-043-0 $48.99
1996